Arthur Young

A Six Months Tour Through the North of England

Vol. 1

Arthur Young

A Six Months Tour Through the North of England
Vol. 1

ISBN/EAN: 9783744754422

Printed in Europe, USA, Canada, Australia, Japan

Cover: Foto ©Andreas Hilbeck / pixelio.de

More available books at **www.hansebooks.com**

A SIX MONTHS TOUR THROUGH THE NORTH of ENGLAND.

CONTAINING,

An Account of the present State of AGRICULTURE, MANUFACTURES and POPULATION, in several Counties of this Kingdom.

PARTICULARLY,

I. The Nature, Value, and Rental of the Soil.
II. The Size of Farms, with Accounts of their Stock, Products, Population, and various Methods of Culture.
III. The Use, Expence, and Profit of several Sorts of Manure.
IV. The Breed of Cattle, and the respective Profits attending them.
V. The State of the Waste Lands which might and ought to be cultivated.
VI. The Condition and Number of the Poor, with their Rates, Earnings, &c.
VII. The Prices of Labour and Provisions, and the Proportion between them.
VIII. The Register of many curious and useful Experiments in Agriculture, and general Practices in Rural Oeconomics, communicated by several of the Nobility, Gentry, &c. &c.

INTERSPERSED

With Descriptions of the SEATS of the NOBILITY and GENTRY; and other remarkable Objects: Illustrated with Copper Plates of such Implements of Husbandry, as deserve to be generally known; and Views of some picturesque Scenes, which occurred in the Course of the Journey.

La seule voie de se procurer un corps complet d'agriculture seroit, sans doute, de rassembler les diverses observations qu'auroient fourni dans chaque province.   ENCYCLOPEDIE.

IN FOUR VOLUMES.

The SECOND EDITION, corrected and enlarged.

VOL. I.

LONDON,

Printed for W. STRAHAN; W. NICOLL, N° 51, in St. Paul's Church-Yard; T. CADELL, in the Strand; B. COLLINS, at Salisbury; and J. BALFOUR, at Edinburgh.

MDCCLXXI.

TO

SUCH OF THE NOBILITY,

GENTLEMEN, FARMERS,

AND OTHERS,

AS WERE PLEASED TO GIVE

INTELLIGENCE TO THE AUTHOR,

DURING THE COURSE OF THIS TOUR;

THIS REGISTER OF IT IS INSCRIBED,

BY THEIR OBLIGED,

MOST OBEDIENT, AND

DEVOTED SERVANT,

ARTHUR YOUNG.

CONTENTS

OF THE

FIRST VOLUME.

LETTER I.

STATE of *husbandry from* North Mims *to* Stamford.——— Mr. Searank's *experiments on burnet at* Hatfield.———*Earl of* Bute's *seat at* Luton.———*Duke of* Bedford's *at* Wooburn.———*Mr.* Bramstone's *experiments on grasses.*———Sandy Gardener's *culture of carrots,* &c.———*Duke of* Manchester's *seat at* Kimbolton. Page 1 to 66.

LETTER II.

State of husbandry from Stamford *to* Rotherham.———*Earl of* Exeter's *seat at* Burghley.———*Mr.* Sisson *of* Casterton's *experiments on burnet.*———*Duke of* Ancaster's

CONTENTS.

at Grimsthorpe.———*Mr.* Middlemore's *experiments at* Grantham *on cabbages, lucerne,* &c.———*Duke of* Rutland's *at* Belvoir.———*Mr.* Lyster's *experiments at* Bawtrey, *on cabbages, carrots, lucerne,* &c.——— *Mr.* Wharton's *experiments at* Doncaster *on cabbages, potatoes, carrots,* &c. P. 66 to 115.

LETTER III.

Husbandry from Rotherham *to* Beverley.— *Manufactures at* Rotherham.——— *Mr.* Tucker's *experiments at* Rotherham *on cabbages,* &c———*Beautiful landscape.*— *Manufactures at* Sheffield.———*Earl of* Strafford's *at* Wentworth Castle.——— *Manufactures at* Wakefield *and* Leeds.— *Town of* Beverley. P. 115 to 150.

LETTER IV.

Agriculture from Beverley *to* Wentworth House.——— *Sir* George Metham's *at* Cave.——— *Mr.* Watson's *shrubbery at* Cottingham.———*Town of* Hull.—*Mr.* Elleker's *experiments on cabbages,* &c. ———*Remarks on the high prices of labour in the* East Riding.———*City of* York.———
Minster.

CONTENTS. iii

Minster.—*Assembly room.*—*Miss* Morret's *beautiful work.*——Dr. Hunter's *experiments.*——*Drill plough.*——*Proposed improvements at* Stillingfleet.—*Mr.* Ellerker's *seat at* Risby.—*Proposed improvements in the* East Riding.—*Inclosing.*—*Remarkable moors at* Thorne.

P. 150 to 245.

LETTER V.

Description of Wentworth House, *the Marquis of* Rockingham's.——*Park, plantations, water, temples, &c.*——*Marquis of* Rockingham's *experiments in husbandry.*——*Sad state of agriculture before his Lordship improved it.*——*His method of executing it.*—*Covered drains.*—*Management of grass lands.*——*Turnip hoeing.*——*New implements.*——*Establishment of a* Kentish *and a* Hertfordshire *farm.*——*Cabbages.*——*Manures, &c.*——*Common husbandry around* Wentworth.—*Remarks.* P. 245 to 317.

LETTER VI.

State of husbandry from Wentworth *to* Ferry Bridge.——*Duke of* Leeds *at* Kiveton.——*Duke of* Portland's *at* Welbeck.——

CONTENTS.

His Grace's experiments on the moory soil, &c.——*Duke* of Norfolk's *at* Workſop.——*His Grace's farm-yard.*——*His experiments on carrots.*——Mr. Hewett's *experiments at* Bilham *on carrots, lucerne, burnet, bird graſs, ſainfoine, cabbages,* &c.——Mr. Farrer's *experiments at* Barnborough *on tillage, barley,* &c.——*Culture of liquorice at* Pontefract.——*Lord* Mexborough's *at* Methley.——*Lord* Irwin's *at* Temple Newſham.——*Sir* John Ramſden's *at* Byrom.——*Sir* John's *culture of turnips and cabbages,* &c.

P. 317 to 360.

PREFACE.

SOME private business carrying me into the south of *Wales*, gave birth to the *Six Weeks Tour*, which I wrote chiefly as an amusement on the road; nor was I sensible that the papers might be of use, till I sat down to consider them again. It then appeared to me, that a view of *English* agriculture would be serviceable.

The public, by a very kind reception of it, has confirmed the idea, and induced me to undertake a more extensive Tour.—But as my time before was limited, and I had other things to regard besides my book, I determined to have no other employment in my new journey, and to take such means of procuring intelligence, as were open to a person, who could command so few advantages.

With this view, I inserted the following advertisement, in many of the *London* papers, and in all the country ones, published near my intended rout.

The AUTHOR of the SIX WEEKS TOUR through the southern counties of *England* and

and *Wales*, propoſing to undertake this ſummer a Tour through The North of England, begs leave to requeſt ſuch of the nobility, gentry, landlords, farmers, and others, as poſſeſs, or are acquainted with, any particular improvements, experiments, cuſtoms, implements, &c. in the agriculture of the following counties, *viz. Hertfordſhire, Bedfordſhire, Huntingdonſhire, Northamptonſhire, Rutlandſhire, Leiceſterſhire, Nottinghamſhire, Lincolnſhire, Derbyſhire, Yorkſhire, Durham, Northumberland, Cumberland, Weſtmoreland, Lancaſhire, Cheſhire, Shropſhire, Staffordſhire, W*orceſ*terſhire, Warwickſhire,* and *Buckinghamſhire,* to inform him of ſuch circumſtances, with exact directions to the places where ſuch improvements, &c. are carried on. He ſhould not take the liberty of this general addreſs to perſons unknown, were it not, that he might probably, without this previous intimation, overlook many improvements and experiments in huſbandry, and return unacquainted with many practices, implements, &c. which deſerve to be univerſally known. And it certainly is of indiſputable conſequence to the welfare of agriculture, that every thing commendable in the practice of it, ſhould not be confined to particular diſtricts, but publiſhed for general good. The Author is not unacquainted with the improvement of waſte lands,

lands by marle, clay, chalk, &c. with the clover, turnip, and carrot husbandry; and the culture of the modern artificial grasses; and shall, with the utmost readiness, impart the little knowledge he possesses to any who may think his opinion of the least consequence, as he travels with the sincerest desire of being serviceable to the interests of husbandry. His principal aim is agriculture; but he shall not pass the seats of the nobility and gentry without visiting them.

Those who favour him with their address, are **desired to direct to THE AUTHOR OF THE SIX WEEKS TOUR**, to the care of Mr. *W. Nicoll, St. Paul's Churchyard, London*.

The effect of this intimation, was not so advantageous as I expected: However, I determined to take every measure that was requisite for procuring intelligence; and marked no certain rout, designing to turn to the right or left, whenever I heard of any thing worthy the least attention. An unremitted industry made some amends for the want of better advantages, and I compensated the loss of such intelligence as gentlemen alone can give, by applications to many farmers.———This was in general the case from *London* to *York*.

I spent

I spent the race-week in that city, which accident brought me acquainted with several gentlemen, famous in the north for their love of agriculture, and the uncommon spirit with which they practise it. I was received by them with much politeness, and the intelligence they gave me is undoubtedly the most valuable part of these sheets.

Now it must surely be apparent, that the value of such a work, as I at present offer to the public, must inevitably depend on the nature of the intelligence I receive; and this in so great a degree, that it would be vanity in me to pretend to any merit from the compilation; for as to the reflections which I subjoin, they are so obvious, that I think no one could have failed making the same; and most certainly many others will occur, which have escaped me. This Tour is therefore useful in proportion to the value of my authorities: Common farmers have given me very sensible accounts of common practices; **but few of** them enter into the spirit of such an undertaking;—some were jealous of my designs;—and none of them try experiments, and register them.—In all these points, I have found many gentlemen extremely satisfactory.——By their means, (in sending for their tenants, *&c.*) I have been enabled to gain complete accounts of common husbandry,——and have been favoured

voured with the particulars of many experiments, that cannot fail of pleasing and instructing. Some registers of this sort I insert, which I am confident will do honour to the age, and be of the greatest use to husbandry.

In several parts of the journey I had not these advantages; it was, therefore, impossible for me to make use of them. The inferiority of such parts of this register is not to be laid to my account;—but to those who could have given me better intelligence, but neglected or slighted the undertaking.

I must confess, that I have dwelt so much on the idea of rendering my general design complete, that I wish for the opportunity of extending the Tour through every part of *Great Britain* and *Ireland*, and presenting the public a complete work.

Were I to receive the encouragement that was necessary, and which consists only in the intimation of designed intelligence, I should proceed with the undertaking—— finish the account of *England* and *Wales*, —travel over *Scotland*, and make the tour of *Ireland*: But I have already found the advantages of the best authority too much, to depend on that alone which chance may throw in my way.

That such an extension of the journey might be of some use, is undoubted:

the

the remaining parts muſt contain many practices that deſerve to be generally known; and likewiſe numerous inſtances of bad huſbandry, that require explanation, in order for a remedy.——The more a man views the agriculture of various ſoils, the readier and better able is he to propoſe methods of improvement. There muſt alſo, in ſuch tracts, be many gentlemen, who have practiſed huſbandry with unuſual attention, and who have noted their experiments and obſervations; ſome would probably conſent to their publication. POLITICAL ARITHMETIC might reap great benefit; for moſt of the points that form the foundation of national calculations would receive a light they never yet had;——the proportion of cultivated and uncultivated land;—the rental;—the value of the ſoil;——the amount of ſtock; —the annual expenditure in huſbandry;— the ſtate of population, dependent on agriculture;——theſe, and many other points of equal importance, would afford to politicians much better grounds for their variety of diſputes, than ſome they at preſent uſe.

But it is here requiſite to explain or apologize for one or two circumſtances concerning this Tour, that may not be ſo clear as they ought.

In the firſt place, I have been aſked more than once, whether I did not think it a
little

little too much, to pretend to instruct others in husbandry, before I had convinced the world of having practised it myself;—— no work that I had yet published displaying any matters of *experience?* Now, as this question may arise in the minds of many of my readers, I think it necessary to hint, that, small as my experience is, yet I have some. I have been a farmer these many years, and that not in a single field or two, but upon a tract of near 300 acres, most part of the time; and never on less than 100. I have cultivated, upon various soils, most of the vegetables common in *England*, and many that have never been introduced into field husbandry; but, what is of much more consequence towards gaining real experience, I have always kept, from the first day I began, a minute register of my business; insomuch that, upon my *Suffolk* farm, I minuted above three thousand experiments; in every article of *culture, expences,* and *produce,* including, among a great variety of other articles, an accurate comparison of the old and new husbandry, in the production of most vegetables: But in this, I would by no means be thought to arrogate any other, than that plodding merit of being *industrious* and *accurate,* to which any one of the most common genius can attain, if he thinks proper to take the trouble.——

From those experiments, I have selected the most conclusive, and propose to lay them before the public, under the patronage of a name auspicious to agriculture. ------This, I think, is sufficient to satisfy such of my readers as may think me so greatly wanting in experience.

In the second place, I should apologize for introducing so many descriptions of houses, paintings, ornamented parks, lakes, &c. I am sensible they have little to do with agriculture, but there is, nevertheless, an utility in their being known. They are a proof, and a very important one, of the riches and the happiness of this kingdom: No traveller can here move far, without something to attract his notice, ------ art or nature will perpetually catch his eye.—An agriculture that even reaches perfection.— Architecture, painting, sculpture, and the art of adorning grounds, every where exhibit productions that speak a wealth, a refinement—a taste, which only great and luxurious nations can know.------I have thought it not improper, to consider them all;------to reject nothing that either art or nature have contributed to render our country beautiful or convenient:—Every reader does not seek for the same entertainment; some hastily pass over the pages that are not dedicated to ploughing and sowing,— others quickly turn over every leaf that

concerns

concerns husbandry, and dwell alone on the description of houses and gardens,—and not a few, perhaps, who seek the latter, are accidentally led to more useful passages, and become undesignedly acquainted with agriculture.—However, if I have been in this respect to blame, it is by no means a matter of consequence;——my farming readers may pass over those sheets; and in the general reflections I offer at last, neither architecture, painting, nor gardening will interfere with rent, crops, and culture.

Thirdly, I should request, that the farmers will not suppose I have been inattentive in such parts of the work as are incomplete in the common articles of intelligence. I put the same questions to every one, but very few were able to answer me all, consequently many gaps must appear: Every article varies in the extent of the intelligence; and this general remark, I think, much better than inserting a string of negatives in every day's journey.

Some of my readers may possibly think I have been too free in inserting the particulars of farms; it would be anticipating my subject to explain fully my motives, but I refer to the general deductions at the conclusion, where I apprehend the necessity of this part of the enquiry will clearly appear.

In refpect to *ſtile* and *accuracy of language*, the candid reader will, I hope, confider the *time*, *places*, and *manner* of writing thefe fheets; the minutes were fo extremely numerous, and of fuch variety, that, had they not been regiftered as faft as they were taken, it would have occafioned an endlefs confufion,——and a work that is partly founded on the *prefent* ſtate of affairs (*viz.* the prices of provifions, *&c.*) will not allow its author that time for correction and polifhing, which more favourable fubjects afford: This plea will perhaps be the readier accepted, when it is confidered, that I pretend to nothing but giving a book of facts.

Indeed the undertaking has been of that laborious nature, that the idea of uniting elegance with utility would be extravagant: For many hundred miles, I had nothing but provincial weights and meafures, totally unknown in the fouth: Thefe were all reduced to the common ftandard;—— the intelligence I received in the moft common points was conceived in fuch uncommon terms, and in fuch barbarous meafures, that had I not gained numerous explanations, my work would have been a volume of contradictions. A practical knowledge of agriculture, is as requifite to fuch

an

an undertaking as plenty of patience. After abundance of explanations, I frequently had such intelligence as would have passed current with those who were unexperienced in husbandry, but which forced me to a most uncommon attention to discover wherein was the mistake. My business was likewise so very unusual, that some art was requisite to gain intelligence from many farmers, &c. who were startled at the first attack. I found that even a profusion of expence was often necessary to gain the ends I had in view: I was forced to make more than one honest farmer half drunk, before I could get sober, unprejudiced intelligence. Nor were such my only difficulties; I met with some farmers who gave me accounts too improbable to credit; whether from ignorance, or an attention to deceive, I know not; but I always repeated my enquiries upon those occasions, until I gained the truth. When the candid reader considers these, and many other circumstances, I flatter myself, he will excuse small errors, and improprieties of stile.

One point remains for me to speak to, whereon I shall ever dwell with pleasure; it is the returning my most grateful thanks to those gentlemen that had the spirit to encourage an undertaking, which has by some been branded as *visionary*. I cannot forego the satisfaction of a slight recapitulation;

lation, to let my countrymen know, that there are men of every rank in husbandry that have given me intelligence; and, I doubt not, *all* with some view to the good of their country. No apology is wanting, for joining peers and common farmers in the same page: He, who is the BEST FARMER, is with me the GREATEST MAN.

I am much obliged to JOHN SEARANKE, Esq; of *Hatfield*, for giving me an account of his burnet. Few have cultivated that vegetable with more spirit, or on a larger scale.

Mr. WHITTINGTON of *Stevenage* has my thanks, not only for the intelligence he gave me, but in the name of the public, for the neat and husband-like manner in which he cultivates a very considerable farm.

Mr. GEORGE SISSON of *Bridge Casterton*, in *Rutlandshire*, merits the like return: He deserves much praise for his attention to burnet, an article of culture unknown in his neighbourhood.

I am much obliged to SAMUEL TUCKER, Esq; of *Rotherham*, for his account of cultivating cabbages. He has carried that part of agriculture to very great perfection.

I had the satisfaction of conversing on the subject of husbandry with Dr. HUNTER of *York*, whose designs shew an inventive genius,

genius, and his writings display no trifling share of knowledge and precision. I am also obliged to him for a hand-drill of his own invention.

My very excellent friend E. M. ELLERKER, Esq; of *Risby*, must allow me to repeat in public what I have so often reflected on with pleasure in private: That no man wishes better to his country, or would sacrifice more to her welfare.——The articles of farming intelligence which I am enabled, through his means, to offer to the public, are particularly valuable;—they concern several very extensive tracts of country in which his estates are situated; and no circumstances in his power to command, were wanting to render them clear and of authority. The time I spent at *Risby* afforded me an opportunity of executing my general design with particular advantage. I am also indebted to him for several recommendations, which proved of much use to me.

I am much obliged to Sir GEORGE METHAM, for the politeness with which he showed me his plantations, and gave me some information concerning the husbandry of his neighbourhood.

If I was not fearful of breaking in upon his attention to matters of greater importance, I should beg the Marquis of ROCKINGHAM to accept my humble thanks

thanks for the great encouragement he gave me, and for the information I received from him; which any one, who views the land his Lordship keeps in his own hands, will soon perceive must have been very instructive. I never saw the advantages of a great fortune applied more nobly to the improvement of a country. Every discovery of other counties,—every successful experiment in agriculture,——every new implement, (and many of his Lordships own invention) introduced at a great expence.—Draining.——The general management of grass-land——and manures, among numerous other articles, are, at *Wentworth*, carried to the utmost perfection. Nor should I forget to observe, how much I was indebted to his Lordship for recommending me to several excellent cultivators.

The Duke of PORTLAND will honour me with the acceptance of my acknowledgements, for my reception at *Welbeck*, as well as the information he was pleased to give me concerning some points in agriculture. The effects of the black moory soil, as a manure and a preservative from the cock-chaffer grub, are curious.

SELWOOD HEWETT, Esq; of *Bilham*, and JAMES FARRAR, Esq; of *Barnborough Grange*, receive my sincere thanks for the
intelligence

intelligence which they were pleased to give me.

I am much obliged to Sir GEORGE STRICTLAND, Bart. for shewing me his manufactory. It is an undertaking that does him honour.

The value of the intelligence, I received from Sir DIGBY LEGARD, Bart. will speak sufficiently for itself; but I cannot avoid acknowledging the liberal manner in which he consented to improve my work. His memoir upon the wolds husbandry, is a piece full of excellent observations.

I beg the Reverend Mr. COMBER of *East Newton* will accept the slight return of thanks for the kind and friendly manner in which he assisted me in prosecuting my design. I gained by his means several valuable articles of intelligence.

I wish I could return my thanks to CHARLES TURNER, Esq; in a manner adequate to the spirit of his agriculture. His undertakings do him much honour: His experiments on cabbages, clover, potatoes, *&c.* cannot fail of being of lasting utility to the public. No one could enter more into the nature of my design or forward it with greater alacrity. The week I very agreeably spent at *Kirkleatham*, these sheets will prove was no idle one.

CHRISTOPHER CROWE, Esq; will permit me to thank him very sincerely for the obliging

obliging reception I met with at *Kiplin*: I is with great pleasure, I reflect on the intelligence he gave me, which is extensive and accurate.——— His own husbandry is spirited; and in several instances uncommon.

I am much obliged to ——— SMELT, Esq; of *The Leases*, for an accurate account of his experiments in agriculture.

It is with great pleasure that I remember the kindness with which WILLIAM DANBY, Esq; encouraged my undertaking. My readers will find, that I was not negligent at *Swinton*, for that gentleman took every measure for my information of the state of husbandry in his neighbourhood;—his attention to the populousness of his extensive estate, and the excellent example he has set in the management of his miners, deserve every acknowledgement which a lover of his country can give. One of them (for whom I have ventured to propose a subscription, see Vol. II. Letter XI.) is almost as great a curiosity in farming as can any where be met with.

I cannot omit acknowledging how much I am indebted to MATTHEW DODSWORTH, Esq; for the important intelligence he gave me; as well as the very friendly manner in which he received me at *Crakehall*.

WILLIAM DALTON, Esq; of *Sleningford*, gave me, with great civility, a full account of of the common husbandry in his neighbourhood; and of many very important experiments he made upon lucerne, burnet, sainfoine, potatoes, &c.

SYMON SCROOPE, Esq; of *Danby*, **must allow me to assert, that** I was particularly **fortunate** in meeting with a cultivator, **whose** experiments do honour, not to himself alone, but to his country. Few works of agriculture extant, contain more judicious, accurate and decisive trials, than many which this gentleman favoured me with.

The intelligence which I received from the Earl of DARLINGTON, was too valuable——his experiments too numerous and accurate, **not to** be mentioned with all possible acknowledgments. I can by no means do justice to that uncommon candour, with which his Lordship honoured me with the particulars of the common husbandry about *Raby Castle*; and his own experience on a most extensive tract of land. No man can be more accurate in the culture of twenty acres, than his Lordship on some thousands. I am particularly obliged to him for the plan and elevation of a farm-yard, which I believe has no equal.

I desire that — CARR, Esq; will allow me to thank him for the civilities I received at *Cocken*.

It is with the utmost pleasure, that I acknowledge the attention of ABRAHAM DIXON, Esq; of *Belford*;—no man could entertain a more favourable idea of my undertaking. The intelligence I gained by his means, was particularly valuable. The extensive county of *Northumberland*, demanded a more accurate view than I should otherwise have been able to offer; and Mr. *Dixon*'s experiments in agriculture, and the active and spirited manner in which he carries on numerous and important undertakings, claim a particular notice.

I am obliged to Mr. CUTHBERT CLARKE of *Belford*, for a drawing of his turnip slicer, and to Mr. JOHN WILKIE of *Hetton*, and Mr. CULEY of *Fenton*, for the civilities I received from them. *Northumberland* owes much to the latter for improving her breed of sheep.

M. PARKE of *Liverpool* has my thanks, for the account of improving a bog in *Lancashire*, that was conducted upon a very original plan with spirit, and does him much credit.

I desire Mr. ARCHIBALD BELL, and Mr. HAMILTON, principal manufacturers at *Manchester*, will accept my thanks for the intelligence they gave me concerning the fabricks of that town *.

* I do not at present recollect having received any letters which are unanswered: I had several invitations from counties through which I did not pass, if I have omitted a due acknowledgment, it has been through error alone; and owing neither to design nor neglect. Should any remain unacknowledged, I beg it may be attributed to my letters having miscarried, as I hold myself too much obliged to all who thought of giving me intelligence, to omit such a return.

It would be endless and tedious to recapitulate every person who was kind enough to afford me intelligence; but I must be allowed in general to assert, that I found a great many farmers who contributed much to my design;— who gave me very sensible accounts of common husbandry, and many of them more void of prejudice and contraction, than some of my readers would suppose. I beg that all such would accept my sincere acknowledgments, which I make with the greater pleasure, as I am certain, from their conversation, that they are good husbandmen in their respective neighbourhoods. No set of people whatever can be more hospitable, or more desirous of obliging, than the farmers in the north of *England*——it is the land of hospitality.

In regiſtering the minutes of a Tour of above two thousand five hundred miles, many errors muſt have crept in :——Many articles of intelligence received not so accurate as could have been given by gentlemen :——Even in the particulars of private experiments, I may have made some mistakes—and not a few omiſsions; whoever obſerves such errors or omiſsions, will lay me under a great obligation by informing me by letter of the particulars; and I shall certainly make the proper use of them, in case this work should see another edition.

——This

———This is the only way to render it perfect———those who wish to see a complete view of *British* agriculture, will take a little trouble of this sort.

The manner in which my undertaking has been promoted, by so many spirited cultivators, claims something more than a mere return of thanks: I shall never omit any opportunity of acknowledging my obligations, and be proud of obeying any of their commands within the reach of my situation.———I have farmed in *Suffolk* and *Essex*; which counties, as well as *Hertfordshire*, in which I at present live, may probably contain something in husbandry that my distant friends may accidentally stand in need of.—If any person has an inclination to transplant good farmers into a soil occupied by bad ones—to hire servants used to the best culture in some of these countries*—to make use of implements more perfect than common in some parts———to procure a change of seed corn———or, in a word, for any thing in which I can assist them; I consider myself (independently of inclination) as bound by gratitude to do it; and I shall accordingly execute their commands with the utmost satisfaction.

* Particularly ploughing with two horses without a driver; and *strait*.

PREFACE

PREFACE

TO THE

SECOND EDITION.

THE favourable reception the first edition of this work has met with from the public, animates me in the strongest manner to render the present impression as perfect as possible. I have corrected it with as much attention as I am able; and applied, I believe, to every person whose experiments are mentioned, for their corrections, and the continuation of their trials, and am happy in being able to insert many such improvements that render the respective registers much more useful than they would otherwise be. The communications of this sort which I have been

been favoured with from several persons, deserve the warmest acknowledgments.

I cannot omit expressing how much I am indebted to the Earl of HOLDERNESSE, for the attention he was pleased to give to the article concerning *Hornby Castle*. I was misinformed of the husbandry of some grass fields; and his Lordship was so obliging as to correct the errors, and at the same time explained the motives of his conduct: His letter is inserted in the proper place, and will speak for itself much more forcibly than any thing I can say in praise of it. It shews him to be an excellent farmer.

THOMAS B. BAILEY, Esq; of *Hope*, near *Manchester*, has favoured me with some particulars relative to the designs and success of the patriotic society of *Lancashire*, for which I am much obliged to him. I should have been able to render the *Lancashire* part of this Tour much more complete through the assistance of this gentleman and Colonel TOWNLEY, the president; but unfortunately I was not known to them before the journey. The spirit with which they encourage and practise agriculture, merits much praise.

The Earl of DARLINGTON, since the first edition of these papers, has favoured me with the product of a crop of drilled turnips, which demands the attention of
all

all correct husbandmen: I believe it is the greatest ever raised in *England*.

Mr. TURNER has been so attentive to render the *Kirkleatham* article complete and accurate, that I cannot but express my acknowledgments in the warmest terms: He has enabled me to continue the register of all his experiments; and the additional ones (particularly on cabbages) now inserted, will shew to what perfection he has carried that culture.

I am much obliged to Mr. DANBY for the corrections he sent me: They shew the attention he has given to render the work accurate, and the judgment with which he read it. His remarks on the calculations of the moory improvements were very useful; as I have from them been able to sketch new ones which are much more decisive than the former.

The letter with which Sir DIGBY LEGARD has enriched this edition, is extremely valuable; the experiments on grasses and turnips are most accurately registered and perfectly satisfactory: I am particularly obliged to this most spirited farmer for so valuable a piece.

Mr. DIXON, Mr. SCROOPE, and the Reverend Mr. COMBER, have been so kind as to favour me with various corrections and additions, for which I am much indebted to them.

I am

I am obliged to Mr. SEARANKE of *Hatfield*, for the particulars he gave me of his experiments on burnet. They are now extremely satisfactory and conclusive.

It is only by communications of this sort, that such an undertaking can be rendered tolerably complete. Nor shall I conclude without again requesting these, and other cultivators, to favour me with a continuation of their trials; from whence the public will find, that real utility has caused an increase of several practices which perhaps curiosity alone began.

JAMES CROFTS.

I Have the satisfaction of informing my Readers, that the Subscription I ventured to propose in the first edition of this work, for this very honest and industrious man, has met with some success.

	£.	s.	d.
His worthy landlord, *William Danby*, Esq; advanced in cash, and additions in buildings and inclosures; for which he generously takes neither interest nor increase of rent during *Crofts*'s life, - - -	50	0	0
Sundry subscriptions, by *Charles Turner*, Esq; - -	21	0	0
Mr. *Lott Knight*, -	1	1	0
Unknown, by ditto, -	0	5	3
Mr. *Roberts*, - -	0	5	3
Mr. *George Hannay*, -	2	2	0
Mr. *Robert Livie*, -	0	5	3
Mr. *Middleton*, (*Suffolk*,) -	1	1	0
Rev. Mr. *Bouchery*, of *Swaffham*, Norfolk, - - -	1	1	0
G. N. - - -	0	2	6
John Arbuthnot, Esq; -	1	1	0
Mr. *John Whin Baker*, of *Laughlinstone*, near *Dublin*, -	1	1	0
A. Y. - - -	1	1	0
W. N. - - - -	1	1	0
J. E. - -	0	10	6
	81	17	9

SUBSCRIPTIONS continue to be received.

Mr. *Danby* informs me, that this very industrious man's labours, last summer, were greatly interrupted by inward complaints, that are, in all probability, the consequence of repeated strains and violence, and of the incessant fatigues he has gone through; but since he has recovered, he has returned to his labours with his usual assiduity.

It is proposed to expend the Subscription in assisting him in Labour, for improving some of his inclosed wastes, and also in the purchase of some cattle. But a further account will be given in the public papers; and the Subscriptions received in the country not yet come to hand will be acknowleged and included in the general account.

A SIX MONTH's TOUR, &c.

LETTER I.

DEAR SIR, *June* 1768.

YOUR remark that the minutes I took of my Six Weeks Tour were by no means complete, in not being extended over each county I passed through, is certainly very just; but at the same time you must allow me to observe, that such perfection is not to be expected from the leisure and fortune of a private person, who has other matters to attend to besides the *public* good. I am very sensible of the advantages which would result from a tour upon this plan through every village in the kingdom; but I do not think we should slight such general views as these I venture to the world, because greater advantages in the traveller would be attended with a more enlarged intelligence. —— In a word, my good friend, I am encouraged to undertake a second tour by the candid, but unmerited notice which an impartial public has taken of my first Essay —— with such a view, accept the following minutes: I hope they will be worthy your attention; I promise that no care and accuracy shall be wanting on my part.

My former minutes extended from *London*, in the north road almost to *Hatfield*; permit me, therefore, to begin the following journal in that neighbourhood.

The first objects I found worthy of attention in husbandry, were several fields of burnet belonging to Mr. *Searancke* of *Hatfield*, for which he obtained a gold medal of the Society for the Encouragement of Arts, Manufactures, and Commerce.

EXPERIMENT, N° 1.

He began his culture at *Bramfield* in the year 1764, on four acres of a poor, cold gravelly loam, on clay and chalk. It was well fallowed and amply dunged. Sown broad-cast in *August*, twelve pounds of seed per acre, at two shillings per pound. The conduct of the trial will best appear from the following minutes which he made of the success, and which are an extract of a letter written on the subject. ——
" As it has been lately much agitated, whether

whether the cultivation of burnet will prove beneficial to the farmer, and consequently to the whole nation? I trouble you with a few particulars on the subject.—In the beginning of *August* 1764, I sowed four acres of poor wet ground with seed bought of Mr. *Rocque* of *Walham Green*, after the rate of twelve pounds per acre. It came up very thick in about ten or twelve days: But the fly beginning to take it, I immediately sent for a load of soot, and strewed over it, about twenty-five bushels per acre: This prevented its receiving further damage. It grew and flourished more than could be expected through the whole winter, which was uncommonly wet. I suffered no cattle of any sort to be turned upon it, least it should receive damage by being poached. My cows once broke into it, and I have reason to believe it was a dainty repast to them; as they seemed to be very desirous of getting in again. By the twelfth of *May*, it was full headed, and fit to cut for hay: Some gentlemen (whom curiosity had led to see it) as well as myself and servants, judged it would turn out two loads of hay (dry in the winter) per acre. It was allowed to be by far the greatest burthen that was known to grow upon the land: In short, it was the only good crop ever known on it.——However, I chose rather to let it stand for feed; mowed it

the third of *July*, and had eighty-four bushels on the four acres. The method pursued in threshing it was as follows: I made a temporary floor in the field of twelve feet three inch deals covered with cloths, and inclosed with herdles hung with other cloths to prevent the seed from flying off the stage. Ten men threshed and were supplied by three others who brought the burnet upon forks. On the outside of the floor I had another cloth for the men to put the straw on, where it was the employment of another man to shake out the loose seed, and then to carry the burnet and spread it on the ground to dry for hay.--- After it is mowed it ought to have two or three days field-room before you begin to thresh it. I hear it has been asserted, that the straw makes very poor hay. I am of a different opinion, for my horses eat it much beyond expectation; and my cows are very fond of it. But one circumstance I should remark, which is, my strewing salt over it when I stacked it, as I did in 1764 with about four loads of after-pasture clover hay, that was damaged so much by rains as to be thought more fit to be made dung of than hay; but this I do aver as a truth, that my horses eat more, and fed more heartily on this damaged but salted hay, than they did upon that which was cut in full sap and stacked without rain: The
experi-

experiment was tried by racking them sometimes with one sort, and sometimes with the other: The nights they were racked with the best hay they did not eat all that was given, but the nights in which they had the salted damaged hay, although a a larger quantity was given, yet in the mornings their racks were found empty*."

Mr. *Searancke* sold the seed at one shilling per pound (except some he kept for his own use); and the eighty-four bushels weighing 2184 lb. came at that price to 109 *l*. 4 *s*. 0 *d*. or 27 *l*. 6 *s*. 0 *d*. per acre; a product that will not often be exceeded. The price of burnet is now three-pence per pound, but suppose it two-pence in quantities, such a crop would produce per acre 4 *l*. 16 *s*. 6 *d*. besides the hay and after feed: This calculation shews that burnet-feed is yet an object of importance in husbandry.

After this crop of seed the land was fed by cows until *October*.

---

* This proof of the efficacy of salt in recovering damaged hay convinced Mr. *Searancke* so much, that he practised it on other occasions. In finishing a stack of common hay the top was making up with some that was almost spoiled by rain; he ordered it to be thrown off, spread on the ground and made again, and then in stacking it strewed it with a good deal of salt; in the winter it was eaten by cows very freely.

The common quantity is a peck of salt to a load of hay.

1766.

This year the crop was mown for hay, the latter end of *May*, product four loads. It was left rather too long; the beginning of that month is a much better feafon; the cows refufed to eat it: Mr. *Searancke* reflecting on the fuccefs of laft year with only the *ftraw*, thought it might be owing to the bruifing the ftalks in the threfhing; he therefore took the hint, and made his men threfh this hay enough to bruife the ftalks, and then trying the fame cows with it, they eat it very freely. After the mowing it was fed by cows, and the milk was always found to be plentiful, and the butter excellent.

1767, 8, and 9.

Throughout thefe years it was paftured by cows; and the former remark verified by experience, that no food gives more milk or fweeter butter.

Prefent State of the Crop.

It is to be obferved, that the natural graffes during the laft two years have arofe pretty much, fo that the field is now a very good common pafture. This opens a view of burnet that is very advantageous; it is a good and cheap way to lay down land for perpetual pafture; the burnet gives immediately

diately a profitable crop, and the grasses increase by degrees until the land is quite matted.——Not however to the exclusion of the burnet, for Mr. *Searancke* thinks there are to the full as many plants of it as in the first year; but the vacancies among them are filled and the general herbage thicker, and more like an old pasture.

EXPERIMENT, N° 2.
1765.

NINETEEN acres were sown at *Bramfield* in *August* 1765: the soil, a cold, wet, strong clay land; fallowed, but not manured: It was kept through the winter without any cattle going in In *April* and *May* 1766, it sprung very thick, but low; It was fed by cows through the year. In 1767 it was also fed in the same manner, but the crop turning out very poor, owing merely to the wetness of the land, Mr. *Searancke* ploughed it up in 1768, and harrowed in oats, of which he got a most excellent crop.

EXPERIMENT, N° 3.
1765.

Ten acres of land at *Hatfield*, the soil an upland poor gravel, and inclinable to wetness, nefs, were fallowed in 1765, and thoroughly manured with black rotten dung: Sown with burnet (a bufhel, or 26 lb. per acre) in *Auguſt*: No cattle turned on it; but it was kept quite clean from weeds, by hand-weeding for fome time, but the chick-weed came up in fuch prodigious luxuriance that it was mown twice and carted away: Some cows got to the dunghill where it was laid, and fed very eagerly on it: Some fattening bullocks did the fame: This was before the whole field was finifhed; Mr. *Scaraneke* took the hint, and ftopping the weeding, turned in his cattle, and they eat up every fprig. This is a remarkable cir-cumftance, and fhould be remembered by thofe whofe lands are fubject to that weed; for the difference is amazingly great be-tween the converting it to dung in one cafe —or to beef and milk in the other.

1766.

May 12th mowed it for hay; the crop about 12 loads: As to the application of the hay in the following winter; horfes would not eat it; it was therefore all cut into chaff, in which ftate they eat it very freely; the price at which it was fold for this ufe was 32 s. per load. After the mowing it was paftured by horfes; who fed very heartily on it. And the quantity of food it yielded was very confiderable.

1767.

1767.

Mown the first week in *May*; produce, about nine loads of hay. This hay was eaten in the winter by cows: Six were kept on it the chief part of the winter; and the butter made from them was excellent. After the mowing the field was pastured by horses.

1768.

May 12th, mowed for hay; but the product not more than five loads: The smallness of which quantity induced Mr. *Searancke* to sow over the burnet, one bushel per acre of ray-grass and six pound of white clover. Both seeds took very well. Since that time the field has not been mown, but every year been fed with horses and cows: The quantity of food it has in that manner yielded is considerable: It is, however, found advisable once a year to mow off the bents, and those spots in the burnet where a great luxuriancy makes cattle neglect it, to encourage the fresh growth. In the winter of 1769, manured it with long dung.

Present State of the Crop.

This field is now a very good common pasture: Equal to the general run of its neighbours. The herbage is very thick,

con-

consisting of burnet, ray-grass, white clover, and much natural grass. And it is worthy of remark, that notwithstanding the ray-grass took so well, yet it has not in the least damaged the burnet, which is so vigorous a plant, that it keeps the superiority over all around it.

EXPERIMENT, N° 4.

1766.

In 1765, five acres of the same soil as N° 3. were sown with barley; and in 1766 with oats, among which a bushel per acre of burnet, and six pounds of white clover were sown. After the oats were cut and carried, the whole field was folded with sheep.

1767.

The beginning of *May*, mowed it; the produce seven loads of good hay, eaten by cows and horses. After the mowing it was pastured by horses.

1768.

It was fed throughout this year by cows and horses, the number of which maintained by it was very great. Plenty of milk and remarkably sweet butter, the constant attendants of cows eating burnet.

1769.

1769.

Fed again this year; in the winter manured, for a trial, half of it with long dung, and half with road fullage; the fandy mud fhovelled up in the turnpike. It fhould be obferved, that the farmers will have nothing to do with this ftuff; fo that Mr. *Searancke* was applied to by the furveyor of the road for leave to cart it into his land, which being complied with, it was fpread on this burnet in Autumn. I viewed the field in *March* 1770, and the different appearance of the two parts of the field I thought remarkable: The part covered with the road fand, exhibited as beautiful a young vegetation of the white clover as ever I beheld:——It formed quite a carpet; whereas very little of it was to be feen in the dunged part. I have no doubt but the fame fuperiority will be found throughout the year. N. B. The dung was long ftable litter.

Prefent State.

The field is now a very good common pafture and exceeds the others that were fown without corn. The herbage very thick, and in general has the appearance of a very good natural grafs field.

General

General Observations.

Mr. *Searancke*, upon the whole, is of opinion, that burnet is a valuable acquisition to husbandry; but as to the *general* and undistinguishing assertions in its favour, he thinks them no more to be regarded than the prejudice of those who insist, that no cattle will eat it. The fact with him has been this:—For hay, he cannot recommend it; the quality is not comparable to common meadow hay, and the quantity by no means an object of importance. By way of pasture for horses, cows and sheep, it is excellent; quite in the same stile as natural grass fields; with this superiority, that the butter made from it has a more pleasant flavour, and in respect to earliness in the spring, it is ready for sheep before any other grass: In general, it has a good bite the beginning of *March*, if it is fed down close in *October.*———That the sowing land with burnet is a very good way to lay it for a constant pasture; and that it mixes extremely well with white clover, with ray-grass, or with natural grass.

I cannot conclude this article without observing, that Mr. *Searancke* has cultivated burnet with unusual spirit; and has given a very clear and impartial account of his success: Good husbandry is never more laudable than when all circumstances, adverse,

as

as well as favourable are related with such candour *.

From *Hatfield* quite to *Welwyn*, the soil continues a light gravel, but most of the occupiers possess some fields of stronger land, upon which they raise better wheat than on their gravels. About *Bishop*'s *Hatfield*, farms run in general from 70 and 80 *l.* to 140 *l.* a year rent, about 12 *s.* at an average. Their course of crops is in general,

1. Fallow
2. Wheat
3. Pease or oats
4. Fallow
5. Turnips
6. Barley,

which is very good. For wheat they plough four times, sow two bushels and an

---

* HATFIELD HOUSE, the seat of the Earl of *Salisbury*, is situated in a very beautiful park close to the town of *Hatfield*. The variety of ground is fine, and the prospects rich and extensive. The house, which is very capacious, is in the stile of the age of *Elizabeth*; and conveys very strongly from its magnitude and a certain air of grandeur, the idea of an ancient and considerable family: It tells the spectator very forcibly, *Here does not reside a family of yesterday.*

Many of the rooms are large, and well proportioned. The following are those I was shewed; they are minuted in the order I viewed them.

The chapel; the glass of the windows finely painted; here are several pictures, much damaged

an half of feed, and reap on a medium 25 bushels. For barley they plough their turnip land generally but once, unless the soil is not in good order, in which case they give two stirrings, sow four bushels, and gain about four quarters. For oats they plough but once, sow four bushels, and get four quarters. The practice of giving but one earth for this or any other grain, ought ever to be condemned. For pease also but once, sow the same quantity and gain about 20 bushels. Beans they very seldom sow. For turnips they stir three times, hoe once, and feed off with
sheep;

---

maged by the damps; some of which seem to display the hand of a master.

Mary and Elizabeth. *Mary*'s attitude and attention are well represented; and *Elizabeth*'s face not inexpressively done.

Christ teaching among the Doctors. The head of the old man in blue drapery is executed in a great stile.

The baptism in the river Jordan. Our Saviour's hands very well done. The figures and the attitude of *Christ* in this piece reminds me of *Albano*'s famous picture at *Houghton*.

The hall 30 by 55, is a good room, but irregular, paved with black and white marble.

In the parlour 36 by 27.

Lord Cranbourn. A portrait touched with great freedom and spirit; the hands, face, and hair are fine.

Sir

sheep; very often sell them to the sheep graziers, the price at an average of years about 50 s. an acre. Particulars of one farm, I heard of, as follows:

150	Acres in all	100	Sheep
120	Ditto arable	4	Servants
30	Grass	2	Labourers
£.120	Rent	20	Acres of wheat
6	Horses	30	Spring corn
5	Cows	31	Turnips

LABOUR.

In harvest, 36 to 38 s. a month and board.
In hay time, 9 s. a week.
In winter, 1 s. and small beer.
Reaping, 5 s. *per* acre.
Mowing,

Sir P. Lely. *Mary in the sepulchre after the resurrection* There is something pleasing in the diffusion of light—in the attitudes— and the angel's drapery.

Cleopatra. What subject so unpleasing as beauty in pain! *Venus* gay and voluptuous, drawn in the car of the Loves;—or appearing in all the grace of motion to *Æneas*, are the painter's subjects;——not the same goddess lamenting over the dead body of *Adonis.* This *Cleopatra* is admirably executed; there is a mellowness in the colouring of the flesh,—a warmness in the tints, extremely expressive.

In

Mowing corn, 1 s. and 1 s. 2 d.
Mowing grass, 2 s. 6 d.
Hoeing turnips, 4 s. and small beer, before harvest; 5 s. in harvest.

IMPLEMENTS.

A cart, 13 l. complete with broad wheels.
A plough, from 3 l. to 4 l.
A pair of harrows, from 1 l. 10 s. to 3 l.

PROVISIONS, &c.

Beef, *per lb.* - 4 d.	Bread, - 2 d.
Mutton, - 4	Candles, - 8
Veal, - 4½	Soap, - 8
Butter, - 7	

Labourers

In the organ-room 28 by 22.
Dutchess of Cleveland. Fine; but the fixed formality, and demureness of the countenance destructive of all grace and elegance.
In the drawing-room 24 by 22. Lord and Lady *Thanet*, two portraits; good.
In the waiting-room 30 by 24, is a curious ebony cabinet. This room opens into a bed-chamber 22 by 20. And that into a closet where is a piece by *Holbein*, representing a masquerade given by *Henry* VIII. in honour of *Anne Boleyn.* It contains many figures, and has some curious attitudes.
In the King's dining-room 60 by 30. Symbolical portrait of Queen *Elizabeth.* In one hand is a snake, in the other a rainbow;

and

Labourers houfe-rent from 50 s. to 3 l.
Wear of their tools *per annum*, 25 s.
Their firing, 40 s. *per annum.*

Sir *Penyftone Lambe*'s park at *Brocket-hall* is extremely well worth feeing: It contains a fine variety of ground, many hills that command noble profpects, and winding hollows very picturefque; the water is large, much of it finely traced and of a beautiful colour: In a word, it is one of the beft fituations in *Hertfordfhire.*

Around *Stevenage*, hufbandry varies fomething with the foil, for in that neighbourhood there is a great deal of cold clay land: The farms are of all fizes, from 50 l. to 700 l. Land in general lets from 8 to 10 s.

---

and the drapery nothing but eyes and ears, defigned to give us an idea of her cunning, her vigilance, and the extent of her empire. Had *Apelles* given an idea of the fortitude, the invincible courage, and daring ambition of *Alexander* only by the fymbols of his picture, the hero of the painter would not have been called *The Inimitable.* Fortitude and heroic conitancy might have fhined in the countenance of *Elizabeth*, as well as meaner virtues in the hem of her garments. —The hands are delicately executed.

In the drawing-room 40 by 20, is a good portrait of the prefent Lord's grandmother; after this come two bed-chambers of 24 by 23, and fome other rooms: Then the

Vol I. C Gallery

10 s. *per* acre; their course of crops with some variations,

1. Fallow
2. Wheat
3. Pease or oats,

and in light lands it goes on,

4. Turnips
5. Barley

They plough four times for wheat; sow two bushels and an half, and reap on a medium 23 bushels: For barley they stir three times, sow four bushels, and gain in return 4½ quarters. For oats they chuse

to

Gallery 105 by 20. Here are several pictures: Among others,

Rubens. *The Last Supper*; but more like a banquet of *Vulcan*.

Bassan. *Abraham and Lot.* Cattle piece; in his rough manner.

Virgin and Child; with a rabbit introduced: It seems to be taken from *Correggio*; the attitude excellent.

Raphael. *Petrarch's Laura*: Very fine finishing; but not the *Laura* of *Petrarch's* poetry.

Bassan. *Christ praying*: In the rough stile: the lights thrown remarkably strong.

A Ruin. Very finely executed.

Abraham's Head. Sketched in a very noble stile.

—— In this room is a table inlaid with marble, pebbles, granate, &c. curious.

In the room over the kitchen.

Charles XII. A portrait. Spirited; the same as in the picture gallery at *Oxford.*

Holy

to plough twice, but cannot always; sow four bushels, and the mean produce they reckon the same as that of barley. For pease they stir once or twice, as it happens; sow 2¼ bushels of seed and gain from 5 to 30 bushels in return. They give two earths for beans; sow them in every furrow after the plough, about 2¼ bushels per acre, never hoe them, and the crop upon an average about 20 bushels. For turnips three or four ploughings are given; hoe them always once, and sometimes twice; feed them off with sheep; and the large farmers, some with black *Scotch* cattle; and reckon the average of crops at

---

Holy Family. Something in the stile of many of *Raphael*'s pieces. It appears to me to be incomparably fine, though an unequal piece. The child is executed with great spirit; his countenance is (like the children of painting) animated; his attitude spirited, his thighs well foreshortened, and the colouring excellent; there is a mellowness in the tints that is fine. The face of the virgin is insipidity itself, as is usual, and not badly adapted to the subject in general. The secondary figures are mean, and the draperies (especially the virgin's) in poor stile.

From the leads of the house, the park and the surrounding country are seen to great advantage; nor will you often see a richer view.

2*l.* 2*s.*

2 *l.* 2 *s.* The product of a cow they lay at 5 *l.* They always use four horses in a plough with two men, and do an acre in a day. The most capital farm in the neighbourhood is Mr. *Whittington*'s, the keeper of the *Swan Inn* at *Stevenage:* the particulars as follow:

1200	Acres in all	90 Turnips
1000	Ditto arable	40 Horses
200	Grass	22 Cows
£.700	Rent	28 Fatting Beasts
150	Acres of wheat annually	800 Sheep
		8 Servants
400	Of spring corn	25 Labourers

Mr. *Whittington* sows a good deal of sainfoine, with barley, after a clean turnip fallow; he finds it lasts from 6 to 8 and 10 years, but after that time he ploughs it up again. This husbandry ought in general to be imitated on the proper soils. I cannot dismiss these particulars without remarking, that I rode over a considerable part of his farm, and not only found his crops very good, but clean, and all his land to lie in a truly husband-like manner.

LABOUR.

In harvest, 35 *s.* and board.
In hay-time, 9 *s.* a week and small beer.
In winter, 1 *s.* a day and ditto.
Reaping wheat, 5 *s.* per acre.

Mowing

Mowing corn, 1 s. 6 d.
——— grafs, 2 s.
Hoeing turnips, 4 s. and 4 s. 6 d.

IMPLEMENTS.

A waggon, 20 l.
A cart, 8 l. to 9 l.
A plough, 5 l.
A pair of harrows, 1 l. 10 s.

PROVISIONS.

Beef, per *lb.*	$3\frac{1}{2}$ d.	Cheefe, -	$3\frac{1}{2}$ d.
Mutton, -	4	Bread, -	2
Veal, -	4	Candles, -	$7\frac{1}{2}$
Butter, -	7	Soap, -	7

Labourers houferent, the medium 2 l. per annum.
Wear of ditto's tools, 1 l. 1 s.

 Firing cofts them but little; break hedges, and fteal moft of it.

 From *Stevenage* I took the road to *Hitchin*, and from thence to *Luton*; in all, twelve as villainous miles as any creature can ever fear travelling, the roads are fo execrably bad. At *Offley* I ftopped for intelligence, and found their hufbandry to vary in feveral particulars from that of *Stevenage*. The foil is a chalky clay; the under ftratum pure chalk ftone; they call it white land. The farms feldom reach more than 140 *l.* a year. The rents run about 5 *s.* an acre since they were inclosed, but before used never to be above 1 *s.* in several farms. Their course of crops

1. Fallow
2. Barley
3. Pease and Oats
4. Turnips
5. Barley

For wheat they plough three times, sow 2½ bushels of seed, and reap about 15 bushels at a medium. For barley they stir three times, sow four bushels, and reap on an average three quarters. They give for oats but one ploughing, sow four bushels, and reap 2½ quarters. They plough but once also for pease, sow four bushels, and gain from 10 to 24 bushels in return. They sow a great many turnips, plough three times, hoe them but once, and reckon the value *per* acre from 35 *s.* to 3 *l.* They feed them all off with sheep. They never plough without four horses and two men, and do but an acre a day; this terrible custom, which is such a bane to the profit of husbandry, cannot be too much condemned; for the whole expence (on comparrison with the common custom) of tillage, might be saved by the farmer, if he would adopt the rational method of tilling with a pair of horses, and one man to hold the plough and drive at the same time. ⸺The product of a cow is reckoned here at 4 *l.* 10 *s.* All these products you will undoubtedly

undoubtedly remark, bear no proportion to the rent of 5 s. which is evidently a favoured one, or dependant on some circumstances unrelated to me. The soil admits not any expensive improvements by marle, &c. The particulars of a farm were

300	Acres in all	£. 70	Rent
280	Arable	6	Horses
20	Grafs	6	Cows
50	Of Wheat	220	Sheep
100	Of spring corn	5	Servants
30	Of turnips	4	Labourers

The husbandry of *Sainfoine* on such of the chalks as are dry, undoubtedly deserves attention in this neighbourhood.

LABOUR.

In winter, 1 s. a day.
In hay time, 1 s. and board.
In harvest, 2 l. a month and board.
Reaping *per* acre, 5 s.
Mowing corn, 1 s. 6 d.
——————Grafs, 2 s.
Hoeing turnips, 4 s. and a quart of ale *per* day.

IMPLEMENTS.

A waggon, 17 l. to 20 l.
A cart, 9 l.
A wheel-plough, 4 l. to 5 l.

A foot

A foot ditto, from 30 s. to 40 s.
A pair harrows, 1 l. 15 s.
A barley roller, 1 l. 1 s.

PROVISIONS, &c.

Bread, near 2 d. per lb.		Mutton, -	4 d.
Butter, -	7	Pork, -	4
Cheese, -	3½	Candles, -	7
Beef, -	4	Soap, -	7
Veal, -	3½		

Labourers house rent, from 35 s. to 50 s. a year.
Wear of their tools, 30 s.
Their hiring (if they buy) 30 s.

If the Earl of *Bute*'s park at *Luton Hoo* was not an inducement, there certainly could be none to visit that town: Notwithstanding the wretched roads I was forced to crawl through, yet the beauties of the hill and dale, wood and water in that park, made ample amends. We entered through the lodge from the town of *Luton*, and drove along the banks of the river, which was naturally a trifling stream, but is now forming, and is made further on, the finest water I have any where seen: the plantations on the top of the of the hills to the right as we entered, are very beautiful; on the left, the winding hollow, which is prettily diversified with scattered trees, is nobly traced for continuing the water; and is a

spot

spot wonderfully capable. Where the lake is finished, which is just before you come to the island, the view is very fine; the stream bends in a noble manner; is seen a long way without wanting irregularity, and from its breadth has a magnificent appearance. The island is large, has many full-grown trees upon it, with young plantations, and adds much to the beauty of the scene. The road winds among some scattered trees towards the right, the river appearing through them in a pleasing manner; there are many very fine beeches as you advance up to the house, from the dark shade of which the water is seen at a distance very advantageously. When you come near the house (which I should remark is now rebuilding upon a more extensive plan) turning to the right, a gravel road leads down to the water; it passes through several clumps of beech and other trees, through the openings of which the opposite hills are viewed in a pleasing stile; at the bottom of these hills the water appears; it is about a quarter of a mile broad, forming a fine bend; two boats, and a sloop with sails and flying colours lie at anchor here, but are by no means equal to the size of the water: Turning a little to the right, the bridge fronts you; it is of wood, and though unornamented, is light, and has here a good effect. A little

little further is the cascade, which yet is but a *capability*; when a little improved, and catched from a proper point of view, it will add to the variety of the scene.

Returning from the water, you take a different road, which leads through a pleasing wood, and gives you a view of the monumental pillar which is seen among the trees in a picturesque manner. It is a plain one of the *Tuscan* order, on a square pedestal, upon which is the following inscription:

In Memory of

Mr. FRANCIS NAPIER.

Upon the top is an urn; and although it is quite unornamented, this pillar is peculiarly beautiful; from the road in the valley it appears to great advantage, with that beautiful simplicity which results alone from an harmony of proportion: The urn rests on it with a lightness that is pleasing. The view from hence is good; the breaks in the woods are fine, and the hollow dales, grouped with beeches, are perfectly rural.

From *Luton* we crossed the country through very bad roads to *Dunstable*; the soil continuing a gravelly loam, and the culture pretty good: At that place is a manufacture of basket-work, which they have carried to a great perfection of neatness, and make of hats, boxes, baskets, &c. a large quantity annually; but not a great number of hands are employed. From this town to *Wooburn,* the soil is various; chalk, clay, loam and sand. At *Houghton* it is chalk on the high grounds, and a black clay in the low lands. The farms are in size from 50 *l.* to 300 *l.* a year; land lets about 14 *s.* an acre: Their course in general is,

1. Fallow
2. Wheat
3. Pease and beans, or oats,
4. Turnips
5. Barley

They plough three times for wheat, sow two bushels, and reap upon a medium about 15 bushels. For barley they plough twice, sow three bushels of seed, and reckon 23 a middling crop. They likewise stir twice for oats, sow 2½ bushels, which is very little, and get on an average 3¼ quarters in return; 24 bushels a middling crop. For pease and beans mixed they plough twice, sow three bushels, and get on an average 32 in return. When beans alone, they stir twice, sow some broad cast, and some after the plough; 2½ bushels *per* acre, but never hoe; twenty-five bushels the medium produce. They give two tilths for turnips, hoe them twice, and always feed off with sheep. So few for this crop cannot be too much condemned. They

plough

plough their land with three horses at length, and use a driver; do an acre and half a day, in light work. The particulars of a farm as follows:

300 Acres in all	60 Sheep
£. 200 Rent	9 Servants
9 Horses	3 Labourers
12 Cows	

PROVISIONS, &c.

Beef, - $3\frac{1}{2}$ d. per lb.	Pork, - 4 d.
Mutton, 4	Bread, - $1\frac{1}{2}$
Veal, - 4	Cheese, 4

Labourers house rent, 2 *l*.
Wear and tear of their tools, 12 *s*.
Their firing, 2 *l*. 10 *s*.

LABOUR.

In harvest, 40 *s*. a month board and lodging.
In hay time, 6 *s*. a week and board.
In winter, 6 *s*. a week and small beer.
Reaping *per* acre, 5 *s*. and 6 *s*.
Hoeing turnips, 4 *s*. and 5 *s*.

I found many variations before I reached *Milton* in the way to *Wooburn*; at that place and neighbourhood the soil is a mixture of clay and gravel; farms are in general much smaller than before, from 50 *l*. to 100 *l*. a year; land lets at an average of about 10 *s*. the arable; and from 15 to 20 the grass grafs. They plough four times for wheat, fow two bufhels *per* acre, and reap at a medium 20 bufhels. For barley alfo four times, fow two bufhels, and reckon three quarters a middling crop. They fow but few oats; when they do, they plough but once, fow four bufhels, and reckon four quarters a middling crop. For peafe and beans mixed they ftir but once, fow four bufhels, and gain in return on an average three quarters. When they fow beans alone they plough but once, fow them broad caft, three or four bufhels *per* acre, hoe them fometimes, but oftener turn their fheep in to feed off the weeds. For turnips they ftir thrice, hoe once, and feed off with fheep. They ufe four or five horfes in a plough at length, with a driver, but do feldom more than an acre in a day.——— This execrable cuftom is pernicious to the profit of farming: It is ftrange the race of landlords are not vigorous in their endeavours to root out fuch miftaken practices. They reckon the product of a cow at 4 *l*. The following are the particulars of a farm here:

150	Acres	100	Sheep
120	Arable	4	Servants
30	Grafs	2	Labourers
£.90	Rent	30	Acres of wheat
9	Horfes	30	Barley, &c.
10	Cows	40	Beans and peafe.

LABOUR.

LABOUR.

In harvest, 35 s. a month and board and carriage of a load of wood.
In hay time, 1 s. 4 d. a day, and small beer.
In winter, 10 d. a day, and small beer.
Reaping wheat, 3 s. to 4 s. 6 d.
Mowing grass, 1 s. 4 d. and 1 s. 6 d.

PROVISIONS, &c.

Bread,	$1\frac{1}{2}$ d. per lb.	Mutton,	$3\frac{1}{2}$ d.
Butter,	7	Pork,	4
Cheese,	4	Candles,	7
Beef,	$3\frac{1}{2}$	Soap,	7

Labourers house rent, 30 s.
Wear of their tools, 6 s.
Firing, 25 s.

IMPLEMENTS.

A waggon, 20 l.   A cart, 11 l.

I have not failed on all opportunities of making many enquiries respecting the general state of the *parishes* I passed through, but was never able until this time to gain the least intelligence. The following particulars of *Milton* are worth minuting; I should however remark that neither in this case or any other, do I obtain answers to *all* my queries, so that a complete description is not to be expected; but I believe the

the following circumstances pretty accurate; in the number of acres perhaps it is not *absolutely* exact *.

1000 Acres	100 Cows
7 Farms	650 Sheep
£. 650 Rent	25 Labourers.
50 Horses	

The Duke of *Bedford* maintains a large stock of cattle in the summer to keep down grass in his park, he found it difficult to keep them in the winter; this occasioned his practising the turnip husbandry upon a large extent of land; and also to raise great quan-

---

* *Wooburn* Abbey, the noble seat of his Grace the Duke of *Bedford*, is in all respects well worth the view of the curious traveller. The house forms a large quadrangle, with a handsome court in the center; the front to the bason is the best. Behind are two large quadrangles of offices distinct from the house, which are very beautiful, plain, and simple, but extremely proper for the destination; they are built like the house, of white stone; in the center of their principal front is a small dome rising over a porticoed center, supported by *Tuscan* pillars, which have a very good effect. Upon the whole, these detached offices appear in a more judicious state, than any I remember to have seen.

In the house you enter, first the hall, which though not a well-proportioned or elegant room, is handsome. It is 40 by 37 and 15 high,

quantities of carrots, which the sandy parts of his farm are admirably adapted for, being of a deep staple and the sand a rich one; it is to be regretted that the neighbouring farmers do not follow so excellent an example.

In the town of *Wooburn*, I had the satisfaction of meeting with a curiosity in agriculture, a most accurate experiment ground, in which many kinds of grasses are tried with a neatness that must please every spectator. Mr. *Bramstone* is the owner, and certainly,

---

high, the cieling supported by eight pillars. The chimnies bas relieves in white stone.

The green drawing room is 22 by 35, between the windows are fine glasses and two very noble slabs of *Egyptian* marble. The chimney-piece is of white marble polished. Here are three large pictures; the plague of *Egypt*, dark; *David* and *Abigail*, ditto; as are the colouring and general expression. Two large landscapes, fine.

The decker worked room 25 by 20: Nothing can be more pleasing than this bed of decker work lined with green silk; the work is exquisite, and the representation of the birds and beasts in it admirable. The chimney-piece very elegant; the scrol of polished white marble in a light taste.

The dining room 35 by 22, a very noble room; the chimney-piece a festoon of flowers carved in white marble, and finely polished. In this room

certainly, from the variety of his trials, must be very underſtanding in the nature of ſeparated graſſes, and very attentive to their culture. This gentleman was not himſelf at home, but I was very civilly received by his brother, who ſhewed me all the experiments, and obligingly reſolved my enquiries.

His prickly-edged *Medica* appears to me a great curioſity: It is an annual, as Mr. *Bramſtone* apprehends, but the luxuriance of its growth exceeds every thing I ever ſaw: two or three plants which ſtand ſingle, ſpread an extent of ſhoots ſix feet diameter,
as

---

room are four large pictures of the battles of *Alexander*. The repaſt is not a diſagreeable one, were the heroes grouped with more taſte, but they ſit at as ſquare a table as any *Dutch* painter could ever have deſigned. The oppoſite piece to it is the beſt; the groupe of three horſemen with a large rock in the back ground is fine; the fire and ſpirit of the horſes well done.

In the yellow drawing room are two portraits by *Reynolds*, one the late Marquis of *Taviſtock*; the other the preſent Ducheſs of *Marlborough*; the latter a very fine one. The chimney-piece is elegant and the pier-glaſs frame finely carved, of plated ſilver: Here is alſo a portrait of the preſent Duke of *Bedford*.

The coffee room 30 by 20; in this room remember to obſerve a ſmall portrait of

as I measured myself; the leaf and yellow blossom give it the appearance of a trefoil rather than a lucerne, as does its trailing shoots, none of them being upright. I cannot but apprehend that this plant might be applied to most excellent purposes in common, by attentive husbandry, in which case, it should certainly be sown very thin, and the plants set out at five or six foot distance from each other with hand hoes; but if it is an annual, nothing of this sort can ever answer.

The purple fescue appears very thick and fine; but Mr. *Bramstone*, who has tried the

---

Francis Earl of *Bedford*, which is exceedingly fine; the face and hands admirably painted.

The grotto is pretty *of its kind*; the rusticks are well cut, but the figures of bas reliefs in shells are strangely incongruous with the idea of a grot. The china jars noble.

The billiard room is hung with very fine tapestry, designed from *Raphael*'s cartoons.

The Duchess's dressing room, hung with embossed work on white paper, which has a very pleasing effect: The chimney-piece a carved scroll in wood, the marble black, and veined: The pier-glass large, and the frame elegant; over the chimney Lady Ossory by *Hudson*. The chairs and sofas painted ta...ta.

The *French* bed-chamber, 26 by 22; the bed and hangings a very rich belmozeen.
The

the folding of two or three sheep upon most of his grasses, finds that they do not at all affect this fescue.

The barren broom grass was two feet high, but neither fine nor thick.

The annual dwarf poa, which I remember Mr. *Rocque* praised much for lawns, is a shabby, beggarly plant: Mr. *Bramstone* has a small plat of it, which is quite ragged, though fed off with sheep.

The great oat; two feet high, but coarse and thin.

The

The chimney-piece light and beautiful; the cornice, festoons of gilt carving on a white ground; and the ceiling the same on a lead ground; the pier-glass and frame, and the frame of the landscape over the chimney pleasing.

The dressing-room of the same dimensions, is likewise hung with the same silk, the ceiling and cornice richly ornamented with scrolls of gilding on a white ground: The chimney-piece all of white marble polished, but not light. The doors, door-cases, and window-shutters, &c. all ornamented like the ceiling, &c. in white and gold. In this room, remember to observe four very large blue and white china jars; the two by the windows are prodigiously fine.

The state bed-chamber is most magnificently furnished. It is 30 by 22, the bed and hangings of very rich blue damask; the ceiling ornamented in compartments of rich gilding

The bird grafs, very fine and thick, and much affected by sheep; this is certainly an excellent grafs.

The meadow fox-tail, coarse, but very early; sheep in the spring of the year eat it greedily.

Crested dog's-tail, made no great appearance, but is well affected by sheep.

Of lucerne, Mr. *Bramstone* has several experiments; broad-cast, drilled at 18 inches asunder, and transplanted at two feet; all two years old, and cut twice this year before I viewed them: I found the drilled above two feet high, and very fine

---

on a white ground. The chimney-piece of marble polished, and the carved and gilt ornaments around the landscape over it in a beautiful taste: The toilette is all of very handsome *Dresden* work, the glass frame, and boxes of gold. An India cabinet on each side of gold japan, with coloured china jars exquisitely fine.

The dressing room 21 by 20, hung with green damask; the chimney-piece very handsome; the pier-glass fine.

The drawing room exceedingly elegant, 33 by 22; the ceiling a mosaic pattern of rich carving on a white ground; the cornice of the chimney-piece supported by double pillars of very fine *Siena* marble. The pier-glasses very large, and in one plate; under them noble slabs of *Siena*. In this room are several excellent paintings; particularly a landscape

fine and thick. The transplanted was 18 inches high, but very thin; it is, however, by no means in perfection yet. The broad-cast eight inches high, thick and fine; cleaned by a strong iron rake instead of harrowing: In respect to the comparison, Mr. *Bramstone* seems to think the broad-cast yields most in quantity, but as the others were so much forwarder, they probably will get a cutting upon it, in which case the drilled must certainly exceed it: No conclusions, he observed, could be drawn from the transplanted, as it was visibly yet

in

---

landscape by *Claude Loraine*, representing a ship partly appearing from behind a building; amazingly beautiful, the diffusion of light, the general brilliancy and harmony of the whole, admirable.

A holy family; very fine, the turn of the boy's head inimitable.

Virgin and child; the air of the Virgin's head, and her attitude most sweetly elegant and expressive.

A *Magdalen*; fine.

The inside of a church; the minute expression of the architecture, and the rays of light, well done.

A rock, with the broken branches of trees hanging from its clefts; (I apprehend by *Salvator*) the expression very noble: The romantic wildness of the scene most excellently caught.

D 3 *A holy*

in an imperfect state; but he apprehended it would last longer than any of them; a remark which is very probable, when the rows are at the distance of three feet four inches, according to the directions of the Rev. Mr. *Harte*, in his *Essays on Husbandry*; but I question whether, at an equal distance, it will last longer than the drilled. Mr. *Bramstone*'s soil is a black rich sand, very light, and of a good depth; carrots would thrive incomparably in it.

From *Wooburn* to *Newport Pagnell*, the soil has a great variety; for some miles it is quite a light sand, and then a gravel

with

A holy family; the child standing in the cradle; very pleasing.

Joseph interpreting the dreams of Pharaoh, by *Rembrandt*; most admirable; in a greater stile than common with this master.

Rembrandt, by himself; inimitable.

Her Grace presenting Lady Carolina to Minerva, by *Hamilton*; a very large picture, and some of the figures not inelegantly done.

The saloon 35 by 22, and of a good height; it is most magnificently fitted up, and elegantly furnished; the ceiling of gilt carving on white; the door-case carved and gilt, the cornices supported by *Corinthian* pillars in a light and pleasing stile; the chimney-piece of white marble beautifully polished. In the center hangs a magnificent

gilt

with some light loams: About *Wanden* the soil is chiefly sand, but few of their farms are very large, they run from 30 *l.* to 200 *l.* a year; their field land lets at an average for about 7 *s.* 6 *d.* an acre, and their inclosures from 10 *s.* to 12 *s.* Their course of crop is,

1. Fallow
2. Wheat or barley
3. Beans and pease
   And

1. Fallow
2. Rye
3. Turnips
4. Barley

They plow four times for wheat, sow tow bushels an acre, and reap on a medium three quarters. For barley they stir four times,

---

gilt lustre. Remember to observe the picture, representing the last supper; it is fine. The drawing in a free and bold stile.

A piece of angels; fine.

Dining room 40 by 22; the ceiling white and gold; the chimney-piece pleasing; over it a landscape, a waterfall, which has merit.

Second drawing room 20 square; this, like the rest, is well fitted up; and among other pictures, contains

Two landscapes, *morning and evening*; by *Moret*; capital.

Lyons, by *Rubens*; fine.

Two battles, like *Porgognone*.

The picture gallery in three divisions 100 by 15, ornamented by a vast number of excellent portraits of the *Russel* family: Among others, remark that of the Countess of *Somer-*

times, sow four bushels, and get in return about three quarters. For oats they plough but once, sow four bushels, and reap at an average three quarters. For pease and beans mixed they likewise plough but once, sow four bushels, their crop not above 2¼ quarters. They give but one tilth for beans alone, sow them broad-cast, never hoe them, but turn in sheep to feed off the weeds, and reckon three quarters a middling crop. This is an execrable custom, and ought to be exploded by all landlords of the country. For turnips they stir three or four times, hoe them twice, reckon the value

---

set, the face and hands very finely done; also *William* Earl of *Bedford* and Lady *Catharine Brook*, excellent. The ornaments of this room are all carving painted white: There are four statues, among them a *Venus* of *Medicis*, but not pleasing; and a *Venus* plucking the thorn out of her foot, but with none of that expression of pain in her countenance which is so fine in the antique at *Wilton*. *Wooburn* park is 10 miles around, and contains variety of hill and dale, with woods of noble oaks; we drove from the house through them towards the south, and looked up the great glade which is cut through the park for several miles, and catches at the end of it a *Chinese* temple; then winding through the woods we came to the Duchess's shrubbery, containing 16 acres of

value at about 40 s. an acre, and feed them off with sheep alone. They use four or five horses at length in their ploughs, and yet do no more than an acre a day. The reader will not forget the soil being sandy, the requisite team is certainly nearer a single jackass than five horses. This miserable management cannot be too much condemned. The product of a cow they lay at near 4 *l.* They let their dairies at 3 *l.* a head. The particulars I gained of a farm are,

100 Acres
£. 60 Rent
8 Horses
12 Cows
200 Sheep (a walk)
2 Servants
3 Labourers

of land beautifully laid out in the modern taste, with many most glorious oaks in it. From thence we advanced to the hill at the north end, from which is a vast prospect into *Buckinghamshire*, *Hertfordshire*, and *Bedfordshire*; turning down the hill to the left, the riding leads to the evergreen plantation of above 200 acres of land, which thirty years ago was a barren rabbit warren, but now a close winter's ride, on a dry soil, with all sorts of evergreens of a growth. About the middle on the left hand, is an handsome temple, retired and pleasing: At the end of this plantation, we came to the lower water, which is about ten acres, and in the center, an island with a very elegant and light *Chinese* temple, large enough for thirty people

PROVISIONS, &c.

Bread,	-	1¼ d.	Veal,	-	3 d.
Cheese,	-	4	Pork,	-	3½
Butter,	-	7	Candles,	-	7
Beef	-	3½	Soap	-	6½
Mutton,		4			

Labourers house rent, *per annum*, 30 s. to 50 s.

Wear of their tools, 15 s.

Their firing they get off the common.

---

to dine in; and in the adjoining wood is a kitchen, &c. for making ready the repasts his Grace takes in the temple. In the front of the house is a large bason of water with several handsome boats; formerly a large yacht swam in it, but rotting, it has not been rebuilt.

This park, which is one of the largest in the kingdom, contains 3500 acres of a great variety of soils, from a light sand to a rich loam, which yields grass good enough to fat large beasts: It is all walled in; was there a greater variety of water, it would be much more beautiful, but the nature of the soil in the low parts makes that acquisition very difficult; but what might be much easier gained, are buildings scattered about it, which would give a pleasing variety to the ridings, and for want of which, most of them are very melancholy.

LABOUR,

LABOUR.

In harvest, 35 s. the month and board.
In hay time, 1 s. a day and victuals.
In winter, from 8 d. to 1 s. a day, and no beer.
Reaping wheat, 5 s. 6 d.
Mowing corn, 1 s. 6 d.
—— Grafs, 2 s. and 2 s. 6 d.

The soil and management both changed much for the better about *Broughton*: The former is there various, but much of it very excellent. Farms are from 100 *l.* in general to 200 *l.* a year; rents about 1 *l.* an acre.

1. Fallow
2. Wheat
3. Beans
4. Turnips
5. Barley
6. Clover

This is an excellent course: For wheat they stir three or four times, sow two bushels, and reap from 20 to 30. They give the same tillage for barley when on a fallow which they manage excellently, for they throw their fields on to the ridge to lie dry in the winter, and then plough and sow early in the spring. Their quantity of seed is five bushels, and their mean crop as many quarters. For oats they plough but once, sow five bushels, and gain in return $4\frac{1}{2}$ quarters: They plough but once also for the mixture of peafe and beans, sow four bushels, and reap $2\frac{1}{2}$ quarters; nor

four

do they give more earths for beans alone, sow them generally broad cast, but sometimes dibble them in, by which method they save near two bushels of seed; broadcast they sow six bushels, but never hoe them; before they blossom, they feed off the weeds with sheep; their crops are extremely various, sometimes none, and at others 40 bushels. For turnips they give four or five tilths, hoe once, and feed them all off with sheep; they generally lay all their manure upon the turnip fallow: They sow some clover, but seldom mow it, feed it with sheep; and mixed with a little ray-grafs, reckon that it will fat an ox in the spring of the year better than natural grasses. This is a circumstance that much deserves attention: Ray-grafs has of late been much exploded——but fashion should never exclude the consideration of all fair circumstances. The product of a cow they reckon at 4*l.* and in a kindly year like this, one acre of their pastures will keep one through the summer.

Like their neighbours, they continue in the absurd custom of three, four, and five horses in a plough at length, with a driver; use none but foot-ploughs, and do an acre a day.

LABOUR.

In harvest, 32 *s.* the month and board.
In hay time, 6 *s.* and board; 9 *s.* without.

In winter, 10 d. a day and small beer.
Reaping wheat, 4 s. to 6 s.
Mowing grass, 2 s.
Hoeing turnips, 5 s.

PROVISIONS, &c.

Beef,	4 d.	Butter,	6 d.
Mutton,	3¾	Cheese,	4
Bread,	1¾	Candles,	7

Labourers house rent 20 s. and keep in repair.
Wear of ditto's tools, 20 s.
Their firing, 50 s.

The following are the particulars of a farm in this neighbourhood:

140 Acres in all	30 Cows
20 Ditto arable	150 Sheep
120 Ditto grass	2 Servants
£.140 Rent	1 Labourer
4 Horses	

Of another:

200 Acres, all grass	80 Sheep
£.160 Rent	3 Servants
3 Horses	2 Labourers
30 Cows	

Of another:

200 Acres, all grass	80 Sheep
£.160 Rent	2 Servants
2 Horses	2 Labourers
20 Cows	

Of another:

200 Acres in all	60 Of arable

140 Grass   30 Oxen
£.180 Rent   400 Sheep
7 Horses   2 Servants
2 Cows   2 Labourers

These four farms compose the whole parish; consequently it contains

740 Acres   82 Cows
80 Of arable   710 Sheep
580 Of grass   9 Servants
£.640 Rent   8 Labourers
16 Horses

From *Newport Pagnel* I took the road to *Bedford*, if I may venture to call such a cursed string of hills and holes by the name of road; a causeway is here and there thrown up, but so high, and at the same time so very narrow, that it was at the peril of our necks we passed a waggon with a civil and careful driver. This is a pernicious and vile practice; it might be expected if thrown up at the expence of the farmers alone; but when found in *turnpikes*, deserves every unworthy epithet which frightened women or dislocated bones can possibly give rise to. The whole way to *Bedford*, I found immense quantities of beans; not a mile passed without several hundred acres. About *Astwick* their course is,

1. Fallow
2. Wheat and barley
3. Beans and pease, or oats.

For wheat they plough three times; sow two bushels, and reap on a medium 15 bushels. They give three stirrings for barley, sow four bushels, and reckon 3½ quarters a middling crop. For oats they plough but once, sow four bushels, and get on an average not above 2 and 2½ quarters. They give but one tilth for beans, sow them broad-cast, four bushels to an acre, never hoe them, but feed off the weeds with sheep. Clover they often sow over their wheat in the spring; generally mow it for hay twice, but seldom feed it.

LABOUR.

In harvest, 40 s. the month and board.
In hay time, 8 s. a week, no beer.
In winter, 8 d. and 9 d. a day.

IMPLEMENTS.

A waggon, 18 l.   A cart, 10 l.

About *Biddenham*, they have all sorts of soil, from very light loam and gravel to clay. Their farms run from 40 l. to 300 l. a year; the open fields let from 2 s. 6 d. to 3 s. 6 d. an acre; and the inclosures from 10 s. 6 d. to 12 s. The principal of their courses are,

1. Turnips
2. Barley
3. Clover and ray-grass. And

1. Fallow
2. Wheat
3. Pease and beans

For

For wheat they plough three times, sow two bushels, and reap on a medium $2\frac{1}{2}$ and 3 quarters. They give three earths for barley, sow four bushels, and reckon three quarters a middling crop: For oats, which is somewhat unusual, they stir twice or thrice, sow four bushels, and three quarters the mean produce. They plough but once for beans, sow two bushels broad-cast, never hoe them, but like their neighbours are slovens enough to trust to their flocks for the weeding of them; the average of crops is three quarters. For pease they likewise stir but once, sow two bushels and an half, and gain in return about two quarters and half.

LABOUR.

In harvest, 40 s. a month and board.
In hay time, 1 s. 4 d. a day for three weeks.
In winter, 4 s. 6 d. a week.

PROVISIONS, &c.

Beef, *per lb.*	4 d.	Butter, -	6 d.
Mutton, -	4	Bread, -	$1\frac{3}{4}$

The particulars of a farm, I enquired after were,

£.40 Rent	4 Cows
5 Horses	2 Servants

The vale of *Bedford*, which is a perfectly flat tract of land for some miles around

around the town, is very rich in soil and excellently managed, if I may judge by the noble crops I saw. The wheat, barley, and turnips, were very fine, and equal to any I have seen, and the beans, in point of height and thickness, made a fine appearance, but I doubt can never turn out equal to the other crops for want of hoeing: The practice through all this country of sowing three, four, and five bushels of beans to an acre, and not hoeing, must for ever exclude capital crops; that quantity of seed, which is more than double of what is requisite, only choaks the earth with straw so very thick, as not to admit the air to forward the production of the seed. In *Suffolk* and *Essex*, they sow only two bushels, and hoe half the plants up, and yet reap much greater crops than the farmers of this country, which, considering the soil of both, can only be owing to a great superiority of management.

The town of *Bedford* is noted for nothing but its lace manufactory, which employs above 500 women and girls. They make it of various sorts up to 25 *s.* a yard; women that are very good hands, earn 1 *s.* a day, but in common only 8 *d.* 9 *d.* and 10 *d.* Girls from eight to fifteen, earn 6 *d.* 8 *d.* 9 *d.* a day. This manufacture is of infinite use to the town, employing advantageously those who otherwise would have no employment at all.

Leaving *Bedford*, I took the road to *Northill*, it was for a few miles the *Bigglefwade* turnpike, but I was astonished to find after I left the turnpike, that the road continued a very fine causeway, of a good breadth and heighth, and very level and free from ruts; I could scarce believe myself upon a byeroad, which induced me to enquire: I found it was the excellent effect of several gentlemen attending much to the business; particularly —— *Howard*, Esq; of *Carrington*, who not only greatly assisted the parish in making a fine causeway through the village, but himself expended above fifty pounds in making one bad piece a good road: Highly deserving of praise are such instances, for had other gentlemen conducted themselves with half this spirit, turnpikes would have been rendered quite unnecessary: A striking contrast to this *by-road* is the *turnpike* between *Newport* and *Bedford*.

Having mentioned *Carrington*, I should not forget to remark, that that village is one of the neatest, best built, and most lively I have seen; most of the houses and cottages are new-built, all of them tiled, and many of brick, which, with white pales and little plantations, have a most pleasing effect. After I left *Carrington*, the road continued extremely good, until I got near *Northill*; owing to the fpirited attention of ―――― *Butcher*, Efq; but it degenerated much over a common, a little before *Northill**.

The parifh of *Sandy* near *Northill* is much noted for its gardens; there are above 150 acres of land occupied by many gardeners, who fupply the whole country, for many miles, with garden ftuff, even to *Hertford*. I examined their grounds with much attention, and inquired concerning the practice of a very fenfible gardener, refpecting two or three articles of their culture, which are, or ought to be the bufinefs of farmers in many fituations.

Their

---

* I would advife any traveller, who paffes through the county of *Bedford* to make *Northill* in their route, were it only for the fatisfaction of viewing two fmall pieces of painted glafs done by *J. Oliver* in 1660, belonging to the Rector, the Rev. Mr. *Maxey*. They are very fmall, but each has a fly, fo exquifitely painted as to exceed the power even of imagination to conceive; the wings are coloured on one fide, and the bodies on the other of the glafs, and are touched in fo lively and fpirited a manner, (efpecially one, which is fuperior to the other, that without fruit) that it is difficult to believe them but painting, and not life itfelf; the light appears through the body at the junction with the tail

Their soil is a rich black sand two or three feet deep. Carrots they sow about new *Lady Day,* upon ground dug one spit deep, hoe them very carefully three times; they do it by the day, and the three cost them from 20 to 30 *s.* an acre, as the crop happens to be; they set them out about eight or ten inches from plant to plant; and get, on a medium, 200 bushels upon an acre. I drew several roots and found them from one foot to 18 inches long. Parsnips they cultivate exactly in the same manner, but the product never equals that of carrots, by forty or fifty bushels. This point of comparison deserves attention, for parsnips have been more than once recommended as superior to carrots; but I apprehend they never will be found even equal. The prices of carrots vary from 1 *s.* to 4 *s.* a bushel, but the first is very low. Potatoes they plant at the same time; 20 bushels plant an acre, at the distance of about one foot every way; they hoe them three times, but not at all before they come up, which is practised in *Essex* about *Ilford.*

---

in the most inimitable manner, and the roundness of the fly, with the lightness of its claws, are represented in the boldest and fullest relief. In a word it is truly admirable: In the chancel of the church, is a very fine painted window in good preservation by the same master.

They reckon the midsummer dun sort to yield best; a middling crop is 250 bushels upon an acre; they always manure for them, either with dung or ashes, about 20 load, but ashes they prefer. This on a sandy soil is, I think, very extraordinary. The price varies from 1 s. 4 d. to 2 s. a bushel.

Of onions, they sow vast quantities;— the time, about a fortnight before *Lady Day*; they hoe and weed them always five times at the expence of four pounds an acre, set them out six inches asunder, and their crops rise to above 200 bushels, but their price from 16 d. (which is very low) to 2 s. They always manure for them with great care. These gardeners give from 40 s. to 5 l. rent per acre, for their land; it is, as I before observed, a rich loose black sand of a good depth, and very favourably protected from adverse winds by several considerable hills. It is a remarkable, and a very pleasing sight, to behold crops of onions, potatoes, *French* beans, and even whole fields of cucumbers, intermixed with crops of wheat, barley, turnips, &c.

It may not be unentertaining, to calculate the profit these gardeners make by the preceding crops, and first with carrots; the expences per acre we may suppose as follow:

Rent	£.3	0	0
Digging	1	0	0
Seed	0	8	0
Sowing	0	0	6
Raking	0	4	0
Hoeing	1	5	0
Digging up	0	10	0
	£.6	7	6

Produce.

200 bushels at 2 s.	20	0	0
Expences	6	7	6
Profit	13	12	6

POTATOES.

Expences.

Rent	3	0	0
Manuring	5	0	0
Digging	1	0	0
20 Bushels sets	1	13	6
Planting, &c.	0	10	0
Hoeing	1	0	0
Digging up	0	15	0
	12	1	6

Produce.

250 Bushels at 20 d.	20	16	0
Expences	12	18	6
Profit	7	17	6

ONIONS.

ONIONS.

Expences.

	£	s.	d.
Rent	3	0	0
Manuring	5	0	0
Digging and raking	1	5	0
Seed	0	15	0
Sowing and raking	0	6	0
Weeding and hoeing	4	0	0
Taking up	0	5	0
	14	11	0

Produce.

	£	s.	d.
200 Bushels at 20 d.	16	13	0
Expences	14	11	0
Profit	2	2	0

At this place, is to be seen a small field of lucerne belonging to Sir *Philip Molyneux*. It was sown broad-cast by itself last spring; the part of it that was uncut I found very thick and fine, about two feet high, but numerous weeds were among it, from which I conjecture, that the land either was not duly prepared by fallowing, or that the crop was not kept clean while young.

From *Sandy* to St. *Neot's* the country is chiefly open, and the crops not equal to those around *Bedford*: I would advise you, if accident should carry you to that town, to view a very beautiful little natural landscape,

landscape, which is seen in great perfection from Mr. *Cole*'s close, at the bottom of his garden; the river winds along at your feet; at one end is the bridge, through the center arch of which, houses are seen in a pleasing manner; on the other side, the stream is lost among the wood; in front are several meadows, which, though flat, are by no means disagreeable; some high trees vary the scene, among which a farm house appears just at the point you would place it; turning a little to the right the houses of the town are seen very prettily intermixed with trees, and the steeple rises from behind a fore ground of wood, which has a good effect. St. *Neot*'s is a clean, well-built town, has a good church ornamented with a handsome organ, and the river not only adds greatly to its beauty, but much enlivens it.

I took the road to *Kimbolton*, the country continuing in general open; about *Hale Weston*, the soil is a gravelly loam, with variations. The open fields let at 7 *s.* and 7 *s.* 6 *d.* per acre, and the inclosed pastures about 17 *s.* Hence we find a profit of 10 *s.* an acre from inclosing and laying to grass: Is it not astonishing that the landlords should allow any part of the country to remain open! The farms run from 40 *l.* to 200 *l.* a year. Their course of crops,

1. Fallow

1. Fallow   And 1. Turnips
2. Wheat   2. Barley
3. Pease, &c.   3. Pease, &c.

They plough four times for wheat, sow two bushels, and reap at a medium fifteen. For summertilth barley they stir four times, and twice the turnip land, sow four bushels, and reckon the mean produce at three quarters. They give but one earth for oats, sow four bushels, and get at an average two quarters. This produce is so low that the crop must unavoidably be a losing one. For pease they plough but once, sow four bushels, and reckon 12 bushels the mean produce. For beans they likewise stir but once, sow them broad-cast, four bushels to the acre, never hoe them, but sometimes hook out the rank weeds, and turn sheep in; fifteen bushels the medium. For turnips they give three earths, hoe them once; reckon the mean value per acre, at 35 s. and feed all off with sheep: They use from three to six horses in a plough at length; and do, after the breaking the fallow, five rood a day. The profit of a cow they reckon at 4 *l.* The particulars of a farm,

  660 Acres   20 Cows
   60 Grass   650 Sheep
  600 Arable   8 Servants
 £. 300 Rent   10 Labourers.
   20 Horses

PRO-

PROVISIONS, &c.

Bread, 1¾ d per lb.   Veal, 4 d.
Cheese, 4   Pork, 4
Butter, 7   Candles 7
Beef, 3¼   Soap, 7
Mutton, 4

Labourer's house rent from 20 s. to 30 s.
Wear of their tools, 20 s.
Firing, 30 s.

IMPLEMENTS.

A waggon, 20 l.
A cart, 12 l.
A roll, 15 s.

LABOUR.

In harvest, 36 s. to 40 s. the month and board
In hay-time, 1 s. 6 d. a day, and beer
In winter, 1 s. a day, and small beer
Reaping wheat, 5 s. to 7 s.
Mowing corn, 1 s.
———— grass, 1 s. 6 d. to 1 s. 8 d.
Hoeing turnips, 4 s. 6 d. to 5 s.
Ditching (the reparation) 4 d. a pole
Threshing wheat, 1 s. a load, or 5 bushels
———————— spring corn, 1 s. a quarter *.

From

---

* *Kimbolton* castle, the seat of his Grace the Duke of *Manchester*, is situated close to the town; it is a quadrangular building. The hall is 50 feet

From *Kimbolton* to *Thrapstone*, the country is in general open, very little inclosed besides their pastures; I should observe to you, that quite from *Newport Pagnel*, to *Thrapstone*, the soil is all ploughed into broad arched lands about a perch and half over, and a yard higher in the center than the furrows. This custom is a very good one, where the water is let clean clean out the furrows, but I have more than once, in winter seen such furrows two feet deep in water. About *Great Catworth*, the soil is very good, clay in general, but some gravelly loams. It lets, the arable for about

14 *s.*

---

50 feet long by 25 broad, and hung round with family portraits, some of which are very good. Out of it you enter on the right hand, the blue drawing-room, 35 by 20, over the chimney-piece hangs a fine picture of *Prometheus*, the horrible expression of which is very great. Between the windows are six small portraits, excellently done, particularly the man and woman in the middle; his face is very expressive, and the finishing in hers the same.

The yellow drawing-room 35 by 22, with a handsome glass lustre in the center: Here are,

A most admirable portrait of *Lord Holland*, with an attendant officer, and a page adjusting his sash; the heads and hands, the drapery and the relief of the figures are all fine.

A virgin and sleeping child. Strange attitude.

Virgin

14 *s.* an acre, and the grass 20 *s.* Farms, from 30 *l.* to 100 *l.* a year. Their course of crops,

1. Fallow
2. Wheat or barley
3. Beans, pease or oats.

They plough three times for wheat, sow two bushels, and reap about 2½ or three quarters. For barley they give the same tillage, sow four bushels, and reckon three quarters the mean produce. For oats they stir but once, sow four bushels, and gain, at an average, two quarters and a half. They sow but few pease, but when they

---

Virgin and child. Eyes very bad.

The saloon is 40 by 27; hung with crimson velvet; the pillars in two corners, I suppose, were necessary to the building, but they are handsome ones; the slabs are of various marbles in *Mosaic*; over the chimney, a picture of *Hector* and *Andromache*, the colours, attitudes and expression of which are by no means pleasing.——The state bed-chamber, 27 by 21, is hung with cut velvet, the pier glass and slab glasses from *Venice*; the border of the first is pretty. In the closet is a *Magdalen*; the expression of pain in her countenance, not amiss; the thought seems borrowed from Lord *Pembroke*'s *Venus.*——Through the staircase is a small room hung with very fine drawings after *Raphael* and *Julio Romano.*

The dining room is 30 by 27.

The library 24 square; the book-cases pretty.

do,

do, they plough but once, sow four bushels and reap on a medium two quarters. For beans they plough likewise but once, sow all broad-cast, four bushels, never hoe, but sometimes feed the weeds off with sheep. They never sow turnips: In their ploughs which are all foot ones, they use from four to eight horses, and after one or two earths, do an acre and half a day. All their dung they lay on their barley lands, but seldom mix it with earth. The particulars of a farm were,

  250 Acres   200 Sheep
£. 100 Rent   4 Servants
   11 Horses   2 Labourers
   20 Cows

PROVISIONS, &c.

Bread,   2 *d. per lb.*   Mutton, $3\frac{1}{2}d.$
Butter,   6   Veal, $3\frac{1}{2}$
Cheese,   4   Pork,   4
Beef,   4   Soap,   6

Labourer's house rent, from 10 *s.* to 30 *s.*
Wear of their tools, 7 *s.* to 10 *s.*
Their firing, 25 *s.*

LABOUR.

In harvest, 30 *s.* a month and board, with carriage of a load of wood.
In hay-time, 1 *s.* 6 *d.* a day, and small beer.
In winter, 8 *d.* a day, and small beer, and a mess of milk of a morning.

Reaping of wheat, 4 *s.*
Mowing corn, 1 *s.*
———— grafs, 1 *s.* 4 *d.*
Ditching, 5 *d.* per pole.
Threshing wheat, 2 *s.* per quarter.
———————— spring corn, 1 *s.*

IMPLEMENTS, &c.

A waggon, 20 *l.*
A cart, 12 *l.*
Oak timber, per foot, 1 *s.* 6 *d.*

The country between *Kimbolton* and *Thrapstone* is extremely pleasant, and more scattered with villages and churches than any I ever saw; from one level plain, which rises above the surrounding country, I counted with ease twelve steeples. It likewise continues very pleasant and well diversified to *Oundle*. About *Aychurch*, between *Thrapstone* and the latter named place, the soil is a strong clay. The farms are small in rent, in general from 20 *l.* to 60 *l.* land lets at 5 *s.* an acre. Their course of crops,

  1. Fallow
  2. Wheat or barley
  3. Beans

For wheat they plough four times, sow two bushels of seed, and get at a medium three quarters. They plough three times for barley, sow four bushels, and reap four quarters. They sow scarce any oats, and
no

no turnips. For beans they plough but once, sow four bushels broad-cast; never hoe, but the slovenly practice of feeding off the weeds with sheep yet continues; three quarters they reckon the medium produce. They manure only for wheat and barley, spread it on the fallows the end of *July* or beginning of *August*, and plough it in. They use three horses at length, and do an acre a day. The particulars of a farm I gained were

 180 Acres all arable   200 Sheep
£. 50 Rent   3 Servants
 10 Horses   2 Labourers
 30 Cows

PROVISIONS, &c.

Bread, *per lb.* 1¼ d.   Beef,   -   3½ d.
Butter,   -   6   Mutton,   -   4½
Cheese,   -   4

Labourer's house rent, 2 s. 6 d. and repairs to 5 s. and few higher; this is surprizing, notwithstanding the many quarries of stone in the country.

Wear of their tools *per annum*, 8 s.
Their firing, 50 s.

LABOUR.

In harvest, 30 s. to 36 s. a month, and board.
In hay-time, 1 s. a day, and board.
In winter 8 d. a day and small beer, and a mess of milk in the morning.

Reaping wheat, 4 *s.* 6 *d.* and 5 *s.*
Mowing barley, oats and beans, 1 *s.*
———— grafs, 1 *s.* 4 *d.*
Threshing wheat, 1 *s.* 4 *d.* per quarter.
———— ———— spring corn, 1 *s.*

IMPLEMENTS.

Waggon, 20 *l.*   A cart, 10 *l.*

In the whole parish are,
1200 Acres of arable land
8 Farms
A large sheep-walk
20 Labourers
1 Poor family that takes of rates
55 Horses
200 Cows
2000 Sheep
About 550 *l.* Rent

This whole tract of country, quite to *Stamford*, is chiefly open and uninclosed, except in small parcels around the villages, which however give a pleasant variety to it in travelling; but it is melancholy to think, that in an age wherein the benefits of inclosing are so well known and understood, such vast tracts should remain in such a comparatively unprofitable state.— *Stamford* is a very pretty well-built town, all of stone, a quarry lying under the whole country; but the infamy of suffering a street to be so vilely bad as that at the north

north entrance, cannot be too severely remarked; the pavement, if such it is to be called, is nothing but deep holes.

As I shall to-morrow morning view the seat of the Earl of *Exeter*, *Burleigh* House *, and am again come into the great North road, after an excursion from it, I shall here beg leave to conclude this letter, remaining,

DEAR SIR,

Your's, &c.

---

* *Burleigh* House is a very antient building, in the form of a quadrangle, very spacious, surrounding a large court, and in the old stile of building very handsomely ornamented with turrets, carving in stone, &c. &c. Many of the rooms are but small, and therefore I have minuted but few of them distinctly; nor have I marked all the paintings as they hang in each room, as it would be difficult to distinguish them by peculiar phrases. Some are little more than closets.

The Billiard Room, newly fitted up, 33 by 21, the chimney-piece of white marble polished, and a rounding of *Siena*; it is light and pretty.

The Chapel, not finished; 33 by 34; besides the Anti-room, which is ornamented with very elegant carved wainscot.

The Bow-window-room, 45 by 33; painted by *Le Guerc*, who, with *Verrio*, painted all the

ceilings,

LETTER II.

ABOUT *Stamford*, particularly northwards, at *Casterton*, &c. the soil is clay, and what they call creech, which is a poor sandy loam; farms are from 20 *l*. to 500 *l*. a year; rents are, for field land, from 5 *s*. to 7 *s*. per acre; and for inclosures, as high as 1 *l*. Their course is,

1. Fallow
2. Wheat
3. Trefoile and clover mixed for two years
4. Barley, sometimes wheat
5. Turnips
6. Barley.

ceilings, &c. in the house. Out of this you enter into another, 50 by 24, with silver sconces around it, and furniture of the hearth the same. Next is a bed-chamber, rich work on a black satin, and lined with yellow silk; the fringe of the counterpane, and ornaments at the head of the bed, are in a pretty taste. In the closet are

Three pieces by *Gieuseppe Chierera*.

Adoration of the Shepherds, by *Bassan*; the colouring good.

Two landscapes, by *Gasper Poussin*; one of them excellent.

In the small closet adjoining are two pieces by *Wright* of *Derby*; boys blowing bladders, and girls

For wheat they plough four times, sow two bushels and an half and $2\frac{3}{4}$, and reap on a medium two quarters and an half. They give four tilths for barley, sow four bushels, and reckon four quarters the average. They plough but once for oats, sow four bushels, and get at a medium five quarters. For pease they give one stirring, sow three bushels, and gain in return about $2\frac{1}{2}$ quarters. For beans they likewise plough but once, sow them broad-cast, never hoe, and get about three quarters or $3\frac{1}{2}$ at an average. They sow many turnips, plough for

    girls dressing a cat; admirable: The diffusion of light strongly expressed, and very striking.

In the dressing-room, 18 by 27,

Two flower-pieces, by *Baptist*, very fine.

Henrietta, King *Charles*'s Queen, by *Vandyke*; the drapery well done.

Two fruit-pieces; *Michael Angelo*; very fine.

A bunch of grapes, by Miss *Grey*, in worsted; inimitable.

Honey-suckles, by Ditto; very pretty.

Landscape, a water-fall, by *Harding*; the water well done.

Here are, likewise a *Chinese* pagoda in ivory and mother of pearl; very pretty; and some fine china jars: Nor should you forget to remark the *India* cabinets in these apartments, and the japan card tables, both

F 2   which,

for them three times, hoe them once, reckon the mean value at two guineas an acre, and feed them with nothing but sheep. They cultivate a great deal of sainfoine, sow it generally with barley that succeeds turnips, 4, 4½, and sometimes 5 bushels of seed to the acre; they reckon that the land cannot be made too fine for it; it lasts twenty years. They always mow it once, and never more, and get for about a dozen years two loads of hay per acre at an average, but for the first year only one load. If they cut it oftener, they reckon that it damages it much. The particulars I gained of a farm were,

£. 100

---

which, with a great variety of furniture, are elegant. In the following rooms are,

Fruit and flowers, by *M. Angelo*; fine.

Venus and Cupid, by *N. Poussin*; fine; but the sky blue a strange one indeed.

Four pictures, by *Carlo Marratt*, but not in his best manner.

Descent of the Holy Ghost, by *Le Brun*; heads amazingly fine.

Virgin and Child; *Correggio*; the colouring, &c. of this picture does not equal the idea one has formed of this great master.

Wisemen's offerings; *Carlo Dolci*. The finishing of this picture is very fine; the airs of the heads noble, the attitude of the child excellent, and the colours and clear obscure of great merit.

Martyrdom

[69]

£. 100 Rent   10 Cows
    200 Acres   160 Sheep
    150 Arable   4 Servants
     50 Grafs   2 Labourers
      6 Horfes

IMPLEMENTS.

A waggon, 18 *l.*
A cart, 7 *l.*
A plough, 1 *l.* 5 *s.*
A pair of harrows, 1 *l.* 5 *s.*
A roll, from 1 *l.* 5 *s.* to 2 *l.* 10 *s.*

LABOUR.

In harveft, 7 *s.* 6 *d.* a week and board.
In hay-time, 1 *s.* a day and board, for carting, &c.

In

Martyrdom of St. Catherine, by *Julio Romano*; a piece containing numerous figures, and is very fine.

Virgin and Child, by *Carlo Cignani*; noble.

A fleeping Chrift, by *Pouffin*; moft exquifite.

Virgin's head, a fketch by *Raphael.*

Jofeph's head, a ditto by ditto. The name of *Raphael* is great; but thefe fketches will not anfwer any one's idea who has feen thefe alone of this mafter.

St. Euftachius's Vifion, by *Albert Durer*; prodigious expreffion of the minute fort.

Virgin and Child; *Correggio*; the attitude fine.

Chrift bleffing the elements, by *Carlo Dolci.* To defire you to make a paufe when you come to this picture, would furely be needlefs; for

F 3   all,

In winter, 1 s. Only three miles off it is 7 d.
Reaping, 5 s. per acre.
Mowing corn, 1 s.
────── grafs, 1 s. 3 d.
Hoeing turnips, 5 s.
Threshing wheat, 1 s. 6 d. to 1 s. 8 d. per quarter.
────────── barley, &c. 1 s.

PROVISIONS, &c.

Butter, per lb. 6 d.	Mutton,	-	3 d.
Cheese, - 3	Veal,	-	3
Beef, - 3			

Labourer's house rent, 20 s. an acre of land included.

A mo-

---

all, from the connoisseur to the clown, must be struck with astonishment at the first entering the room: Sure never piece was finished in so perfect a manner The divine resignation,────attention to the moment,──── religious complacency of soul;────all is most exquisite: There is not only a picturesque beauty in this piece, but an *ideal* one, and in a noble stile; for the sentiments in the countenance of our Saviour, are rather those of an imaginary existence, something superior to humanity, than a representation of what is ever beheld. The finishing and colouring, down to the bread and napkin, are inimitable; the general glow and brilliancy; the bold relief of the right hand ; the hollowness of the

A modern improvement in this country is the laying their lands down with clover and trefoile for two years, and keeping it fed well down with sheep, by which means many pernicious weeds which used to trouble them greatly are got under, and their lands kept clean and in good order.

Mr. *Sisson* of *Casterton*, a very considerable farmer, and a most understanding, intelligent man, was so obliging as to give me the above particulars: He is noted for his good husbandry in general, and for his freedom from all prejudices against new methods of culture. He once tried lucerne, broad-cast, upon a clean fallow, but met with no success in the attempt. Burnet he has

---

the open'd mouth all surprizingly touched. In a word every part of this great work proves that *Carlo Dolci* deserves to be ranked among the first of painters.

Adoration of the Shepherds, by ditto; amazingly fine.

Christ in the garden; *Bassan*. The strong reflection of the light very striking, but the stile of painting coarse, and almost like tapestry.

Martyrdom of St. Catherine, by *Parmegiano*, after *Correggio*; most sweetly elegant.

Virgin and Christ's body; *Hani. Carrache*; very fine.

Holy Family; *Andrea del Sarto*; fine. The old female head excellent.

F 4 *Head*;

has an experiment on, which turns out very advantageously; the field has now a fine after-crop, the first mowed for hay; but I forbear a particular account, as the following paper contains Mr. *Sisson*'s own register of the experiment. I copy it from one he gave me, which was in his own hand.

" *George Sisson* of *Bridge Casterton* in the county of *Rutland*, farmer, did, in *May* 1767, sow upon an acre of light creech land in *Ingthorp* lordship in the same county (properly cultivated as for turnips) 14 *lb.* of burnet in an inclosure, which was sown with turnips, cultivated in the same manner. After the turnips were hoed, the burnet was laid, and not meddled with till the

---

Head; a sketch by *Correggio*; disagreeable.
Morning and Evening, two landscapes, by *Tempesta*; fine.
Venus and Adonis; *Gieuseppa Chierera*: *Venus*'s flesh is well painted; clear, but natural.
The dressing-room hung with green cut-velvet, with elegant gilt papier maché borders, is very handsomely fitted up: The chimney-piece a small bas relief let into the center, with a border around the whole of *Siena* marble; very elegant.
Christ's head; *Carlo Marratt*; very fine.
Adoration of the Shepherds; *Ferara*. This picture is a good one, but the principal action strangely

the time the turnips were stocked for eating, which was in *March* 1768; it grew to about 18 or 20, and some 22 inches in length, having received no damage by the inclemency of the weather, although the turnips rotted much; and I verily believe it did as much service to the sheep, as the best acre of turnips in the ground. They being remarkably fonder of the burnet than the turnips, I was under a necessity of eating of it until all the turnips were eaten off, and the turnip land sowed with barley, which was the first week in *April*, Old Stile.

" It grew, and was a tolerable good crop to all appearance, but (being a stranger to it) I believe it stood two or three days longer

---

strangely absurd; the Virgin holds the Child in her lap, as a crier would a parcel of oranges.

Virgin supporting the dead body of Christ; *Vandyke*; A small but astonishing picture. The body is painted in the most admirable stile; the expression exact, but great; the colouring exquisite; the group and general effect surprizingly fine. In a word, this piece is truly capital.

Virgin, by *Ferrato*; fine.

Holy Family.—These four by *Carlo Marratt*, and very fine.

Virgin,

longer than it ought: It began to shell very much as I mowed it, which was in the beginning of *July*; the weather being favourable after it was mowed prevented it shelling much after that. After it was properly in order as hay or sainfoine, I carried it into a barn, and threshed it out; and to my astonishment, when winnowed, there were 23 bushels or two quarters and seven bushels, which when weighed, was $562\frac{1}{2}$ *lb.* from 14 only being sowed: the fodder the horses eat much like the sainfoine after it was threshed.

"*N. B.* The 14 lb. cost me $7\frac{1}{2}d.$ per lb. which amounts to 8 *s.* 9 *d.* and the $562\frac{1}{2}$ lb. after the same proportion amounts to 17 *l.* 11 *s.* $3\frac{3}{4}$ *d.*

"This

Virgin, copied by *Patours*; attitude, colour, and turn of the shoulders, good.

The offering the tribute money, in two colours, by *Vandyke*. The group, airs of the heads, and attitudes, admirably fine.

Elisha; *Carlo Dolci*; prodigious fine. The colouring, expression, and general effect, great.

Assumption; *Hanibal Carrache*.

Virgin at our Saviour's tomb; *Carlo Marratt*, after *Raphael*; very fine.

Virgin and Child; *Correggio*; a fine, but an unpleasing picture; the faces very ugly.

"This being my first experiment of the burnet grass, the good success I have had, will induce me to make a further experiment. I intend, (God willing) to sow 12 acres of land in the same lordship properly cultivated in *March* 1769, with a crop of barley, in order to find out the best and most advantageous method of dealing with the said seed, and shall endeavour to introduce it in another lordship in the same county, and more of my family intend doing the like upon different soils.

"Witness my hand,

Bridge Casterton,
Rutland.

"GEORGE SISSON.

Flight into Egypt; *Carlo Dolci*. The thought, manner, colours, and expression, very beautiful.

A Satire on the Capuchines; *David Teniers*; very great expression.

Adoration of the Shepherds, and Offering of the Wise Men; two pieces by *Polenburgh*; colouring, finishing, and design of the heads very fine.

St. John, by *Parmegiano*; very fine.

Centaur and Dejanira; *Jordanus*; finely expressive. The female flesh soft and beautiful, and well contrasted with the rougher is of the Centaur.

St. Sebastian and St. Lucia, by *Carlo Dolci* fine.

"*N. B. John Gervis*, farmer of little *Casterton*, has tried the same experiment with the like success."

This trial is very important; let the reader remember that it is a farmer,—not a theorist that speaks. It is evident from his relation, that burnet is of uncommon use for feeding sheep; which is an application of so much importance that it alone serves strongly to recommend it. The value of a food is determined by the season in

---

A cat and dead birds, and pigeons in a basket, by *Dav. Conich*; extremely well done.

Venus rising from the Sea, by *Titian*; very capital. Most of the pictures I have seen of this master are either in bad preservation, or the colouring gone off and hard. We look in vain for that glowing brilliancy of pencil, of which we read so much in many works on painting: But in this exquisite piece, the colours are admirable; nothing can can be more beautiful than the expression of the naked; the roundness and elastic softness of the breasts are inimitable; the beauty of the face very great, and most elegantly painted; her attitude very pleasing: In a word, you will view this picture with uncommon pleasure.

Albano; *Amphytrite*; fine.

Roleant Savary, landscape; very fine. It is painted in the stile of *Salvator Rosa*.

In the blue damask drawing-room are several exquisite pieces; and the glasses, frames, &c. very elegant.

Carlo

in which it can be procured: an acre of food in *April* is worth five acres in *November*.

Returning to *Stamford*, I took the road to *Grimsthorpe*; the country mostly open, and the roads execrably bad; about little *Byten*, their husbandry is but indifferent, however their soil is the same; it is clay and gravelly loam; farms run from 40 *l.* to

---

Carlo Marrat. Our Saviour and the Samaritan Woman; fine.
Celesti. Adam and Eve lamenting over the dead body of Abel; very fine.
Guido. The Persian Sybil; prodigiously fine; the colouring and expression wonderfully great.
Jordanus. Isaac blessing Jacob; amazingly fine. The dying expression in *Isaac*'s face, and that of the whole piece, very capital.
Carlo Marratt. Virgin with the dead body of Christ; noble.
Salutation. The colouring fine; but the clear obscure appears to me very faulty.
Jordanus. Tobit; exquisite.
Carlo Marratt. Magdalen; inimitable.
Titian. Virgin and Child; the colouring a good deal gone off.
Girendo de la Notte. The reconciliation of St. Peter and St. Paul; the heads and hands very fine.
Ludovico Carrache. Virgin, Christ, and John; extremely fine.
Carlo Marratt. Magdalen.

In another drawing-room, 30 by 27, is a most noble

to 80 *l.* a year; rent of land about 4 *s.* an acre: Their course,

1. Fallow
2. Wheat
3. Beans, pease or lentils.

They plough five or six times for wheat, sow from four to six bushels per acre: *N. B.* their measure is random work, some acres very large, and others small, but the largeness of the above quantity made me observe

---

noble chimney-glass in one plate 7 feet by 4; it is hung with crimson damask: Here are several very fine pictures.

Jordanus. Jupiter and Europa.
Marcus Curtius.
Fortune.
Death of Seneca.

These four pieces are all fine; but the last most inimitable. The expression in the whole of *Seneca*'s figure is wonderfully great; nothing can be truer than the representation of the muscles.

Guerchino. Christ, the Virgin, and St. John; very fine.

The dining-room is an excellent one, 40 by 25, richly fitted up; the recess is within some very elegantly carved and gilt pillars. Here are, by

Ferrara. Passage of the children of Israel over the Red Sea; fine.

Morellio. Diogenes dashing his cup to the ground;
pro-

obferve their fields, and enquiring the fize believe by my eye that their acres in general contain near one and half or better, but ftill the quantity of feed is very great: they reap on a medium about two and half quarters. For barley they ftir three or four times, fow five or fix bufhels, and gain in return, two quarters. For oats, they plough but once, fow three bufhels and

---

prodigioufly fine attitude and expreffion. It is life itfelf.

Jordanus. The *beheading St. John*; fine.

Genario. *Armida enchanting the fword of Rinaldo*; extremely pleafing.

Jordanus. *Diana and Acteon*; the figure of *Diana* great; the naked backs inimitably done; the clear obfcure excellent, and the general effect very ftriking.

A Head in Mofaic; the only piece in that noble invention that I remember having feen; at a fmall diftance the colours are natural and fine; but near, the effect is by no means good.

This collection, upon the whole, will afford any fpectator the greateft entertainment; for here are pictures that muft kindle raptures in thofe who remark nature alone; and others fufficient to afford the moft noble enjoyment to the moft learned eye. The pieces are extremely numerous; very few of them indifferent, and many exquifitely fine. The collection of the works of *Jordanus* is moft capital; they are in great numbers, and of amazing expreffion. The death of *Seneca* is one of the fineft pieces of this mafter

and do not get above one and half or two quarters at an average; from which it is plain their foil does not suit them, and I observed the crops (even this good year) to be very poor. They plough twice for peafe, fow four bushels, and gain in return two quarters: They cultivate but few beans: plough once for what they do fow in the broad-caft manner, and never hoe, nor have any idea of feeding the

---

mafter that is any where to be feen. *Carlo Dolci* is likewife feen here in furprizing perfection; his pieces in this collection are all good, and fome of them fuperlatively fo; particularly our Saviour blefling the elements. The two hiftoric pieces by *Vandyke* are particularly valuable, as that painter did fo few of them: The dead *Chrift* is of moft capital merit. Of *Carlo Marratt* we find many very fine pieces, but not upon the whole equal to thofe feen at *Houghton*. *Titian* is exhibited in the *Venus* rifing from the fea, to very great advantage, confidering how few of his capital pictures are to be found in *England*. *Guido*'s Sybil is worthy of the higheft admiration; and *Pouffin* appears to advantage in feveral pieces. In a word, many of the greateft painters are here to be ftudied with profit and delight, in works that will remain the lafting admiration of every fpectator. Among fuch a number of exquifite pictures, it is difficult to draw comparifons; but I believe you will be beft pleafed with *Chrift blefing the elements*, by *Carlo Dolci*, the dead *Chrift* by *Vandyke*, and *Seneca* by *Jordanus*.

weeds

weeds off with sheep, which slovenly custom I have minuted so long; their mean crop two and half quarters; scarce any turnips sown. Their clover they commonly sow over wheat in the spring, and if it takes well, let it lie a year, mow it twice for hay, the second of which they reckon best, contrary to general ideas; but their reason is the number of weeds, they cut with the first crop, a proof of bad husbandry; at *Michaelmas* they plough up the sward, and harrow in wheat, which is running the land to impoverishment; but this is not however universal. Their dung they never mix with earth, but carry it directly on to their wheat fallows; they fold their sheep likewise on them, and reckon that 1000 will fold an acre and half, never on the same spot twice; 160 sheep they calculate will in a summer fold 20 acres. They plough with four horses at length, and sometimes six, and do an acre a day *.

PRO-

---

* The Duke of *Ancaster*'s park at *Grimsthorpe* is of very great extent; the road leads through it for the course of about three miles; the house appears at first view (as well as afterwards, as you proceed) extremely magnificent; being admirably situated on a hill with some very fine woods stretching away on each side; many hills and slopes seen in different directions, and all

PROVISIONS, &c.

Cheese, - 4 d. per lb. Mutton, - 3½ d.
Butter, - 4   Veal, - 3½
Beef. - 4   Candles, - 7

Labourer's house rent, 19 s.
Their firing, 30 s.

LABOUR.

In harvest, 6 s. a week and board.
In hay-time, 1 s. 6 d. a day.
Reaping *per* acre, 5 s.
Mowing corn, 1 s.
Threshing wheat, 1 s. 6 d.
——————— spring corn, 1 s. 6 d.

---

pointing out as it were an approach to the dwelling. In the vale before the house is a noble piece of water, with two pretty yachts upon it, the banks are boldly indented with creeks in a fine stile, and the breadth and length considerable, but two circumstances are much wanted to render it complete; the principal end of it appears in full view, instead of being lost behind a hill or a plantation which this might easily be, and would add infinitely to its beauty and magnificence, for the *conclusion* of a water being seen, is painful at the very first view: The other point is, the break in the water by the road, for in fact it is two lakes, and one being higher than the other, a *real* bridge cannot be thrown over; at present it is a causeway; but might it very easily be made to appear so like a bridge, as to deceive even

From *Grinsthorpe* to *Coltsworth* are eight miles, called by the courtesy of the neighbourhood, a turnpike; but in which we were every moment either buried in quagmires of mud; or racked to dislocation over pieces of rock which they term *mending*: A great house must be great indeed to answer the fatigue, pain and anxiety of *such approaches!* No environs are so truly magnificent as *good* roads in a country which abounds with *bad*. Pity that the tolls are not trebled. The country is chiefly open, disagreeable and badly cultivated.

It

---

even those who pass it, and this would be attended with a great effect.

The house is a very convenient, and a good one, and some of the apartments very elegantly fitted up. The hall is 50 feet long by 40 broad, and of a well proportioned height; at each end is a stone stair case parted from the room by stone arches; but these are heavy. The chapel is neat: The tea room with a bow window is pretty; the chimney-piece of marble dug out of the park. Returning through the hall you are conducted up the staircase, into the principal apartment; the first is a tea room richly ornamented with fluted pilasters of the *Corinthian* order, finely carved and gilt, the ceiling, cornices, &c. in a most light and elegant taste, gilt scrolls on a light lead colour. Next is the dining room 40 by 27, with two bow windows fitted

It is very picturesque and beautiful, all the way from *Colsterworth* to *Grantham*, and all inclosed on the right hand. About *Paonton*, the soil is a loamy gravel, lets from 5 s. to 15 s. an acre; farms from 20 l. to 100 l. a year, their course,

1. Fallow
2. Wheat
3. Pease
4. Turnips
5. Barley,

which is excellent. They stir twice or thrice for wheat, sow 10 pecks, and reap on a medium, $3\frac{1}{2}$ quarters. For barley, they plough twice, sow four bushels, and gain $3\frac{1}{4}$ quarters in return: For oats but once,

---

fitted up with gilt ornaments on a blue ground. The ceiling ditto on white in compartments. The festoons of gilt carving among the pictures, &c. is in a light and pleasing taste. The chimney-piece one of the most elegant in *England*; under the cornice three basso relievos in white marble, (but not polished) the center a man pulling a thorn out of a lion's paw, well executed; these are upon a ground of *Siena* marble, and have a fine effect; they are supported on each side by a fluted *Ionic* pillar of *Siena*. In this room are several family portraits, and

King Charles and his family, by *Vandyke*; a large picture and fine.

The next is a bad proportioned room, being much too narrow and low for its height, but the fitting up is handsome. Here are,

Cocks

once, sow four bushels and get four quarters. For pease they give two earths, sow four bushels, and reap three, four, and five quarters. They sow few beans, but their method is to plough once, sow them broadcast, four bushels, never hoe, and get about three quarters. For turnips they stir thrice, hoe once; value from 1 *l.* to 3 *l.* feed them with sheep alone. They mix ray-grass with their clover, and sow it both on barley and wheat, mow it once, and seldom get more than $1\frac{1}{4}$ load per acre: Their dung they lay on their turnip land.

PRO-

Cocles defending the bridge. His attitude is a very tame one; nor is there any great expression in it.

Two Landscapes, in a showy stile, containing each a large trunk of a tree, pretty.

A fire at night in a town, fine; the figures in the front ground are numerous and well grouped, and the light not badly expressed.

Christ crowned with thorns, the minute expression good; but never were ideas more truly *Dutch.*

A battle; fine. I suppose by *Borgognone.*

Two large pieces of cattle; I apprehend by *Bassan.* The diffusion of light is in his stile, and likewise the roughness of the tints.

A Dutch fair.

The blue damask bed-chamber is elegant, it is hung with blue paper upon which are painted

PROVISIONS, &c.

Cheese, - 4 d. Mutton, - 3½ d.
Butter, - 6   Candles, - 7
Beef,   - 3½ Soap,   - 6

Labourer's house rent, 50 s. with commonage.
Their firing, 40 s.

IMPLEMENTS.

A waggon, 22 l.   A cart, 12 l. 12 s.

LABOUR.

From the beginning of *June* to *Michaelmas*, 9 s. a week.
In winter, 1 s. a day.
Reaping, 4 s. 6 d. to 5 s. 6 d.
Mowing grass, 2 s.

---

many different landscapes in blue and white, with representations of frames and lines and tassels in the same; the toilette in a bow window, all blue and white. Out of this room you enter the breakfasting-closet, which is extremely elegant; quite original, and very pleasing. It is hung with fine *India* paper, the ceiling in arched compartments, the ribs of which join in the center in the gilt rays of a sun, the ground is prettily dotted with coloured *India* birds; the window shutters, the doors and the front of the drawers (let into the wall) all painted in scrolls and festoons of flowers in green, white and gold; the sofa, chairs, and stool frames of the same. Upon the whole, it is in real taste.

Hoeing

Hoeing turnips, 4 s. to 5 s.
Ditching 24 yards, from 8 d. to 20 d.
Threshing wheat, 2 s. a quarter.
——————— spring corn, 1 s. 2 d.

It is a common practice around *Grantham*, to pare and burn their old turf when they convert it into arable land. The operation costs about twenty shillings an acre.

Mr. *Middlemore*, at a farm about three miles from that town, has for some years tried a series of experiments on many acres of land, a complete register of which would undoubtedly be highly acceptable to the Public. The following particulars I gained of his bailiff, as he is himself abroad. Near the farm-yard he has a close of about three acres with lucerne; a rood was transplanted in rows two feet six inches asunder, last *March* twelvemonth; it was cut but once last year, once this year, and I found the plants about 18 inches high: They were for their age fine and vigorous, but many of them had failed, and the intervals were quite overrun with weeds, insomuch that I wondered at the luxuriance of the plants while so surrounded. The rest of the close is broad-cast, seven years old: It has been always cut three times a year; once this year, and when I saw it, was two feet high, in blossom, and very thick, but had many weeds among it. It had been always

always harrowed after each cutting, with a machine, of which I took the draught. See plate I. fig. 1.

1. 1. Two bars of wood 7 feet long.
2. 2. 2. Cross-bars, 1 foot 5 inches.
The teeth 1 foot long. Drawn by one horse.

Sometimes he uses that represented by fig. 2. which is a solid piece of timber, about six or eight inches thick, and about a yard square. The last cuts the deepest, but is apt to choak. The lucerne has frequently been made into hay, and yielded a load an acre at each cutting; nor has the making it been found more troublesome than with sainfoine or clover. The bailiff calculates, that an acre will last three horses at soiling the summer round; but I apprehend this is a *very* large supposition, for the appearance of the crop spoke no such matter in three cuttings. He thinks it will last four or five years longer, and this I believe may be the case, if the harrowing is well executed, and the strongest weeds were dug out. All sorts of cattle have been fed with it, but none affect it so much as horses; and it yields in general more than any other grass in that country, more than either sainfoine or clover.

This gentleman has likewise cultivated large quantities of cabbages for feeding his sheep, (of which he keeps some hundreds) bullocks,

bullocks, &c. He has used them four years, and notwithstanding the lightness of the soil, which is a red sand, called here *creech*, has found them of incomparable service. The sorts he has planted most are the turnip, the *Battersea*, and the winter green globe *; the first have rose to 5 *lb.* weight, the second to 10 or 12 *lb.* and the last to 14 *lb.* The bailiff informed me, that the last was much the best; for besides the superior quantity, cattle like it better, and it lasts longer good in the spring. It has generally been reserved for the sheep in the month of *April*, and it stands the sharpest frosts. The turnip cabbage, though well affected by sheep, is not liked by oxen, it being extremely hard, and sometimes flocky. The seeds of these sorts are sown in the beginning of *March*, and when four inches high, pricked out into a well dug bed. About *Midsummer* they are transplanted into the field in rows four feet asunder, and one foot or eighteen inches from plant to plant. If the weather holds dry, they are watered with a water-cart, and at a small expence. Six thousand are generally allotted to an acre; they horse-hoe them according as the weeds rise. The turnip cabbage-seed cost † 7 *s.* 6 *d.* per *lb.* and the pricking out the plants of either sort,

* I apprehend, the great *Scotch*.
† It is now only 3 *s.* or 4 *s.* per *lb.*

1 *s.* a thousand, and the transplantation into the field the same: A man sets 1000 or 1500 in a day, and a gardener 3000. I made enquiries into the product, but could learn nothing explicit; however, if the weight per cabbage is only 4 *lb.* the amount is above ten ton, which, considering the season of the year they last to, is a most valuable crop.

Turnips are here cultivated in large quantities, but in an imperfect manner: Their soil about *Coldharbour* is so light, that they do not half pulverize it, even for this crop, saying, that they should get scarce any crops; but their hoeing is very bad. I walked over several closes in a farm adjoining Mr. *Middlemore*'s, belonging to a farmer who rents 550 *l.* a year; and although they had been hoed, they were quite thick, and irregularly set out. Mr. *Middlemore* uses for hoeing them a machine, which I apprehend is his own invention. See plate I. fig. 3.

 1. Three feet five inches.
 2. Five feet six inches.
 3. Nine feet.
 4. The wheels 18 inches diameter.

The teeth are about 18 inches long, and stand nine inches asunder. It is a good plan, and loosens the soil well; but then the breadth of the shares (which is not above three inches) is too small to serve by way

way of hoeing; the great use of it must be instead of harrowing, which is by some farmers in the east of *England* much practised. In a field, just by the homestall of 50 acres, wherein I saw that machine, Mr. *Middlemore* has several curious experiments. This close of 50 acres was a few years ago let at one shilling an acre in *Sward*; but Mr. *Middlemore* taking it into his own hands, broke it up, and has kept it in tillage ever since with great success. There are a few acres of it occupied by a crop of pease in drills equally distant of one foot: They were never hoed, but were well corned; however, the crop was by no means equal to those of the neighbourhood broadcast, nor to what the land would in that manner have produced.

In this field I likewise found a remarkable experiment on barley: Observing a large breadth of it, with a great difference between one side and the other, I enquired the reason; and the bailiff informed me, that the best part (which I apprehend will be full five quarters per acre) succeeded cabbages, and the other part (which does not promise above $3\frac{1}{2}$ quarters) turnips. Adjoining this barley is a good crop of wheat, with sainfoine drilled among it in one part, and sown broad-cast in another; the latter was harrowed in spring, and benefited the crop; both rise very finely. In the

the latter method, the common allowance of seed to the acre is about four bushels. Here is likewise an extraordinary fine piece of oats, sown with a peck of seed which Mr. *Middlemore* had from *Flanders*; each stalk bears a very large quantity of grains; and the species seem to prove greatly in the change of climate and soil.

Throughout all this country, and much I have already described, is found a stratum of stone at a small depth from the surface, which precludes the improvement by clay, chalk or marle, and yet their land much wants something further than farm-yard manure and the fold. Paring and burning in so shallow a soil can be practised but once in many years, and when done, lasts but few. Lime was once tried by Mr. *Middlemore* upon turnip land, but the crop failed just where the manure was spread; and a strong proof now exists, that this is no improvement; for opposite this gentleman's fields are some turnip closes of the farmer above-mentioned. One of 40 acres was manured from the farm-yard; another adjoining of 40 was limed; the first is well spread with plants, and would prove a good crop, had they been well hoed; those upon lime are nothing. These fields I viewed with particular attention, and I am confident from their appearance, that the lime is absolutely good for nothing on this soil;

and

and yet how numerous are the *general* advocates for liming? It is much to be regretted, that some accurate cultivator does not try the real efficacy of this manure on various soils, that the merit of it might be known with precision.

Mr. *Middlemore* has a spiky roller, which I should apprehend of excellent use in strong clays, but of none in this sandy country; it is 7 feet 6 inches long, 14 inches diameter; the spikes ½ths of an inch square, and 4 long, 100 in number. Also a moveable sheep-rack, upon an improved construction, for feeding flocks with hay, bran, malt-combs, oats, &c. See plate I. fig. 4.*

---

* My road not laying by *Belvoir-castle*, I went thither purposely to view it. About three miles from *Grantham*, in the way the road rises up a small hill, at the summit of which suddenly appears an immense prospect over a prodigiously extensive vale, which those who delight in *extent* will be highly pleased with. It is not however equal to that from *Belvoir-castle*, which is seen almost in the clouds on the top of a vast hill, for many miles around. From the rooms may be seen *Lincoln* minster at 30 miles distance perfectly clear; *Newark* appears in the center of the valley; and *Nottingham* is easily discerned.

The house is old, and the fitting up and furniture the same; insomuch that I may venture to advise all who, being at *Grantham*, and having

The country between *Grantham* and *Newark* is all open; about *Foffen* the foil is a rich clay, which flacks after rain like lime; a ftrong mark of excellent land. Farms are fmall, from 20 *l.* to 36 *l.* a year; they do not hire or reckon by the acre, but by what they call *orfe-fkins*, which generally contains nine acres, but varies; the rents generally from 4 *l.* to 6 *l.* Their courfe,

1. Fallow
2. Wheat or barley
3. Beans.

For wheat they plough four times; fow two bufhels, and reap from 24 to 30. For barley

---

fome inclination to fee it, but not a determined one, to give up the fcheme, for the road is dreadfully bad, and the profpect exceeded in real beauty by many in *England*. I remarked the following pictures:

Two pieces of fruits and flowers, with a china bafon in one, well done, in the ftile of *Michael Angelo*.

Landfcape, a rock, and a water-fall; good.

Virgin and Child; pleafing.

Portraits of the hereditary prince, the count de la Lippe, and duke Ferdinand; very good ones, efpecially the laft.

Landfcape; the glowing light behind the trees fine.

Storks; good.

A witch's

barley plough four times, sow four bushels, and gain about the same quantity as of wheat. They sow no oats, considering their land as too good. For beans they stir but once, sow them broad-cast, four bushels to the acre, never hoe them, but sometimes hand-weed the largest; mean crop 20 bushels. Their manure they lay all upon their barley fallows. In their ploughs they use four horses at length, and do an acre a day. I must venture particularly to recommend to such of these farmers as have inclosed lands, to sow beans

---

A witch's cave, in the *Dutch* stile; romantic ideas, and expressive execution.

A cattle piece; good.

The setting sun, a large landscape; the glowing warmth of the sky is fine; and the architecture and trees well done.

The holy Virgin; a large picture, in the manner of *Guido*; the turn of the head admirable, and the general attitude fine.

Gods and Goddesses, I apprehend by *Rubens*; but not in his best manner.

The inside of a church; the architecture and light very fine.

Miracle of the five loaves; the figures numerous, and well grouped; the finishing and colours good.

Landscape, in a dark stile, but good.

Two small ditto; pleasing.

Cards; not so *Dutch* as in common.

the firſt crop in the courſe, and hand hoe them completely; then to ſow barley, and with it lay down to clover, and upon the clover ſow their wheat. This precludes a fallow which upon ſuch land is quite unneceſſary, and would enſure great crops of all ſorts; but all would depend on giving the beans excellent tillage: Of that crop they would certainly gain five quarters an acre inſtead of 20 buſhels; of barley as much inſtead of 27 buſhels; and of wheat four quarters. One hundred acres upon this plan would much exceed 200 as now managed; their crumbling clays are particularly adapted to this huſbandry. The particulars of a farm I gained were,

  81 Acres in all   9 Horſes
  20 Acres graſs   (a ſurprizing number)
  61 Arable   72 Sheep
 £. 36 Rent   3 Servants
   6 Cows   2 Labourers

    In the pariſh are,
  1080 Acres   60 Cows
  20 Farms   960 Sheep
  80 Horſes
 2 s. 6 d. in the pound poor rates.

IMPLEMENTS.

A waggon, 16 l. 16 s.
A cart, 9 l. 9 s.
A plough, 1 l.

LABOUR.

In hay and harvest, 1 s. a day, and board.
In winter, 6 d. to 8 d. a day, and board.
Reaping wheat, 5 s. to 7 s. 6 d.
Threshing wheat per quarter, 2 s. to 2 s. 6 d.
———— spring corn, 1 s. 6 d.

PROVISIONS, &c.

Butter,　　　　6 d.　Beef,　—　3½ d.
Cheese,　—　4　　Mutton,　—　3
Labourer's house rent, when no land, 15 s.
Their firing, 30 s.

 Newark is a very clean, and well built town; remark, when you see it, particularly the steeple, which, for some miles around, appears light and beautiful: There is likewise a new street worth viewing; although the houses are very small, yet each side of the whole street forms but one front, and in a very neat taste. How much is it to be lamented, that this is not the method in all the towns of *England!*

 From *Newark* the country is mostly inclosed to *Tuxford*, and appears to be pretty well cultivated: Around *Cromwell* the soil is sandy; but lets from 10 s. to 20 s. per acre; farms from 20 l. to 100 l. a year: Their course is,

  1. Turnips
  2. Barley or oats
  3. Rye

They

They plough three or four times for turnips, hoe them once or twice; value a crop at about 40 s. and feed them off with sheep. They give the turnip land but one stirring for the barley, sow four bushels, and reap about four quarters. Oats they manage in the same manner, and gain at an average four quarters. The few pease they sow they plow once for, sow three or four bushels, and get in return three quarters. When they sow beans, which is not often, and only upon particular pieces of land, they sow them broad-cast four or five bushels an acre, never hoe them, and get about three quarters per acre. These crops are in general good, and speak better management than common in many of these parts.

LABOUR.

In hay-time and harvest, 1 s. a day, and board.
In winter, 8 d. and board.
Reaping per acre, 4 s. to 6 s.
Mowing corn, 1 s. 3 d.
——— grass, 1 s. 6 d. to 2 s.
Threshing wheat, 2 s. to 2 s. 6 d.
——————— spring corn, 1 s. 4 d. to 1 s. 6 d.

PROVISIONS, &c.

Butter,	-	6 d.	Mutton,	-	3 d.
Cheese,	-	4	Candles,	-	6½
Beef,	-	4	Soap,	-	6

La-

Labourer's house rent, 25 *s*.
———————— firing, 20 *s*.

The road from *Newark* to *Tuxford* is excellent, and very well kept. The practice of ploughing on to broad-arched lands, continues yet on all but the lightest soils; but the farmers in this long tract of country have little idea of draining off the water which lodges in the deep furrows; a circumstance of very bad management.

At *West-Drayton* I was fortunate enough to meet with a very intelligent occupier, who gave me a clear and consistent account of the husbandry of that neighbourhood. The soil is a rich sandy gravel; the arable lets from 10 *s*. to 12 *s*. an acre, and the grass from 15 *s*. to 20 *s*. The farms are not large, being in general from 40 *l*. to 100 *l*. a year. Their principal course is,

1. Turnips
2. Barley
3. Clover one year
4. Wheat

which, for land rich enough for wheat, and light enough for turnips, is an excellent course. They lay all their dung upon their turnip land, but never mix it with turf or clay. They very often lime their lands for all sorts of crops; sow four quarters on an acre; which cost 1 *s*. 10 *d*. per quarter, and the carriage they reckon as much more; but it lasts only one year. Sometimes they pare and burn the old sward, which is done

done for 10 *s*. 6 *d*. to 15 *s*. an acre, sur-prizingly cheap. For turnips they plough three, four, and five times, hoe once, reckon the mean value at 35 *s*. an acre, and use them for feeding sheep and rearing young cattle. They give the **turnip** land two earths for barley, sow **three** bushels, per acre, and gain on a medium 4½ quarters, sometimes six, and even seven quarters. For oats they plough once, sow five bushels, and five quarters the average produce; **have now** and then ten quarters. For pease they give two stirrings, sow three bushels of **seed**, and get from two to four quarters. They sow few beans, but plough once, use four bushels of seed, never hoe them; the crop about 2½ quarters; clover at two cuttings gives three loads of hay. Their land I am confident must be of a very **fine and fertile nature from** these crops, which are uncommonly good. The particulars of a farm as follow:

55 Acres in all	6 Horses
12 Of grass	7 Cows
40 Of arable	1 Servant
£.40 Rent	1 Labourer

Has annually

8 Acres of wheat	7 Of turnips
14 Of spring corn	

In the whole parish are,

250 Acres	20 Cows
	3 Farms

3 Farms   £. 200 Rent
18 Horses   £. 20 Poor's Rate

LABOUR.

In hay-time and harvest, 1 s. a day, and board.
In winter, 8 d. and ditto.
Reaping per acre, 4 s. 6 d.
Mowing corn, 1 s.
———— grass, 1 s. 6 d.
Hoeing turnips, 4 s.
Ditching, 1 s. 2 d. the acre, or 28 yards.
Threshing wheat per quarter, 1 s. 11 d.
———————— spring corn, 1 s. 4 d.

PROVISIONS, &c.

Butter,	7 d.	Mutton,	3 d.
Cheese,	4	Candles,	7
Beef,	2½	Soap,	6

Labourer's house rent, 20 s.
Repairs of their tools, 14 s.
Their firing, 35 s.

IMPLEMENTS.

A waggon, 20 l.   A roller 1 l. 1 s.
A cart, 7 l. 10 s.   A pair of harrows,
A plough, 5 l.   1 l. 1 s.

BUILDING.

Bricks per thousand, 12 s.
Oak timber per foot, 16 d. and 18 d.
Ash ditto, 14 d.

They use in this country three or four horses at length in a plough, with a driver, and do about an acre a day.——The product of a cow they reckon at 3 *l.*

Shirewood forest was the first large and continued tract of *waste* land that I have met with since I left *Hertfordshire*.

At *Bawtry*, hearing that —— *Lyster*, Esq; had several experiments in agriculture of the modern kind, I desired to view them, and his clerk shewed me them in an obliging manner, and gave me a very intelligent account of them. Mr. *Lyster* has cultivated cabbages as food for cattle four years; the sort he prefers is the large *Scotch* cabbage; he has raised them frequently to 16 and 20 lb. weight, which is a vast size. The uses he generally applies them to, are the feeding of cows both dry and milch; the rearing of young cattle which are excessively fond of them, and the feeding of sheep. I viewed the crop of this year, which made an excellent appearance; it is of two acres in rows, four feet asunder and two feet from plant to plant. Mr. *Lyster* has the seed sown the latter end of *January*, or the beginning of *February*; he used to transplant them twice before they were set out for a crop in the field; but this year he set them into the field directly from the seed-bed; they were transplanted the middle of *June*,

but

but if the weather comes wet sooner by a fortnight or three weeks, he never omits making use of it. The number set on an acre is 6240, and six men plant an acre in a day; the mean produce about 10 lb. per cabbage; which is a very considerable produce of above 27 tons per acre; but Mr. *Lyster*'s clerk informed me that cabbages are by no means so substantial a food for cows or beasts as turnips, for that any given number of cattle will eat up many acres of cabbages in the time that they will consume a few turnips. In *October*, they begin to burst, and by *Christmas* must be all fed off. The soil upon which Mr. *Lyster*'s cabbages are sown is a very light sand, which surprized me greatly, for a strong clay is what we find commonly recommended for the culture of this vegetable; but I take these sands to be naturally of a very rich and fertile nature; indeed, the land lets in general at 10 *s.* or 12 *s.* an acre, which speaks no barrenness. The rows are always horse-hoed three times, and I found the crop in an excellent order without a weed in the field. Mr. *Lyster*'s clerk was in general of opinion that the crop was not upon the whole advantageous; for although all the cattle tried with them, seem very much to affect them, yet they consume them so quick, that a large produce of cabbages does not equal a small one of turnips. In addition to this, I should observe that the landlord of the *Crown Inn* at *Bawtry*, who rents a large quantity of land, has made the same remark in fatting oxen with them.

Upon this culture of cabbages, it is in general to be observed, that turnips have in many parts of *England* been found of excellent use in fatting of beasts, and even adequate to the purpose; but the great fault of a turnip crop is the rotting by frosts early in the spring, so as to leave part of *March*, all *April*, and in some counties part of *May*, quite without spring provision: The vegetable therefore wanting as a succedanum to supply the place of turnips at that season of the year, is one that will abide the severity of the winter frosts: but from the preceding account, it is plain, that the cabbages Mr. *Lyster* has cultivated, will by no means answer that purpose as they are gone by *Christmas*; but we are not therefore to conclude against cabbages in general, for other sorts may be more lasting and hardy than the large *Scotch*, paarticularly the turnip cabbage, and perhaps others. For this reason, I much wish that Mr. *Lyster* had cultivated other sorts as well as the *Scotch*, as I doubt not but the spirit with which he conducts his inquiries in agriculture, would have cast new lights on on the benefits of the advantageous cabbage culture.

Besides this vegetable, Mr. *Lyster* has cultivated carrots; laſt year he had a ſmall piece which was of incomparable uſe in feeding a large quantity of ſwine; this year he has ſome acres which I viewed, I found one field juſt weeded and the other weeding; the crop exceedingly fine in point of regularity and growth but *infinitely* too thick; in weeding, the weeds alone were pulled out by hand, but the carrots not thinned, inſomuch that every foot ſquare preſented knots of three or four, and often more within an inch or two of one another; no hoeing given them: If carrots anſwer ſo managed, what would they not do if *hoed* three times as in *Suffolk?*

Besides theſe experiments Mr. *Lyster* has an acre of lucerne ſown five years ago in drills two feet aſunder. It is upon the ſame ſandy ſoil; he has generally cut it thrice a year, and finds it of uſe in ſoiling horſes; but the clerk informed me, that it by no means anſwered natural paſtures or clover in real value. It is however vigorous, and promiſes to laſt many years longer.

This ingenious cultivator laid down a great many acres with *Dutch* clover, and what is here called ribbed graſs, which I take

take to be the narrow leaved plaintain, and finds it anfwer very well, even to producing in favourable feafons two loads of hay per acre; he fows 4 lb. of *Dutch* clover and 6 lb. of rib grafs feed: The firft at 6 *d.* per lb. the laft at 4 *d.* and finds that all cattle much affect both. One piece he laid with them after a fallow in autumn and without corn, and found it to anfwer much better than in common.

I obferved in one of the fields an inftrument for levelling: See plate I. fig. 5. If it is placed againft a ridge of earth and held down by a man by the handle (*a*), the edge (*b*) let againft earth, and fix horfes fixed to the chains (*c*), it cuts up the earth until the machine is full, when it is moved and emptied, and applied frefh to the work, but as the breadth is not above two feet and the length about four, it muft ftrike any one, that the trouble of moving it fo often as would be requifite in a few perches would, with the great expence of fo many horfes, equal, or probably exceed the price of common digging; and then there is the difference of throwing the earth in the latter method directly into the carts, whereas in the former it will, after the operation, be to be thrown into the carts: fo that I much queftion whether any thing would be faved by the ufe of this machine; however, I have given

it,

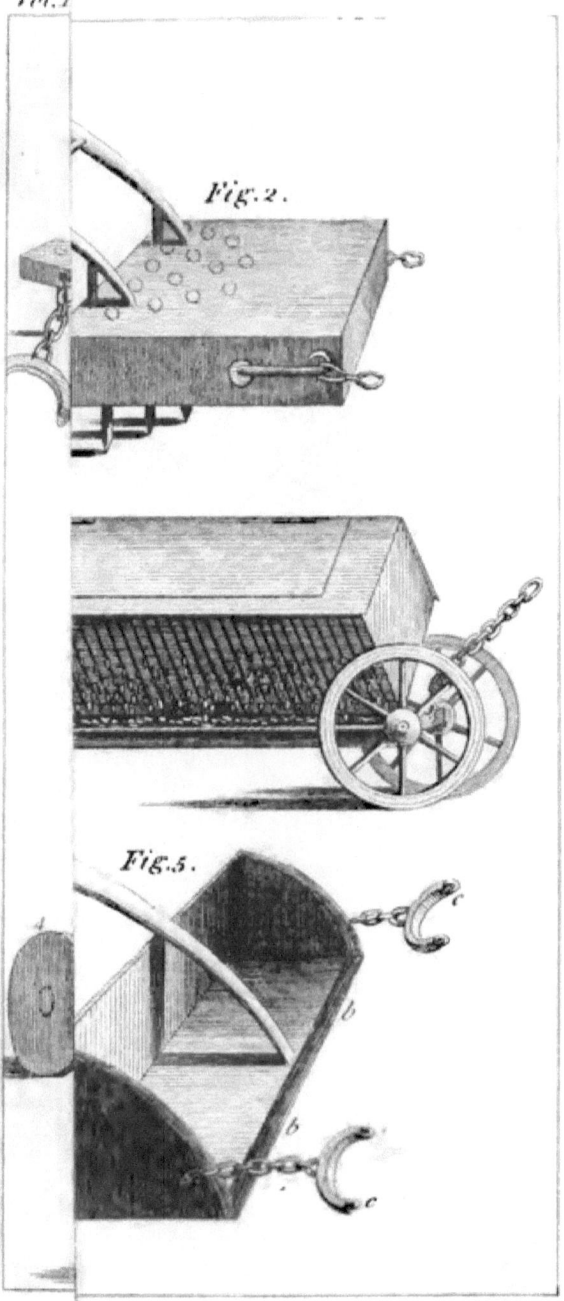

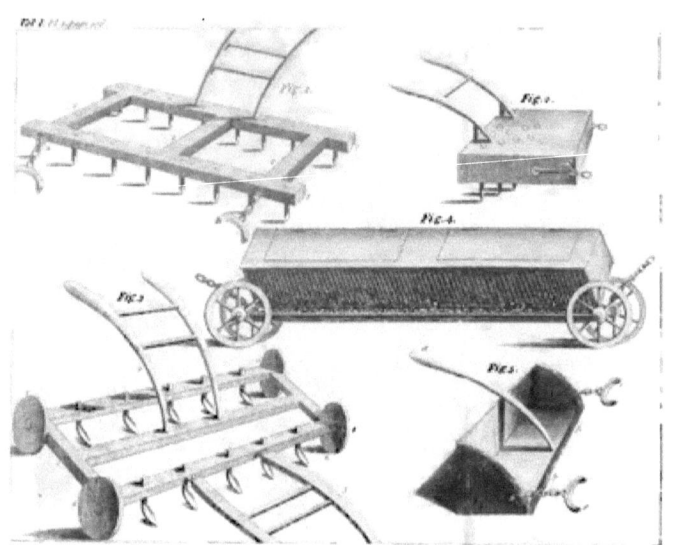

it, that if others are of a different opinion, they may try the experiment.

Mr. *Lyster*'s clerk gave me one piece of information, which was very surprising indeed; That the butchers of that neighbourhood prefer turnips that never were hoed, to those that are managed with the utmost attention, and will give more money for an acre, the apples of which are not larger than a double fist, than for one whose products are as large as a peck loaf: and their reason for this strange preference is this; cattle, they assert, when feeding upon turnips in a field, bite large ones, and if the flavour does not please them, leave them for others, when the first presently decay and are rotten; but this objection holds proportionally to all sized turnips, small in such cases will rot as well as large ones; but to answer such ridiculous notions by reasoning is absurd, facts speak infinitely stronger; ask a *Norfolk*, a *Suffolk*, or an *Essex* grazier, whether he has any objection to large turnips? Why do some of them take the pains to raise large ones to have the trouble of slicing them to pieces? Will ten tons of a vegetable fat as many beasts as thirty tons of the same? The *Bawtry* butchers must be capital fools indeed! —— and the farmers equally ridiculous, if such preju-

dices

dices ever become a rule in their management.

From this town to *Doncaster*, the road leads through a very light sandy country, greatly resembling the western parts of *Norfolk*. About *Cantler*, the soil is chiefly sand; lets at various prices, but all are low. Farms run from 20 *l.* to 40 *l.* Their course is,

1. Turnips
2. Barley
3. Clover
4. Rye, and some wheat.

They plough four or five times for their turnips, never hoe them, value a crop at about 25 *s.* or 30 *s.* and feed them off with both sheep and beasts. Upon so good a turnip-land, this low price can proceed, I should apprehend, from nothing but the villanous custom of not hoeing. For barley they stir twice, sow three bushels, and gain at a medium a crop of $3\frac{1}{2}$ quarters. Their clover they mow twice in the year, and get about two loads of hay at the two cuttings. For wheat they give the clover land but one stirring, sow three bushels of seed, and reap at an average about two quarters. For rye, they likewise plough but once, sow two bushels, and have in return about the same quantity as of wheat. For oats they give but one tilth, sow four bushels, and get in return about three quarters. For pease, they plough twice or thrice, sow three bushels; the mean crop

12 or 16 bushels; they lay all their manure on their turnips; use three horses at length, sometimes two a-breast, and do an acre a day.

LABOUR.

In hay-time and harvest, 1 s. a day, and board.
In winter, 10 d. a day, and ditto, (very high!) formerly but 6 d.
Reaping, per acre, 4 s. 6 d. or 5 s.
Mowing corn, 1 s. to 1 s. 2 d.
——— grass, 1 s. 2 d. to 1 s. 6 d.
Ditching, 1 s. 5 d. the acre, of 28 yards.
Threshing wheat, 8 d. the 3 bushels.
——— barley, &c. 1 s. 4 d. per quarter.

IMPLEMENTS.

A waggon, 20 l.   A plough, 12 s.
A cart, 10 l.   A harrow, 12 s.

PROVISIONS, &c.

Beef,	-	4 d. per lb.	Soap,	-	6 d.
Mutton,		3	Butter,	-	7
Veal,	-	2	Cheese,	-	4
Candles,		7			

Labourer's house rent, 30 s.
Wear of their tools, 5 s.
Their firing, 20 s.

  The particulars of a farm, were
£. 50 Rent   3 Servants
 6 Horses   1 Labourer
 5 Cows

Doncaster

Doncaster is a clean, well built town; ths streets broad and well paved. The town hall is a handsome building, the pillars very elegant, but the door in a heavy and an ugly taste. A little out of the town ———— *Wharton*, Esq; has two or three fields of experiments, which I examined with much pleasure; particularly three or four acres of cabbages, very large and fine for their age; they had not been planted above six weeks, and their leaves almost met; the rows were three feet asunder, and the plants two between each; but this distance was evidently too small, as the horse-hoe must be shut out long before the wetness of the winter would render it necessary to stop. The plantation was very clean from weeds, having been hand-hoed once or twice. Mr. *Wharton* has tried cabbages several years, and found them of excellent use in feeding all sorts of cattle, particularly fatting beasts. They are greatly preferred to turnips for the latter use; it is reckoned that two acres will completely fat three large beasts: I was likewise informed, that they will last late into the spring, even to the time of turning out to grass. This product is very great, and particularly for a sandy soil; cabbages I should apprehend to require much stronger land. As I gained these pieces of information of a neighbouring farmer,

I was

I was not able to discover the sort, but believe it the common large *Scotch*; and if so, the account is very different from the last I received at *Bawtry*.

Besides cabbages, I found in Mr. *Wharton*'s experiment field two prodigious fine pieces of potatoes, one in rows 18 inches asunder, and the other two feet; as good crops as ever I saw; the soil light loose sand, and I apprehend very rich; the cabbages, &c. grow on the same. They raise a great many of these roots about *Doncaster*, and reckon the mean produce of an acre at 250 bushels, and the common price is 1 *s.* 4 *d.* and 1 *s.* 6 *d.* a bushel: There have been some wagers betted this year, that that quantity is gained from off three roods.

The same gentleman has a small experiment on carrots, which, like those I have before mentioned at *Bawtry*, have not been hoed, but stand quite thick on the beds; they were very poor ones, nor could they possibly be otherwise, notwithstanding the excellency of the soil for this root: One of the common carrots now growing in the fields of the sandy gardeners (already mentioned) would outweigh 40 of the best that can be picked out of the plantations either of Mr. *Lyster* or Mr. *Wharton*, and yet their soils appear to be as nearly allied as possible to that of those gardeners; but

the

the want of proper cultivation makes this immense difference.

I beg leave earnestly to reccommend all the gentlemen of this neighbourhood to enter largely into the culture of this excellent root. I never beheld land better adapted to it; but they must act in the most spirited manner relative to hoeing; and not let two carrots in the field be nearer to each other than 12 inches: they will certainly gain crops upon an average worth 25 *l.* per acre.

There cannot be a more pleasant ride, than from *Doncaster* to *Rotherham*; from every part of the road various and agreeable prospects are seen, which vastly enliven the country. But one is peculiarly pleasing; it is a view of *Coneysborough* and the castle, with the adjoining lands. In the front is a prodigious fine break between two large hills, which lets in a noble view of a tract of fertile fields bounded by distant hills, and over them a very extended distant prospect. The hill on the right hand is rough and uncultivated, and contrasts admirably to the opposite one, which is divided into beautiful inclosures, with a great quantity of wood hanging on bold slops, down to the edge of the valley; the castle, which seems almost complete, rises in a most picturesque manner from one of these woods, and in another part of them,

appears

appears the town upon the side of the hill, with the houses one above another, in a manner which adds greatly to the beauty of the landscape. A broad river winds in a charming stile through the irriguous valley, breaking upon the eye in such a pleasing stile, that it is impossible not to be struck with rapture at the view.

Around this neighbourhood the soil is chiefly a sandy gravel; but under the surface through all this country the rock is presently found; in some places it rises quite to the view like an artificial pavement, in broad patches of several yards. Land lets from 6 *s.* to 12 *s.* an acre; farms are from 20 *l.* to 100 *l.* a year. Their course,

 1. Fallow   3. Beans
 2. Barley   4. Wheat

For the latter they plough but once, sow three bushels, and reap on a medium about 20 bushels. For barley, they plough four times, sow four bushels, and reckon four quarters the average produce. They stir but once for oats, sow four bushels, and gain in return about four quarters. In their clay lands, they sow some beans, plough once for them, sow four bushels, and reckon the average produce at 18 bushels. They sow but few turnips; but their culture is, to plough four or five times for them, hoe them once, and sometimes twice, value a crop at about 30 *s.* and use them

Vol. I.   I   in

in feeding both sheep and beasts. The particulars I gained of a farm were,

£.50 Rent   3 Servants
6 Horses   1 Labourer
5 Cows

PROVISIONS, &c.

Butter, *per lb.* 6 d.   Mutton, - 3¾
Cheese - 4   Veal, - 3
Beef, - 3
Labourer's house rent, 30 s.
Wear of their tools, 1 l. 1 s.
Their firing, 24 s.

IMPLEMENTS.

A waggon, 20 l.   A plough, 1 l.
A cart, 10 l.   A roller, 15 s.
A pair of harrows, 12 s.

LABOUR.

In hay-time and harvest, 1 s. a day, and board.
In winter, 1 s. and drink
Reaping wheat from 3 s. to 4 s. 6 d.
Mowing corn, 1 s. 6 d.
———— grass, 1 s. 4 d.
Hoeing turnips, 5 s.
Threshing wheat, 9 d. the five bushels.
———— ———— spring corn, 1 s. 6 d. the quarter.

As am now come into the region of manufactures, and my road running thro' it for many miles, I shall here make a pause in my narrative, and conclude myself your, &c.

LETTER III.

*R*Otherham is famous for its iron works, of which it contains one very large one, belonging to Mr. *Walker*, and one or two smaller. Near the town are two collieries, out of which the iron ore is dug, as well as the coals to work it with; these collieries and works employ together near 500 hands. The ore is here worked into metal and then into bar iron, and the bars sent into *Sheffield* to be worked, and to all parts of the country; this is one branch of their business. Another is the foundery, in which they run the ore into metal, pigs, and then cast it into all sorts of boilers, pans, plough-shares, &c. &c. &c. The forgemen work by weight, and earn from 8 *s*. to 20 *s*. a week, but 12 *s*. or 14 *s*. the average; the foundery men are paid by the week, from 7 *s*. to 10 *s*. No boys are employed younger than 14, such from 3 *s*. to 4 *s*. a week. In the collieries, the men earn from 7 *s*. to 9 *s*. a week. There are few women employed; and only in piling old bits of scrap iron (which are brought to *Rotherham* by way of *Hull* from *Holland*, *London*, &c.) into the form of small pyra-

mids,

mids, upon round pieces of stone, after which they are set into the furnace till they become of a malleable heat, and are then worked over again.

Besides the iron manufactory, they have a pottery, in which is made the white, cream-coloured *(Staffordshire)* and tortoise-shell earthen-ware: It employs about two or three and twenty men and 40 boys; the men are paid 9 *s.* a week for day work, but much is done by the piece, in which case they all earn more, up to 15 *s.* a week. Boys of nine or ten years old have 2 *s.* and 2 *s.* 6 *d.* a week. There is also a very large quantity of lime burnt in this town, which constantly employs about 20 hands, that earn at a medium 9 *s.* a week.

PROVISIONS, &c.

Bread, *per. lb.*	1½ *d.*	Veal, -	3 *d.*
Butter, -	6	Pork, -	4
Beef -	3½	Cheese, -	4
Mutton, -	3½	Candles, -	6

Manufacturer's house-rent, from 30 *s.* to 50 *s.* a year.

Coals sold by the waggon-load, calculated at two ton, for 10 *s.* 6 *d.*

But what gave me much greater satisfaction than the iron works of *Rotherham*, was the cabbage culture of *Samuel Tucker*, Esq; who lives just out of the town. This spirited and accurate cultivator has, I apprehend,

prehend, carried that branch of farming to its *ne plus ultra:* He was pleased to receive my enquiries with the utmost politeness, and answered all my questions with the greatest candor. He has planted them with great success three or four years, but never before had so large a crop as at present, upon three acres of land.

The soil is a light sandy loam, but very rich, and sufficiently strong to throw out any crop that is sown in it; it is not in many places above six or seven inches, and in others eight or nine deep, before the rag stone appears, under which lies a quarry of building stone: This sandy loam is in all seasons dry and healthy, and may be ploughed soon after rain throughout the whole winter. This and the adjoining fields could all be let at from 40*s.* to 50*s.* an acre. It bore wheat last year; was manured for the cabbages in the same manner as is usual for turnips, about 10 loads of rich rotten dung per acre. The wheat stubble was turned up in the autumn, and a part of the field, upon which seven rows of the plants stand, received four ploughings more, before the cabbages were set; the rest of the field received five and six more.

The seed from which those seven rows were planted, was sown the 16th of last *August,* pricked out of the seed-bed the middle

middle of *October*, and transplanted into the field the last week in *May*; it happening to be a dry time, they were watered till rooted. I observed scarce a gap in the rows throughout the whole field. The seed for the rest of the field was sown in the spring, some of which were transplanted into the field directly out of the seed-bed, and viewing them attentively, I could perceive scarce any difference between such, and the others that had been pricked out: Mr. *Tucker* was of opinion, that it is the best way to make two transplantations; but observed, that the plants which were taken directly from the seed-bed, rooted much sooner, and with less watering, than the others. A circumstance which undoubtedly deserves much attention. All the seed for the whole field did not exceed half a pound, was sown on three or four perches of ground in the garden, and produced plants enough for ten acres of land.

The seven rows from the autumn sowing are much the finest; many of them cabbaged largely; some I examined that weigh, I guess, 10 or 11 *lb.* at present, and when in perfection must amount to near 20 *lb.* The rest of the field, however, is inferior to these rows alone, but the whole a most noble crop. The plants on one side of it are much smaller than the rest, owing however to no other cause than a later

later planting, Mr. *Tucker* purposely varying the season, that they might not all come to perfection at once. And in this, I apprehend, he judged right; for I have no conception that cabbages, which at the beginning of *August* weigh above even 6 *lb.* can possibly last longer than *October*; whereas those which are now much less, may abide the winter much better; however this is merely my own conjecture.

The whole field is planted in rows four feet asunder, and the plants at two feet and two feet six inches from each other; consequently an acre holds about 5000 cabbages. But here I must be allowed to differ in opinion from the practice of this very ingenious cultivator; the plants are now so spread, as quite to shut out a horse from the intervals, and in the rows they perfectly crowd one another, which in the nature of things cannot permit single cabbages to grow to so great a weight, as if they enjoyed the full space and air that nature demands. Perhaps it may be said, that the greater number of cabbages gained in this way, will more than make up for such a loss: It may possibly be so, but experiment can alone decide it. Was I to plant cabbages on ground as rich as Mr. *Tucker*'s, I should place the rows six feet asunder, and give each plant three feet in the rows; and from the surprising size of that

that gentleman's plants at this time, I am confident the cabbages would join in a month or six weeks. But such a conduct would undoubtedly be improper upon land of inferior fertility.

The whole plantation has been horse-hoed twice, and I found it as clean from weeds as a garden. In the transplantation, three men in half a day set 3000 plants.

Two years ago, Mr. *Tucker*'s cabbages weighed, he calculates, about 10 *lb.* each at an average: Many of them 23 *lb.* Last year, being on a much worse soil, they were not so good.

In respect to the uses of them; he begins to cut about *Martinmas.* His method is to take up three or four rows at different distances in the field to admit a cart, and then to pick such as require cutting from the whole, by which means the crop lasts vastly longer than if the cabbages were regularly drawn. The quantity which requires cutting before *Christmas,* is not considerable, that being the time when they chiefly come in. They have every year lasted till the end of *March,* and some till the beginning of *April.* They have been of excellent service in feeding milch cows, weaned calves, and fatting beasts. If the cows are confined totally to cabbages, the milk has a rank taste; but
if

if they have other food besides, and depend on these but in part, no such effect is perceived. Last year two acres and a half, much worse than the present crop, kept twelve cows (with some straw) the principal part of the winter. The oxen Mr. *Tucker* has fatted on them, have proved excellent beef. His pigs eat them very greedily.

The vast crops of corn he raises after this vegetable, prove that it by no means exhausts the soil, notwithstanding he constantly draws them, and never feeds in the field. He has raised more than ten quarters of oats per acre, the first crop after them, and eight quarters the second crop without any fallow intervening, which is a surprising produce, considering that his farm never receives any other fallow than the cultivation of *fallow* crops, *viz.* turnips and cabbages.

This gentleman has a very curious experiment on wheat; it is a crop sown with seed from *Dunstable*; it is an excellent one, and the grain much improved. It is pity that seed is not changed often, and from a greater distance than is common*.

From

From *Rotherham* to *Sheffield* the road is execrably bad, very stony, and excessively full of holes.

Sheffield contains about 30,000 inhabitants, the chief of which are employed in the manufacture of hard-ware: The great branches are the plating-work, the cutlery, the lead works, and the silk mill. To give

---

field, situated on the top of a hill. I would at any time, with the utmost pleasure, ride forty miles to view such another. You look down a very bold descent upon an extensive valley, most exquisitely beautiful; chiefly meadows of admirable verdure, and all intersected with hedges and scattered trees. Three rivers wind through it in different directions, in the most pleasing manner imaginable; lost in some places among the trees, and breaking upon the eye in others, in a stile of picturesque elegance, easier conceived than expressed. They appear in eighteen different and almost unconnected spots, insomuch that the whole valley is ornamented with them in a most charming manner: It is every way bounded by hills, waving one above another, scattered with villages, and cultivated to their tops. You look immediately down on one side upon *Rotherham*, and *Sheffield* is seen in the vale at the distance of six miles. There is distant prospect enough to give a variety to the scene, and not sufficient to fatigue the eye, which commands every part of this bewitching landscape with ease and delight.

a clear

a clear and distinct account of these articles, would require infinitely more time than any one can suppose a farming observer could give them.

In the plated work some hundreds of hands are employed; the men's pay extends from 9 s. a week to 60 l. a year: In works of curiosity, it must be supposed that dexterous hands are paid very great wages. Girls earn 4 s. 6 d. and 5 s. a week; some even to 9 s. No men are employed that earn less than 9 s. Their day's work, including the hours of cessation, is thirteen.

In the cutlery branch are several subdivisions, such as razor, knife, scissar, lancets, flems, &c. &c. Among these the grinders make the greatest earnings; 18 s. 19 s. and 20 s. a week, are common among them; but this height of wages is owing in a great measure to the danger of the employment; for the grindstones turn with such amazing velocity, that by the mere force of motion they now and then fly in pieces, and kill the men at work on them. These accidents used to be more common than they are at present; but of late years they have invented a method of chaining down an iron over the stone on which the men work in such a manner, that in case of the abovementioned accidents, the pieces of stone can only fly forwards; and and not upwards; and yet men by the force of of the breaking, have been thrown back in a surprising manner, and their hands struck off by shivers of the stone. The mechanism of these grinding wheels is very curious; many grindstones are turned by a set of wheels which all receive their motion from one water-wheel, increasing in velocity from the first movement to the last; in the finishing wheels it is so great, that the eye cannot perceive the least motion. In the other branches of the cutlery, workmen earn from 1 *s.* 6 *d.* and 2 *s.* to 10 *s.* 6 *d.* a day: The first are common wages, and the last easily earned by the polishers of the razors. Surprising wages for any manual performances! All the hands in these branches have constant employment.

Here is likewise a silk mill, a copy from the famous one at *Derby*, which employs 152 hands, chiefly women and children; the women earn 5 or 6 *s.* a week by the pound; girls at first are paid but 1 *s.* or 1 *s.* 2 *d.* a week, but rise gradually higher, till they arrive at the same wages as the women. It would be preposterous to attempt a description of this immense mechanism; but it is highly worthy of observation, that all the motions of this complicated system are set at work by one water-wheel, which communicates motion to others, and they to many different ones, until

until many thousand wheels and powers are set at work from the original simple one. They use *Bengal*, *China*, *Turkey*, *Piedmont*, and *American* raw silk; the *Italian* costs them 35 *s.* a pound, but the *American* only 20 *s.* it is a good silk, though not equal to the *Piedmont*. This mill works up 150 *lb.* of raw silk a week all the year round, or 7800 *per annum*. The erection of the whole building, with all the mechanism it contains, cost about 7000 *l*.

I would advise you, in case you take this place in your way to the more northerly parts, to view all the mills in town: among others, do not forget the tilting-mill, which is a blacksmith's immense hammer in constant motion on an anvil, worked by water-wheels, and by the same power the bellows of a forge adjoining kept regularly blown: The force of this mechanism is prodigious; so great, that you cannot lay your hand upon a gate at three perches distance, without feeling a strong trembling motion, which is communicated to all the earth around.

Upon the whole, the manufacturers of *Sheffield* make immense earnings: There are men who are employed in more laborious works, that do not earn above 6 or 7 *s.* a week, but their number is very small; in general they get from 9 *s.* to 20 *s.* a week; and the women and children are

all

all employed in various branches, and earn very good wages, much more than by spinning wool in any part of the kingdom. The poor's rates in this town generally run at about 4 *s.* in the pound. All I conversed with assured me, that their business has never been so great since, as it was during the war: Every branch was then strained to an unusual briskness.

The country between *Sheffield* and *Barnsley* is fine; it abounds with the beauties of landscape, and has a pleasing variety. The soil is in general good, and the crops the same. At *Ecclesfield* I conversed with a sensible farmer, whose account of their husbandry was this:

Farms run from 20 *l.* to 80 *l.* and the rent of land from 14 *s.* to 20 *s.* an acre. Their course of crops,

1. Fallow
2. Wheat
3. Clover
4. Wheat.

This is very bad husbandry. Another is,

1. Fallow
2. Wheat
3. Oats

They plough five times for wheat, sow ten pecks, and reckon the mean produce at 20 bushels. For barley they give five tilths, sow 3½ bushels, and get on an average 4 quarters. For oats they stir but once, sow five bushels, and get in return four quarters. For pease they likewise give but one earth, sow three bushels, and

reckon

reckon the medium at 20. They plough but once for beans, sow them broad-caſt 3¼ buſhels, never hoe them, and reap about 30. For turnips they ſtir five times, hoe them once or twice, value an acre at about 40 s. and uſe them for ſheep, and ſtall-feeding bullocks. They drain their lands with much attention, being in many places of a wet ſpringing nature. They cut them from two to ſix feet deep, according as the ſprings are found, which damage the land; the price is about 1 s. a perch; but this relates only to good farmers, who copy it from the Marquis of *Rockingham*. They lay a conſiderable quantity of lime upon their lands, about four quarters an acre, and do it for all ſorts of crops. Their yard manure they never mix with earth, lay it on wheat and turnip land. They ſow ſome rye, plough for it five times, ſow two buſhels, and reap on a medium 30 *.

They

---

* The Earl of *Strafford*'s ſeat at *Wentworth-caſtle*, near *Barnſley*, is very well worth ſeeing. The new front to the lawn is one of the moſt beautiful in the world: It is ſupriſingly light and elegant; the portico, ſupported by ſix pillars of the *Corinthian* order, is exceedingly elegant; the triangular cornice incloſing the arms, as light as poſſible; the balluſtrade gives a fine effect to the whole builiding, which is exceeded by few in lightneſs, unity of parts, and that pleaſing ſimplicity which muſt ſtrike every beholder.

The

They use three and four horses in a plough, at length, and do an acre a day. They let their cows at 45 *s.* for twenty weeks in summer. The particulars of a farm:

70	Acres in all	4	Turnips
25	Ditto grass	4	Horses
45	Arable	6	Cows
£.50	Rent	8	Oxen
24	Acres of wheat	3	Servants
18	Spring corn	1	Labourer

LABOUR.

In harvest, 1 *s.* a day, and board.
In hay-time, 1 *s.* a day, and board, for mowing.

In

The hall is 40 by 40, the ceiling supported by very handsome *Corinthian* pillars; and divided into compartments by cornices handsomely worked and gilt; the divisions painted in a pleasing manner. On the left hand you enter an antichamber, twenty feet square, then a bedchamber of the same size, and thirdly a drawing-room of the like dimension; the pier-glass is large, but the frame rather in a heavy stile. Over the chimney is some carving by *Gibbons*.

The other side of the hall opens into a drawing-room, 40 by 25. The chimneypiece exceedingly elegant; the cornice surrounds a plate of *Siena* marble, upon which is a beautiful festoon of flowers in white; it is supported by

two

In winter, 1 s.
Reaping wheat, 4 s. 6 d. and 5 s.
Mowing grafs, 1 s. 6 d.
Hoeing turnips, 4 s. and 2 s. the second.
Ditching, 2 s. for 28 yards the acre.
Threshing wheat, 8 d. the load of three bushels.
Barley, 1 s. a quarter.
Oats, 8 d. ditto.

---

two pillars of *Siena* wreathed with white, than which nothing can have a better effect. The door-cases are very neatly carved and gilt. Here are three fine slabs, one of *Egyptian* granate, and two of *Siena* marble; also several pictures.

Carlo Maratt. David with *Goliah*'s head, supposed by this master; fine.

Salvator Rosa. Two cattle pieces, exceedingly fine, and in a more finished and agreeable stile, than what is commonly seen of this master.

Guido. Diana, copied from this master; the naked body is painted well, but the arms in the blue drapery very ill done; it is not at first sight clear, whether the figure has a right arm or not.

Paulo Matea. Abraham.

Dining-room, 25 by 30. Here is found the great Earl of *Strafford*, by *Vandyke*; the expression of the countenance and the painting of the hands very fine.

Going up stairs, (the stair-case is so lofty as to pain the eye) you enter the gallery, which is

PROVISIONS, &c.

Bread, $1\frac{1}{2}$ d. per lb. Butter, 8 d.
Oat ditto 1 (This price muſt be owing to the neighbourhood of *Sheffield*)
Cheeſe, $3\frac{1}{2}$ Veal, - 3
Beef, $3\frac{1}{2}$ Pork, - 4
Mutton, $3\frac{1}{2}$ Candles, $6\frac{1}{2}$

Labourer's houſe rent, 40 s.
Wear and tear of their tools, 6 s.
Their firing, 20 s.

---

one of the moſt beautiful rooms in *England*. It is 180 feet long by 24 broad, and 30 high. It is in three diviſions; a large one in the center, and a ſmall one at each end. This circumſtance renders the breadth not of a bad proportion, which would otherwiſe be much too narrow: The diviſion is by very magnificent pillars of marble, with gilt capitals: In the ſpaces between theſe pillars and the wall, are ſtatues.

Apollo.
An *Egyptian* Prieſteſs.
Bacchus, and
Ceres.

This noble gallery is deſigned and uſed as a rendezvous-room, and an admirable one it is; one end is furniſhed for muſic, and the other with a billiard-table: This is the ſtile in which ſuch rooms ſhould always be regulated. At each end is a very elegant *Venetian* window, contrived (like ſeveral others in the houſe) to admit the air by ſliding down the pannel under the center part of it. The cornices of the end-diviſions

IMPLEMENTS, &c.

A waggon, 14 *l*.   A harrow, 1 *l*. 10 *s*.
A cart, 7 *l*. 10 *s*.   A roller, 10 *s*. 6 *d*.
A plough, 1 *l*.   Bricks per 1000, 10 *s*.

The country between *Sheffield* and *Barnsley* is in general good and well cultivated: About *Wooley*, the soil is chiefly clay, and lets from 10 *s*. to 15 *s*. an acre; farms run from 20 *l*. to 200 *l*. a year. One of their courses is,

1. Fallow   3. Beans
2. Wheat   4. Oats

They

---

divisions are of marble, richly ornamented. Here are several valuable pictures.

Borgognone. Two battle pieces.
Vandyke. Charles I. in the Isle of *Wight*; very fine.
Bassan. Wisemens Offerings.
Carlo Maratt: Himself, and a *Turkish* lady kept by him; the lady is beautiful and graceful: *Carlo* had a better taste than *Rubens*.
Titian. Miracle by St. *Paul*; group and colouring very fine.
Carlo Maratt. Christ in the garden, and the bloody issue cured; good.
Michael Angelo. Two sharpers cheating a gentleman at cards; expressive. Vision of St. *John*; the colouring and attitude bad.

Lord *Strafford*'s Library is a good room, thirty by twenty, and the book-cases well disposed.

They plough five times for wheat, sow two bushels, and reap at a medium about 22 bushels. They stir three times for barley, sow four bushels, and gain three quarters and half. For oats, they give but one tilth, sow four bushels, and gain in return five quarters, sometimes seven, eight, and nine, which are vast crops. For pease, they plough but once, sow three bushels; and 15 the medium produce. One earth likewise for beans, sow them broad-cast three bushels; the average crop 18 bushels. They stir five times for turnips, hoe them once, value a crop at about 40 *s.* and generally feed

---

Her ladyship's dressing-room is extremely handsome, about 25 feet square, hung with blue *India* paper; the cornice, ceiling and ornaments, all extremely pretty; the toilette boxes of gold, and fine.

Her ladyship's reading closet is elegant, hung with a painted sattin, and the ceiling in Mosaics festooned with honeysuckles; the cornice of glass painted with flowers: It is a sweet little room, and must please every spectator. On the other side of the dressing-room is a bird closet, in which are many cages of singing birds: The bed-chamber 25 square, is handsome; and the whole apartment very pleasing.

But *Wentworth-castle* is more famous for the beauties of the ornamented environs, than for those of the house, though the front is superior to many. The water and the woods adjoining, are

feed them off with sheep. Their clover they sow on spring corn, mow it twice, and gain three loads an acre. They plough sometimes with two horses a breast, and at others with three or four at length, and do an acre a day. The particulars of a farm I gained were,

50 Acres in all	10 Ditto of barley
7 Grass	5 Horses
43 Arable	1 Cow
£.62 Rent	60 Sheep
14 Acres of wheat generally	1 Servant
	1 Labourer

PRO-

---

are sketched with great taste. The first extends through the park in a meandring course, and wherever it is viewed, the terminations are no where seen, having every where the effect of a real and very beautiful river; the groves of oaks fill up the bends of the stream in the justest style. Here advancing thick to the very banks of the water; there appearing at a distance, breaking away to a few scattered trees in some spots, and in others joining their branches into the most solemn brownness. The water, in many places, is seen from the house between the trees of several scattered clumps most picturesquely; in others, it is quite lost behind the hills, and breaks every where upon the view in a stile that cannot be too much admired.

PROVISIONS, &c.

Butter,	6 d.	Mutton,	3½
Cheese,	4	Candles	7
Beef,	3½	Soap,	6½

Labourer's house rent 30 s.
Their firing, 12 s.

LABOUR.

In harvest, 1 s. 4 d. a day.
In hay-time, 1 s. 4 d. ditto for mowing.
In winter, 9 d. and 10 d.
Reaping and mowing corn and harvesting it 5 s. an acre, one with another.
Mowing grass, 1 s. 6 d. to 2 s. 6 d.
Hoeing turnips, 4 s. 6 d.

Threshing

The shrubbery that adjoins the house is disposed with the utmost taste. The waving slopes dotted with firs, pines, &c. are pretty, and the temple is fixed on so beautiful a spot, as to command a sweet landscape of the park, and the rich prospect of adjacent country, which rises in a bold manner, and presents an admirable view of cultivated hills.

Winding up the hill among the plantations and woods, which are laid out in an agreeable manner, we came to the bowling green, which is thickly encompassed with evergreens; with a very light and pretty *Chinese* temple on one side of it; and from thence cross a dark walk catching a most beautiful view of a bank of a distant wood. The next object is a statue of *Ceres* in a retired

Threshing wheat, 6 *d.* or 8 *d.* the load, of three bushels.

────── barley, 1 *s.* 6 *d.* the quarter.

IMPLEMENTS.

Waggon, 16 *l.*   A plough, 1 *l.*
A cart, 12 *l.*   A roller, 12 *s.*

Wakefield is noted for the dressing trade: The cloths come to this town to be dyed, &c. and go through their last hands. The men earn from 6 *s.* a week (in winter) to 14 *s.* boys till their apprenticeship or 14 or 15, 1 *s.* 6 *d.* and 2 *s.* a week. Around the town are many collieries; the men employed in them, earn 10 *s.* or 12 *s.* a week.

---

retired spot, the arcade appearing with a good effect, and through the three divisions of it, the distant prospect is seen very finely. The lawn which leads up to the castle is elegant, there is a chump of firs on one side of it, through which the distant prospect is caught; and the above mentioned statue of *Ceres*, in the hollow of a a dark grove, one among the few instances of statues being employed in gardens with real taste. From the platform of grass within the castle walls (in the center of which is a statue of the late earl who built it) over the battlements, you behold a surprizing prospect on whichever side you look; but the view which pleases me best, is that opposite the entrance, where you look down upon a valley which is extensive, finely

PROVISIONS, &c.

Bread, *per lb.*	1¼d.	Cheese, —	6½
Mutton, —	3½	Soap, —	6
Beef, —	3½	Butter, —	7
Veal, —	3		

Manufacturer's house rent, from 40 s. to 50 s. Their firing, 20 s.

The trade of this place, is at present very dull; it has been so ever since the peace.

The country between *Wakefield* and *Leeds* continues very beautiful; but the roads stony and very ill made. At this town, but more in the neighbourhood, is carried

---

finely bounded by rising cultivated hills, and very complete in being commanded at a single look, notwithstanding its vast variety.

Within the menagerie, at the bottom of the park, is a most pleasing shrubbery extremely sequestered, cool, shady, and agreeably contrasted to that by the house from which so much distant prospect is beheld: the latter is what may be called *fine*; but the former is *agreeable*. We proceeded through the menagerie (which is pretty well stocked with pheasants, &c.) to the bottom of the shrubbery, where is an alcove in a sequestered situation; in front of it the body of a large oak is seen at the end of a walk in a just stile; but on approaching it, three more are caught in the same manner, which, from *uniformity* in such merely rural and natural objects, dis-

carried on a vaſt manufacturing trade: *Leeds* cloth market is well known, and has been often deſcribed. They make chiefly broad cloths from 1 *s.* 8 *d.* a yard to 12 *s.* but moſtly of 4 *s.* 6 *d.* and 5 *s.* Good hands at this branch, would earn about 10 *s.* 6 *d.* a week the year round, if they were fully employed; but as it is, cannot make above 8 *s.* This difference of 2 *s.* 6 *d.* is a melancholy conſideration. A boy of 13 or 14, about 4 *s.* a week, ſome women earn by weaving as much as the men. The men, at what they call offal work, which is the inferior branches, ſuch as picking, rinting, &c. are paid 1 *d.* an hour.

Beſides

---

diſpleaſes at the very firſt ſight. The ſhrubbery, or rather plantation, is ſpread over two fine ſlopes, the valley between which is a long winding hollow dale, exquiſitely beautiful; the banks are thickly covered with great numbers of very fine oaks, whoſe noble branches in ſome places almoſt join over the graſs lawn which winds beneath them; at the upper end is a Gothic temple, over a little grot, which forms an arch, and together have a moſt pleaſing effect; on a near view, this temple is found a light and airy building. Behind it is a water ſweetly *ſituated*, ſurrounded by hanging wood in a beautiful manner, an iſland in it prettily planted; and the bank on the left ſide riſing from the water, and ſcattered with fine oaks. From the ſeat of the river God; (the ſtream by the by is too ſmall

to

Besides broad cloths, there are some shalloons, and many stuffs made at *Leeds*, particularly *Scotch* camblets, grograms, burdies, some callimancoes, &c. The weavers earn from 5 s. to 12 s. a week; upon an average 7 s. Boys of 13 or 14, 5 s. a week. But they are all thrown out in bad weather; men in general at an average the year round, about 6 s. or 6 s. 6 d. a week. They never want work at weaving. Dressers earn from 1 s. to 3 s. a day, but are much thrown out by want of work. The women by weaving stuffs, earn 3 s. 6 d. or 4 s. a week. Wool-combers, 6 s. to 12 s. a week. The spinning trade is constant,

to be sanctified) the view into the park is pretty, congenial with the spot, and the temple caught in proper stile.

Before I leave this very agreeable place, let me remark to you, that in no great house which I have seen, have I met with more agreeable treatment, from all who show the several parts generally seen as a stranger, nor will you perhaps esteem it wrong to hint, that Lady *Strafford* retired from her apartment for us to view it; I mention this as an instance of general and undistinguishing politeness, a striking contrast to that unpopular and affected dignity in which some great people think proper to cloud their houses—such as the necessity of gaining *tickets*—of being *acquainted* with the family—of giving notice before-hand of your intentions; all which is terribly inconvenient to a traveller.

women

women earn about 2 *s.* 6 *d* or 3 *s.* a week. Girls of 13 or 14, earn 1 *s.* 8 *d.* a week. A boy of 8 or 9 at ditto 2½ *d.* a day; of six years old, 1 *d.* a day. The business of this town flourished greatly during the war, but sunk much at the peace, and continued very languid till within these two years, when it began to rise again.

PROVISIONS, &c.

Much oat bread eat, 10 or 11 ounces for 1 *d.*
Butter, - 8 *d. per* lb. 18 or 19 ounces.
Cheese, - 4 Pork - 4 *d.*
Mutton, - 4 Bacon, - 7
Beef, - 4 Veal, - 2½
Milk, a pint in summer ½, in winter 1½ *d.* and 1 *d.*

Manufacturer's house rent, 40 *s.*
Their firing, 20 *s.*

The country from *Leeds* to *Tadcaster* is fine, and to *Winmoor*, a strong blue clay soil, with noble crops on it. Around *Kiddel*, land inclosed lets at about 8 *s.* or 9 *s.* an acre; it is generally limestone with a covering of various sorts, but chiefly clay: Farms from 10 *l.* to 150 *l* a year; the course,

1. Fallow   3. Oats
2. Wheat or barley 4. Barley, &c.

They plough three or four times for wheat, sow three bushels, and gain in return 18 or 20. For barley they plough

five

five times, sow four bushels, and reckon the medium produce at four quarters. They stir but once for oats, sow better than four bushels, and reap from three to eight quarters. For pease they likewise stir but once, sow three bushels, and gain from eight to 20. They give but one earth for beans, sow four bushels broad-cast, never hoe them, and reap from 12 to 40 bushels. They reckon their soil in general too heavy for turnips, but plough five, six, or seven times, hoe once; value them at from 35 *s.* to 50 *s.* an acre, and use them for sheep and oxen. Clover they sow on wheat and barley, and get at one mowing on good land near three load of hay an acre. Mr. *Rooks,* from whom I have this account, has introduced the husbandry of feeding the clover; he mows it for hay, or feeds the first crop, and lets the second stand for seed, gets from 4 to 12 bushels per acre: They manure with rape dust, lay three quarters per acre on wheat, and four on barley, costs them 13 *s.* 6 *d.* a quarter besides carriage of nine miles. They use two horses double, in their light lands; in their strong, four oxen and one horse, or two oxen and two horses; oxen reckoned best for ploughing. The particulars of a farm,

    283 Acres all   213 Arable
     70 Ditto grass   £.120 Rent
                                      9 Horses

9 Horses
4 Cows
180 Sheep
12 Oxen for ploughing
12 Ditto young, to succeed ditto
7 Servants
2 Labourers
Sows 70 acres wheat
50 Barley, &c.

PROVISIONS, &c.

Butter, $6\frac{1}{2}$ d. per lb.   Mutton, - $3\frac{1}{2}$ d.
Cheese, - 4   Veal, - $2\frac{1}{2}$
Beef, - 3   Candles, - 6

Labourer's house rent, 18 s.
Wear of their tools, 5 s.
Their firing, 20 s.

IMPLEMENTS, &c.

A waggon, 16 l.   A harrow, 14 s.
A cart, 8 l. 10 s.   A roller, 10 s.
A plough, 1 l. 5 s.

LABOUR.

In harvest, 1 s. and board.
In hay-time, 1 s. 4 d. for mowing.
In winter, 1 s. a day.
Reaping wheat, and getting it in, 5 s.
Mowing spring corn and getting it in, 2 s. 6 d.
———— grass, 1 s. 6 d.
Hoeing turnips, 5 s. 6 d.
Ditching, 1 s. the 28 yards.

Threshing

Threshing wheat, 10 *d.* the load of three bushels.

——————— barley, &c. 1 *s.* 4 *d.* a quarter.

About *York* I remarked large quantities of potatoes planted in the open fields. Beans, potatoes, and clover, they reckon a fallow, and sow winter corn after the latter two; sixty bushels they reckon a middling crop; they plant generally in rows, two feet asunder, and earth them up by hand hoes. The fields in which they are set, let at about 12 *s.* an acre.

I omit speaking of the city of *York* at present, as I purpose returning to it in the race week, and expect then to view the public buildings with greater advantage. I took the road to *Beverly*.

About *Wilbersfort*, the soil is general clay and some sandy loams, the commons let at 5 *s.* an acre, the field lands at 10 *s.* and the grass inclosures at 20 *s.* This plain state of the rents shew what great improvements might be made, an advance from 5 *s.* to 20 *s.* Farms from 20 *l.* to 60 *l.* a year. Their course

    1. Fallow
    2. Wheat or rye, or barley
    3. Oats or beans.

They plough four times for wheat, sow ten pecks, and reap at a medium 30 bushels. For barley, they plough five times, sow three bushels, and reap from 30

30 to 40. They give four earths for rye, sow two bushels, and gain 25 in return. For oats, they stir but once, sow four bushels, and gain from 30 to 80. They sow some pease, plough but once for them, use four bushels of seed and reckon from 15 to 20 about the mean produce. For beans they likewise plough but once, sow them broad-cast, four bushels to the acre, never hoe, and gain about the same crop as of pease. Some few turnips are sown upon the lands that are fresh burnt, plough but once for them, never hoe, and eat them with cows and sheep. They lime their lands a good deal; lay 64 bushels upon an acre, reckon that it lasts two years; the expence 20 $s.$ The grand improvement which they practice on their new land is paring and burning; they give 5 $s.$ an acre for stubbing up the whins, 10 $s.$ for paring, and 5 $s.$ for burning. They sow clover on their barley lands, mow it for hay, and get surprising crops, two load each mowing, and they sow wheat after it. In a plough they use two horses double, stir an acre a day. The product of a cow they reckon at 3 or 4 $l.$ The particulars of a farm I gained as follow,

  80 Acres in all   40 Grass
  40 Arable   £. 30 Rent
   2 Horses   1 Servants
  10 Cows   1 Labourer.

PRO-

PROVISIONS, &c.

Cheese, 2 d. per lb. Mutton, - 3½ d.
Butter, - 7   Candles, - 6
Beef, - 3½   Soap, - 6

Labourers house rent, 20 s.
Their firing, 30 s.

IMPLEMENTS.

A waggon, 12 l. to 15 l. (very narrow bodies)
A cart, 8 l.   A plough, 1 l.

LABOUR.

In harvest, 1 s. 3 d. a day, and board.
In winter, 8 d.
Reaping, 4 s. 6 d. and 5 s.
Mowing grass, 1 s. 6 d.
Threshing, all by the day.

A vile custom I remarked in some of the new inclosures here, was the sowing common clover in laying down land for five, six, or seven years; that grass lasts in their land but two years, so that you see some fields in which it is wearing out, in others it is quite gone and nothing but couch grass and rubbish succeeding. The white thorn plants in the new hedges were all full of weeds, and of a stinted growth.

At *Hatton*, and the neighbourhood, I found several variations, which require fresh minutes; their soil is chiefly gravel, lets from 5 s. to 20 s. an acre; their course

1. Fallow

1. Fallow
2. Wheat and rye
3. Barley
4. Peafe.

They give four ploughings for wheat, fow two bufhels, and fometimes more, and gain from 15 to 20. For barley they give five earths, fow three bufhels, and get about 15 in return. They plough four times for rye, fow two bufhels, and reap at a medium 20 bufhels; they fow clover on their barley lands, cut it twice for hay, and get three loads at the two mowings. For oats they plough once, fow four bufhels, and get four quarters. They ftir once for peafe, fow two bufhels, the crop from nothing to twenty bufhels. For beans they give but one ploughing, fow them broadcaft, three bufhels to the acre, never hoe, and reckon the mean crop at three quarters. Very few turnips fown. The particulars I gained of a farm were,

140 Acres   4 Oxen
£. 70 Rent   3 Servants
4 Horfes   1 Labourer
16 Cows

PROVISIONS, &c.

Beef, - 4 d.   Cheefe, - 2½ d.
Mutton, - 3   Candles, - 6½
Butter, - 7 18 oz. Soap, - 6

Labourers houfe rent, 20 s.
Wear of their tools, 10 s.
Firing, 20 s.

LABOUR.

In harvest, 9 s. a week and board.
In hay-time, ditto.
In winter, 6 d. a day and board.
Reaping per acre, 4 s. 6 d. and 5 s.
Mowing grafs, 1 s. 8 d. to 2 s.
Threshing wheat, 1 s. 8 d. to 2 s. a quarter.
———— Barley, 1 s. 6 d.
———— Oats, 1 s.

IMPLEMENTS, &c.

A waggon, 16 l. 10 s.
A cart, 5 l. to 10 l.
A plough, 1 l.
A harrow, 6 s.
Bricks, 11 s. a thoufand.
Oak-timber, 1 s. 6 d. a foot.
Ash ditto, 1 s.

They use three, four, and five horses in a plough, and do an acre a day. The product of a cow well fed, from 5 l. to 6 l.

I remarked the whole way from *York* to *Beverley*, that they used many oxen in their husbandry works; all the waggons I met had two oxen and two horses in them. At *Barnby* Moor they informed me, that oxen were much the best, and exceeded horses in every respect; would out-draw and out-plough them. A point much worthy the attention of their landlords; for the same superiority has been acknowledged in many other parts of the kigdom, and yet they have been suffered to wear out

of

of use. The adjoining moors are common to the houses around them; would let, if inclosed, at 3 s. 6 d. or 4 s. an acre, without further improvement, and might be made, with nothing but good husbandry, worth 10 s. an acre. What a scandal that they remain in their present condition! The soil in this country is chiefly sand and gravel. The inclosures let at 20 s. an acre, and the open fields at 7 s. 6 d. Their course of crops,

1. Fallow
2. Wheat
3. Barley

They pare and burn a little, and sow rape on it: They have a little sainfoine in their gravelly inclosures. Between *Market Weighton*, and *Beverley*, I observed several warrens, which must raise the wonder of every traveller, to see such good land left to so woful an use; the turf is exceedingly rich and fine, and the plentiful crops of thistles scattered about it, prove the natural goodness of the soil; for the thistle is so luxuriant and exhausting a vegetable, with so strong and penetrating a tap root, that it is scarce ever found on bad soils.

About *Bishop*'s *Burton* is some of the most extrordinary open field land I have met with; for it let while open at 18 s. and 20 s. an acre; and now a bill of inclosure has passed, it is said to be raised to near 30 s.

30 s. per acre. They raise sometimes six quarters per acre of wheat, and six, and even seven of barley, which are immense crops upon any land, but especially in open fields that do not admit of the most beneficial treatment *.

But

---

* *Beverley* is a very pretty town, well and regularly built, very clean, and well paved; the streets broad and handsome. The Minster, for *Gothic* architecture, is a very light and beautiful building, and kept in good repair; but its *modern* decorators appear to have had ideas of neither beauty nor propriety; for, with true taste, they have given the venerable pile just such an entrance as you would imagine for a cakehouse; a *new-fashioned* iron rail, and gate *handsomely* adorned with gilding, and a modern stone wall with two urns of white stone, which, with a few reliefs cut on them, would do tolerably well for the decoration of a shrubbery. But these gentlemen, not content with this stroke of genuine propriety, have carried their *Grecian* ideas into the very choir of a *Gothic* cathedral. At the entrance, under the organ, they have raised some half a dozen (if I recollect right) Ionic pillars and pilasters; and built an altar-piece in the stile of, I know not what. It is an *imperium in imperio*; the bird of *Jove* certainly flutters her lofty wings to command the attention of the spectator, and call it off from the barbarism of *Goths* and *Vandals* to six curious fluted *Corinthian* pillars, raised *merely* to support the pedestal whereon appears the king of birds.

You

But as I shall have the pleasure of residing some days in this neighbourhood, I shall here make a pause in my journal, by assuring you how much I am, &c.

You will not quickly meet with a more capital piece of absurdity; and yet (if you could suppose a use for it) this altar-piece, as high as the cornice of the pillars, has something light and well proportioned in it, but rendered heavy and unpleasing by the eagle's pedestal. Close adjoining is a monument in memory of one of the *Percy*'s, near 700 years old, adorned with a profusion of carving in stone, very light and airy. Behind the altar-piece is a modern one, by *Scheemaker*, (Sir *Michael Wharton*'s) which is in a heavy unpleasing taste.

LETTER IV.

AT *Risby*, near this town, the seat of my very excellent friend, *E. M. Ellerker*, Esq; I fixed my quarters some time, and took the opportunity of viewing the adjacent country*.

From

---

* In the way to *Cave*, the seat of Sir *George Montgomery Metham*, from the hills is a very fine view of the river *Humber*, with the *Trent* falling into it on one side, and the *Ouse* on the other; the high grounds of *Lincolnshire* heightening the prospect greatly. Sir *George* assured me, that when he came to his estate, he found his house in the middle of what deserved the name of a bog; the ground all very flat, the offices close to every window of the mansion, and all in the midst of an open country, with not an acorn planted. His designs are not yet completed; but what is done, gives a very pleasing specimen of judgment and taste. Behind the house is an agreeable sloping fall, down to a very fine irregular sheet of water, the banks of which are waved in taste, with a just medium between the slight trivial bend, (which looks like an old streight line turned into a waved one) and the strong, bold, and sudden indentures which should ever be surrounded with natural woods, or wild unornamented

From *Risby* towards *Hull*, the soil improves in richness, great quantities of beans are sown in the open fields; but I should not forget to remark, that the crops are all over-run with weeds, to a greater degree in general than I remember to have seen; but when beans are never hoed, it is surprizing there should ever be found a clean crop.

---

mented ground; a grass-walk waves along the banks, which is close shaven, and kept in neat order, and this is bounded by a thick plantation; so that the whole being in the stile of a pleasure-ground, no other plan of forming the water would have had so great an effect. The head at the great end of the water appears at present full in view from both sides; but Sir *George* designs to give the corner opposite to the house a sweeping wave around the new plantation, which will take off the effect, and be a great improvement; when the plantations get up, the other end will be quite hid, and the whole have no other appearance than that of ornamented nature. Adjoining are many new plantations, sketched with much taste, with zig-zag walks through them in an agreeable stile; a paddock is paling in around the whole, which will be well surrounded with wood. Besides these improvements, here are numerous and complete offices, both for the house and farm, newly built of a light-coloured lime-stone, dug almost on the spot. The following estimate of walling with this stone, Sir *George* was so kind as to give me.

L 4 A

crop. At *Cottingham* they plant a great quantity of potatoes, chiefly for *Hull* market; their soil is a rich loam, or a mixed clay; lets at 3 *l.* an acre; 70 or 80 pecks of setts plant an acre of land, and they reckon the return upon a medium at ten for one, or from 700 to 800 pecks; the price from 4 *d.* to 6 *d.* a peck. They hoe them several times according to the quantity of weeds, but never before they are up †.

At and about a farm colled *Hottenprice*, belonging to Mr. *Ellerker*, adjoining to *Cottingham*, I remarked a peculiar kind of soil, which is found very troublesome to cul-

---

A rood of seven yards in length, and one in depth, takes three waggon loads of stone, the digging of which is, — — 1 *s.* 6 *d.*
 Workmanship, — — 3 6
 Chipping and pointing, — 4 9
In a wood where there was once only a paltry stream, Sir *George* has made a beautiful lake, and instead of being totally open to every wind, he has disposed on all sides numerous and thriving plantations.

† At this place Mr. *Watson* has a pleasure-ground, which is very well worth seeing; it consists of shrubberies with winding walks, and the imitation of a meandring river through the whole. The grass plot in front of the house surrounded with ever-greens and shrubs, with a *Gothic* bench on one side, is very pretty, and the clumps

cultivate; it is a very loose moory land, to the depth of about six or seven inches, and under it a stiff clay; they get very poor corn upon it, especially barley; beans suit it best. It is, like all the other land in the country, kept on broad high ridges, and as the clay is stiff and retentive of water, which finds no drains to carry it off, the furrows in winter are half full of it. I apprehend it is to this cause the poverty and looseness of the land is owing; if the surface was ploughed down, and well drained with hollow drains, by lying dry in the winter, it would become firmer and more sound; this effect I have often ob-

---

clumps to the water's edge well disposed: From thence, passing by a bridge, you follow the water through a pasture ground, with walks and benches around it; the banks closely shaven, the bends of them natural, and quite in the stile of a real river. About the middle of the field it divides and forms a small island, which contains two or three clumps of shrubs, and is a very great ornament to the place; the walk afterwards leads to the other winding ones around the field, which is certainly laid out in general in a good taste. There are, however, one or two circumstances, that cannot fail of striking every spectator, which, if they were a little altered, would be a great improvement. Directly across the whole runs a common foot-way, which, though walled in, cuts the grounds too much;

observed in *Suffolk*. This land lets at about 9*s.* per acre. I should not forget to remark, that over all this country I saw none but very slovenly husbandry; no turnips hoed; the beans all full of weeds; much barley and oats the same; and all their lands wanting draining even to the being over-run with rushes, flags, sedge, &c. &c.

For some miles around *Hull*, the land is all flat, and intersected by dykes alone, which seem full of water, notwithstanding its being the middle of summer; but the part from *Cottingham* to *Hull* is now draining, and will probably be laid so dry as to take the water from out those dykes. No soil

---

much; a broad arch or two thrown over it, well covered with earth and planted with shrubs, would take off the ill effect of crossing this path. In the water is the imitation of a rock, every kind of which is totally unconsonant with the pleasing and agreeable emotions of the gently-winding stream, and smoothly-shaven banks; besides, any rock worth seeing would swallow up this water. In the next place here are some urns, an ornament, when properly disposed, of great efficacy; but close, shaded and sequestered spots, whereon the eye falls by accident, as it were, are the places for urns, and not open lawns, full in view, and to be walked around. It is surprizing, that the ideas of imitating nature, in rejecting a strait line for the water, and giving its banks the wave of a real stream, should not be extended

foil can ever be of a wholesome dryness, the ditches of which are nearly full of water. These flat lands are chiefly meadow ground, and let from 30 *s.* to 35 *s.* an acre. One piece of œconomy I observed with pleasure, not remembering to have seen it before, which is, the cultivating the earth thrown out of the ditches with oats and potatoes: you see a narrow stripe of fine oats, &c. around many of the pasture fields; and as this earth was thrown out but last winter, and undoubtedly of a most wet and sour nature, it shews the rank luxuriance of that grain and root to flourish so well in a soil but just turned out from the bottom of a ditch usually full of water; this management was pursued upon the cleansing of the old ditches, as well as the moulds of the new ones. But two remarks, no spectator of

---

extended to hiding the conclusion, by winding it among the wood where it could not be followed; and it would have been a great improvement, to have given the stream in one place a much greater wave, so as to have enlarged it to four times its present width; this would have added much to the variety of the scene. Lastly, I might remark, that the circular bason near the end of the river has a very bad effect; any water so very artificial, should not be seen with the same eye that views the imitation of a real stream.

these

these newly drained lands can avoid making, viz. the immense breadth of the bye-roads, many of which lead only to a single farm-house, or to about a dozen inclosures; they are all by Act of Parliament 60 feet broad. For these purposes it is preposterous to lose such quantities of strong rich clay land of 30 s. an acre, when half the breadth would be equally useful. High-roads, it is not to be regretted the Parliament should insist on that breadth for; but for such as these, which have so very slight a traffic, it is a striking absurdity. Secondly, it must surely be observed, that many of these new inclosures are over-run with rushes, and other aquatic weeds, and are in many places so wet, as to poach with the tread of cattle, even at this season; what therefore, must they do in winter? Now it is evident from this circumstance, either that the true *fall* is not taken to carry off the water, (so much of which we see stagnating in the ditches) or that the ditches are not of a sufficient depth to drain the land. But supposing either of these, or both, or neither, to be the case, yet there appears the greatest reason to apprehend, that these inclosures cannot be perfectly drained without the assistance of hollow drains, such as are used in common in *Suffolk* and *Essex*; if the ditches are found of a sufficient depth, (of which, however,

ever, I have no conception) drains laid into them of about 30 inches deep, 4 inches wide at bottom, and 10 at top, filled 12 inches deep with stones, bones, horns, or wood, covered thinly with straw or broom, and then the molds and turf laid in again: these cut across the lands, about a perch and half asunder, would be a prodigious improvement, even to nearly doubling the value of the land, for they would kill all the aquatic rubbish, and make the grass surprizingly sweeter and finer, both for feeding and hay.

Hull is a large, and in general a close-built town, but some of the streets are wide and handsome; all of them, down to the narrowest alley, excellently paved and perfectly clean; but in winter I suppose the latter circumstance not so great, although there are scavengers publicly appointed for cleaning them. The houses in general are well built, and great numbers of them new, but I saw few large ones. The trade carried on here is very great, for a number of the most considerable manufacturing towns in *England* being situated on the rivers that fall into the *Humber*, are infinitely advantageous to the commerce of this place; enabling its merchants to export largely to most parts of the world, a variety of manufactures at the very first hand; and the same

same rivers, particularly the *Trent*, the *Ouze*, the *Rother*, &c. &c. which bring them these fabrics, likewise give them a vast share of the corn trade, and then the return by wine, deals, coals, iron, hemp, *American* products, &c. &c. form together a prodigious traffic. They have even entered into the *Greenland* fishery, which was supposed to be lost to this kingdom when given up by the *South-Sea* Company. Three large ships, of above 500 tons each, made the voyage this year, one of which caught four whales and an half*, and 150 seals. The merchants of *Hull* deserve much commendation for entering into a business so extremely expensive, hazardous, and so often disadvantageous; but from which our neighbours, the *Dutch*, have made such astonishing profit. There are about 150 sail of ships belonging to *Hull*, rising from small craft to 600 tons. The harbour is small, but very secure; at its entrance from the *Humber* is a regular fortification, garrisoned, but of no great strength, from which you have a fine view of the river and its mouth to the sea; it is here three miles broad.

* If two ships join in the taking a whale, they divide it, which occasions the halves, which, without explanation, appear so odd.

They reckon in *Hull* that the number of fouls is 24,000; but from the fize of the town, I have no conception they can amount to 20,000*.

The

---

* Among the public buildings of the town, thofe I found moft worthy of notice were, 1. The Trinity-houfe, a very ancient eftablifhment for the maintenance of captains widows: There is nothing ftriking in the building, but in one of the rooms is a modern fea-piece, reprefenting the battle between Sir *Edward Hawke,* and the *French* fleet off *Quiberon* bay, by D. *Serres.* It is a good picture; the fmoak in a variety of colours and expreffions, the clouds, and the clear obfcure of the whole, are pleafing. In one of the paffages, remember to obferve the effigy of a man in a boat, who was taken up at fea, alive, but died in three days. The following is the infcription:

" *Andrew* Barker, one of the mafters of this houfe, upon his voyage from *Greenland, Anno Domini* 1613, took up this boat and a man in it, of which this is the effigy, the coat, bag, oars, and dart the fame.

The boat is only 18 inches broad and 10 feet long, covered over, fo as juft to admit the man to fit in it, and joins round his waift, it is amazing it fhould live a fingle day at fea.

2. The new theatre is well contrived and handfome; contains a fmall orcheftra, a pit, and

The soil about *Risby* is generally a pretty strong loam from four to eight inches deep, and then a vast stratum of chalk stone. In some fields the chalk stone is covered with a surface of clay. The farms are in general small, they rise from 10 *l.* a year to 150 *l.* but are generally from 50 *l.* to 100 *l.* In the open fields which are much more

---

and three ranges of boxes and galleries; but the balustrade fronts of the boxes being lead coloured, have not a good effect; they had better have been pannelled, unless carved and guilt; the stage has not half a sufficiency of extent in front of the house.

3. The assembly-room is handsome and well contrived; it is 50 by 27 and 25 high; the card-room (32 by 20) is parallel with it, so that at the entrance you see through the doors of each, upon a large handsome pier-glass at the further side of the latter, catching the principal glass lustres in a proper manner: Of these there are eight in the assembly-room, and one in the card-room. The former of these is walled with a most disagreeable red clouded coloured stone, which destroys the beauty of the room: It is ornamented with Ionic pilasters. The music gallery is a coved recess on one side, the front of which being parallel with the side of the room, the proportions are not damaged by it, nor has it that bad effect, which we always observe in projecting galleries of every kind.

in quantity than the inclosures, the lands let at various prices. In *Walkington* field, where the soil is chiefly clay, so as to yield wheat and beans, it lets at about 7 s. 4 d. an acre, whereas in *Little Weighton*, which is barley land, and stands in need of being manured now and then with rape dust, it is not above 4 s. Some of the open land, however, lets as high as 11 s. and 14 s. but it is not much. Inclosures of grass that are not low and rich from 12 s. 6 d. to 18 s. The arable ditto from 9 s. to 10 s. In some neighbouring towns however, rents run much higher, as 5 s. 6 s. and to 10 s. in general for open field; and from 15 s. to 25 s. old inclosures.

The course of crops in the open lands, clay soil,

   1. Fallow
   2. Wheat
   3. Beans

In others not so strong,

   1. Fallow
   2. Barley
   3. Pease or lentils; or if the soil is very thin, grey oats.

For wheat, they plough 4 times, sow 2 bushels and a peck, and reckon 17 or 18 bushels in the open fields a middling crop. In the inclosed ones, three quarters two bushels.

For barley they plough four times, fow three bufhels and an half; and gain in return, in their open lands four quarters and an half, and in the inclofures five quarters.

They plough but once for oats, fow three bufhels and an half; and the mean produce they reckon at four quarters in the open fields, and five quarters and an half in the inclofures. At *Cottingham* one farmer afferts the having raifed twelve quarters from off an acre.

For beans, they give but one ftirring, fow three bufhels and half broad-caft, never hoe them, nor feed the weeds with fheep: They get about three and half in the open fields, and four quarters in the inclofures.

Of peafe they fow but few; plough for them but once, fow three bufhels and an half, and reckon the mean produce at two quarters, or two and a bufhel.

For lentils they likewife plough but once, fow two bufhels and a peck per acre; the crop about two quarters and half, or three quarters.

Very little rye fowed here.

Turnips are but coming in, they make their land pretty fine for them, fcarce any farmer hoes them; but thofe whofe are run over, are done in fo flovenly a manner, that little good refults from the operation; they ufe them only in feeding of fheep.

Clover

Clover and ray-grafs, and fainfoine unknown among the common farmers.

In a few of the neighbouring parifhes, fome rape is fown both for feeding of fheep, and for crops of feed; it is generally thrown in upon new broke-up land, and with good fuccefs, having produced from three to five quarters per acre.

They are throughout this tract pretty attentive to the manuring of their land: Lime, after being long unknown, is coming into ufe, and thofe who have tried it find great advantage from the practice.

Soap-afhes they buy wherever they can, and find nothing to exceed them.

All forts of manure is bought at high prices at *Hull*, and carried nine or ten miles around. Rape-duft from the oil mills is a capital article with them, having found it of prodigious benefit to all forts of land; but it is chiefly laid on their barley lands. All other forts of manure, fuch as coal-afhes, horfe, hog, and cow dung, the fullage of the ftreets, &c. &c. &c. is purchafed at about 2 *s.* 6 *d.* or 3 *s.* a waggon-load of 50 bufhels, and fpread on the fields to great profit. About 50 years ago, the manuring from *Hull* was begun by a poor man who hired a clofe of grafs; he had four affes which he employed conftantly in carrying away afhes and dung, and fpreading them upon his pafture, the improvement of which was so manifest, that his neighbours followed the example; whoever brought away manure for many years, were paid for taking it; 25 years ago, it was to be had for 6 d. to 1 s. a load, but the country around by degrees, all coming into the practice, the price has arose to its present height; extraordinary good stuff will sell for 5 s. a load.

They are very sensible of the benefit of folding their sheep; their folds rise from 120 to 200.

Scarce any paring and burning. Their farm-yard manure is carefully spread on the soil, but never mixed with earth.

There are several warrens in this neighbourhood, which (like those I mentioned on the other side of *Beverley*) appear from the luxuriance and verdure of the grass, and from the multiplicity and height of the thistles, to be excellent land——indeed, the soil must be naturally good, or it could not yield such a spontaneous growth: But yet these large tracts of country are suffered to remain in their present state, which is comparatively that of wastes, to what they might easily be converted to: Their rents are about 6 s. an acre; and when I enquired the reason of not turning them into arable farms, I was told that the farmers would not give above 9 s. or 10 s. an acre for a few years, after which the rent would fall

fall below what it is at prefent: This is the ftrongeft proof imaginable of wrong ideas of hufbandry, for it fhews that the farmers here have no other notion of breaking up old grafs, but that of immediately ploughing out its very heart, and trufting to chance for a renewal of fertility; whereas fuch a rich furface as thefe warrens fhould be managed with the greateft caution, very little corn taken from them, but much turnips, clover and ray-grafs, and fainfoine, by which means the foil would be for ever in heart, the rent greatly raifed, and the value more at the end of a leafe than at the beginning.

Mr. *Ellerker*'s fteward has in his farm ftruck out a better hufbandry than that of his neighbours; inftead of remaining like them ignorant of the clover hufbandry, he has judicioufly introduced it into a courfe which cannot be exceeded,

1. Turnips
2. Barley
3. Clover two years
4. Wheat

This is very different from the courfes I gave above, and infinitely preferable to them; but I fhould remark, that as the foil has no complete fallow, the turnip hufbandry fhould be managed with the utmoft attention, or a worfe courfe cannot be fixed on. If the preparation for the turnips is not very complete by such a number of ploughings, and harrowings, as not only to reduce the soil to garden fineness, but totally divest it for the time of weeds; and if the hoeings do not set the plants at a due distance from each other, so as to admit a 10 or 12 inch hoe around every one, for the utter extirpation of the remaining weeds, and for carrying on the vegetable to its utmost growth, as well for the thorough covering of the land to raise a fermentation, as for the value of the crop: If these points are not well attended to, this very beneficial course will prove by no means advantageous; for a crop of spring corn following them with grasses amongst it, and another of wheat upon them, and all without the intervention of more than one or two ploughings, the land, if not thoroughly cleaned in the turnip fallow, must give a crop of wheat full of weeds. And every course, the last crop of which is weedy, may be pronounced either bad or badly managed: No land is well conducted, that is not *always* clean: It is almost needless to add upon the course of crops in question, that the turnips ought on every account to be fed off the land by sheep.———But to return.

Mr. *Ayer* (the steward) hoes his turnips always once, and generally twice, and feeds them off with sheep. He finds his clover

of

of incomparable use to him both in mowing for hay, and feeding, and the wheat he gets after it on one earth, is generally a fine crop. If the clover turns out an indifferent or a weedy crop, he sows beans upon it instead of wheat; manages them like his neighbours, except in sowing a smaller quantity of seed about two bushels and half; and in this way without hoeing, he gets stalks with about 40 pods: he brought me one of last year, that had 46, but such stalks cannot be common, but must grow in an open vacant spot.

Cabbages he has cultivated these four years. The large *Scotch* cabbage: Sows the latter end of *February*, pricks them out once before they are set in the field. He never gives the land a whole year's fallow for them; only from *November* till the time of planting, which is the beginning of *June*; but always manures for them with about 10 loads of yard dung: The large strong plants he sets directly from the seed-bed into the field. His rows are three feet asunder and the plants two feet in the rows, he never watered any but once; however, that must ever remain accinental, in very dry seasons they would not strike root without watering. A man plants an acre in three days. He horse-hoes them according as the weeds rise from once to thrice; begins to cut the latter end of *November*, and has always found them to last till the end of *April:* He generally uses them for the fatting of oxen; both for finishing the large ones of 70, 80, and 90 stone (14 lb.) that have been fatting through the summer, and also for the total fatting of others of 36 or 40 stone, taken lean from work in *November*, put directly to cabbages, and made fit for the butcher by the middle of *April:* And he finds them to carry the beasts forward in an excellent manner: They are stalled in a house, and have a little hay given them every day. As I did not apprehend cabbages to be a food sufficient to finish the fatting of a large ox, I repeated my inquiries on that head; and he assured me, that he had sold oxen from cabbages at 23 *l.* each. An acre of good plants has with him completely fatted two beasts of 36 stone each. His sentiments upon the crop in general, are highly in its favour; he thinks it pays much better than turnips, and affords not only a surprizing quantity of food, but is a very profitable crop.

Mr. *Ayer* has limed more than any of his neighbours. He lays 12 quarters on an acre when alone; but sometimes mixes it with other manure, then only eight, generally on to turnip land, and finds great benefit from it; the effect of it being plainly visible seven years after: Plate II. fig. 3

fig. 1. is the sketch of a machine invented by this ingenious cultivator for cutting up mole and ant hills, which he has found to answer greatly.

(1.) The beam nine feet long and four inches square.

(2.) The two flat shares of iron four feet long and five inches wide.

(3.) The side pieces five feet long, and five inches broad, by four thick.

(4.) The handles four feet six inches long.

(5.) The four standards, two feet high from the ground, same size as beam.

I forgot to tell you, that all the tillage of this country, is performed by horses which are much preferred to oxen for that purpose; but the latter are chiefly used in the waggon for bringing home the crop, or for carrying manure, &c. but generally two oxen and two horses. They all assert, that two oxen at a draught are much stronger than two horses, and will carry out a much greater weight. In the heavy lands they plough with four horses abreast; in the light ones with two, and do an acre or an acre and half a day; and what is very astonishing, and to me unparalleled, is their ploughing with four horses, without a driver; there is no such thing as a driver known in the country: A lad ploughs, and drives the four horses by two lines, with great ease. I should likewise
inform

inform you, that it is here much the custom to mow their wheat; they do it with a common scythe, and cut *to* the standing corn, not *from* it as with spring corn: A woman follows every mower, to gather the corn, and lay it in order for binding; and a man follows every two scythes to bind after the women: A man will mow from an acre and half to two acres a day; it is reckoned a slovenly method, for it takes in great quantities of weeds at the bottoms of the sheaves, and the ground is obliged to be raked.

The particulars I gained of two farms, one inclosed, and the other open, are as follow. In the first,

200 Acres	4 Working oxen
130 Grafs	4 Cows
70 Arable	70 Sheep
£.120 Rent	2 Servants
7 Horses	2 Labourers

In the second,

70 Acres all arable	3 Cows
£.40 Rent	150 Sheep (a common right)
10 Horses	
4 Oxen besides young beasts	4 Servants
	2 Labourers

IMPLEMENTS.

A waggon, 15*l*. to 17*l*.   A plough, 17*s*.
A cart, 10*l*.   A harrow, 12*s*.

Oak

Oak timber, 1 s. 4 d. and 1 s. 6 d. a foot.
Ash, ditto.
A run of wheels of ash, 3 l. a year ago, but now raised to 3 l. 15 s.
Bricks, 11 s. a thousand.

LABOUR.

From *Midsummer* to *Michaelmas*, 12 s. a week, and small beer.
In winter, 7 s. a week.
Reaping, 6 s. 6 d. to 7 s. 9 d. an acre.
Mowing spring corn, 2 s. 9 d.
——— grass, 1 s. 9 d. on the wolds to 4 s. 6 d. in low lands.
Hoeing turnips, 5 s. 6 d.
Repairing hedges, the ditch five feet broad and three deep, 1 s. 6 d. the rood or seven yards.
Threshing wheat, 2 s. 6 d. a quarter.
——— barley, lentils and pease, 1 s.
——— oats, 9 d.
Wages of farming servants for all sorts of work, 12 l.
Ditto plough lads, 7 l.
Dairy women, 5 l.

PROVISIONS, &c.

Beef,	- 3 d.	Cheese,	- $2\frac{1}{2}d.$
Mutton,	- 3	Butter,	- $5\frac{1}{2}$
Veal,	- 4		

Labourer's house rent, 20 s.
Labourer's wear of tools, 15 s.

Their

Their firing, 5 *s.* (whins chiefly.)
Poor rates, 6 *d.* in the pound rack rents.
Surveyors rate, 3 *d.* in ditto sometimes.
Tythes generally gathered.
Lands upon a medium sells at 35 years purchase.

These prices of labour are most of them extremely high; and the occasion is supposed by all I conversed with on the subject to be owing to the public works which have been for some time, and yet continue to be carried on in the neighbourhood, such as draining, inclosing and making turnpikes: Such works must and will have hands by giving something above the common amount of wages, which obliges the farmers also to raise their pay until somewhat of a competition ensues, insomuch that very lately (since harvest begun) the commissioners of a neighbouring drainage cried in *Beverley* streets, 2 *s.* 6 *d.* a day for common spadesmen. These high wages, the gentlemen and farmers all assert, to be of no service to the poor families, but to affect the price of labour out of proportion to the number of hands taken from husbandry; because the men that earn 3 *s.* or 4 *s.* a day, scarce ever work above three days in a week, but drink out the rest; and thus no great number being publickly employed makes the labourers in winter so saucy, faucy, that they are forced to be almost bribed to threfh.

Perhaps there is no part of the kingdom which can furnifh a ftronger inftance of *employment* creating *hands*, than that of the works, I have juft mentioned. It has been afferted, by abundance of writers, that the kingdom wants people to carry on the undertakings publick and private, which are always in agitation. Thofe circumftances which either prove or difprove this affertion, however feemingly trivial, ought not to be overlooked: Several of the gentlemen, and many of the farmers of this neighbourhood affert, that the war carried off fo many men, that it was with difficulty the harvefts could be got in; but I never heard, here or any where elfe, that a fingle field of corn was ever left to fpoil for want of hands to cut and carry it; nor do I remember any where the mention of one barn of corn, that remained full for want of men to threfh it: General complaints have been, and are very common, but thofe inftances which prove the affertions, will be found extremely rare; the war might occafion a fcarcity of hands ufually employed, but that fcarcity in the nature of things will bring forth others not ufually employed until the increafe of employment will be found to raife men like mufhrooms.

The scarcity of hands in this country, is at present loudly talked of; and attributed to the drainages, inclosures, and turnpike roads, carrying on; these public works act like a war in taking from the farmers abundance of hands they used to employ: But if employment does not create industrious people, how comes the present harvest to be in such forwardness? From whence these troops of hands I see in the fields; The instance of this angle of country is peculiarly strong, as they employ no travelling *Scotch* or *Irish* harvestmen; common in many other places. Here I behold some hundreds of men employed by public works, the commissioners of which carry one their business so eagerly, that before the harvest began, they cried 2 *s*. 6 *d*. a day, for a common spadesman: Now how can such works be carried on, at a time that all the business of husbandry is seasonably performed, and yet hands be really wanted? It is impossible.

But here I am aware it will be urged, that the reality of the scarcity of men is proved by the rise and height of wages and pay, which are very great: But this proves nothing; for sure every one must be sensible, that if men were not in being, money could not buy them; a rise of wages is a contingency, a circumstance that operates we know not how, and is founded,

founded, in a multiplicity of cafes, on we know not what: But the exiftence and increafe of the *working* hands are vifible; the progrefs of all public and private works at the fame moment fufficiently prove this. Thus it is of no confequence to either fide of the prefent argument, to talk of wages and pay; whether they are immenfely high, or unreafonably low, it makes no kind of difference; the number of induftrious hands is the fingle point to be attended to as proof: If we recur to the chain of *caufes* of an increafe of induftry, we fhall there find the rife of wages coming in for its fhare, and forming one material link.

Two fhillings and fixpence a day, will undoubtedly tempt fome to work, who would not touch a tool for one fhilling. A fellow that has been ufed to lounge at home, in an idle cottage, may be tempted out by high wages, though not by low ones: Another that in cheap times ufed to bafk himfelf all day in the fun, holding a cow by a line to feed on a balk in dear ones, betakes himfelf to the pick-ax and the fpade. In a word, idle people are converted by degrees into induftrious hands; youths are brought forward to work; even boys perform their fhare, and women at the profpect of great wages clap their hands with cheerfulnefs, and fly to the fickle.

fickle. Thus a new race of the induſtrious is by degrees created, and its increaſe is proportioned to its creation; an effect ſo undoubted, that any village in this country might by an increaſing employment be preſently raiſed to a *Sheffield*, or a *Birmingham*. But who is weak enough to ſuppoſe, that the ſurrounding farmers would therefore want hands.

But there is another circumſtance, which is a ſtrong additional proof, that the increaſe of the induſtrious, occaſioned by an increaſe of employment, muſt be immenſe, and even more than apparent; and that is the effect which great pay is attended with, of making men idle: This now appears a ſtriking contradiction to what I have before aſſerted; but a very few words will ſufficiently explain it.

Great earnings operate, as I have already explained, in bringing people to work who otherwiſe would have continued idle; but they at the ſame time have a ſtrong effect on all who remain the leaſt inclined to idleneſs or other ill courſes, by cauſing them to work but four or five days, to maintain themſelves the ſeven; this is a fact ſo well known in every manufacturing town, that it would be idle to think of proving it by argument.——The operation of great wages therefore is this; they prodigiouſly increaſe the number of the induſtrious;

strious; but at the same time take away the necessity of working a day, for a day's maintenance, which, though it cannot be supposed to render all at times idle, yet must affect a great number.

Thus it is evident, that the increase of employment raises wages, and the rise of wages increases the number of the industrious, the latter effect, must be much greater than apparent; for not increasing *the quantity of labour*, proportionally to the *number of hands*; the increase of the latter must be out of proportion to the increase of employment, or some of the demands would be unsupplied. For instance, 500 hands are employed by husbandry, public works are set on foot, which would take 300, upon the average of work done by labourers among the farmers; but as the increase of wages occasions a new species of idleness, the works would be at a stand, if only 300 new industrious were drawn forth, so that 350, or 400, must possibly be created by the rise of wages, to do the work of 300.

It is for these reasons, which are founded upon the most simple of all principles, the common emotions of human nature, that no industrious nation need ever fear a want of hands for executing any the most extensive plans of public or private improvement; it would be false to assert, that such plans could any where be executed at a given expence, or at a certain rate of wages; but wherever employment exists, that is, money to be expended; workmen can never wanting. A new war may draw off some hundred thousand men, turnpikes may at the same time be greatly extended; marshes may be drained; open fields be inclosed; harbours opened, and new cities raised, without any prejudice to husbandry: Let but the requisite money be found, men can never be wanting:——It is no paradox to assert, that money will at any time make men.

The *East Riding* of *Yorkshire*, is one proof of these assertions among others; for the inclosures and turnpikes were carried on with great spirit, during the latter years of the war, notwithstanding the great scarcity of hands so often talked of *.

Dr.

---

* In my excursion ro the races at *York*, I took the opportunity to view such of the public buildings, &c. as I heard were worth seeing: The Minster claimed the first notice; it is an immense pile, and considering its enormous size, not heavy; though the lightness is not so striking as in many others I have seen. The dimension of it are as follows,

	Feet.
The whole length besides the buttresses is,	524½
Breadth of the east end,	105
Breadth	

[179]

Dr. *Hunter* of *York*, whose polite and obliging conduct I cannot avoid to acknowledge, made known to me several points of husbandry with which I was before unacquainted; particularly, a discovery of his own, which merits great attention; the invention of a drill, the principle and mechanism of which is so extremely simple and plain, the expence so trifling, and the reparation, in case of accidents, so easy, that it cannot be too much commended. It distributes the seed regularly into the furrows made to receive it: These furrows he makes at

	Feet.
Breadth of the west end,	109
Length of the cross isle from north to south,	222
Height of the lanthorn steeple to the vault,	188
Height of it to the top of the leads,	213
Height of the body of the church,	99
Breadth of the inside isles, north and south,	18
Height of the side arches north and south,	42
From the west end to the choir door,	261
Length of the choir from the steps ascending to the door of the present altar table,	$157\frac{1}{2}$
Breadth of the choir,	$46\frac{1}{4}$
From the choir door to the east end,	222
Height of the east window,	75
The breadth of it,	32

The

at such distances as are thought proper, by putting in some broad iron teeth into the common harrow, in place of the sharp ones. These drills the seedsman carefully follows; and, if he is a good servant, the whole field will come up in rows, at such distances as the harrow teeth were set for; a bush-harrow is usually employed to cover the seed. The following is a sketch of it. See plate II. fig. 2.

1 to 2. An oiled-skin bag, 8 or 9 inches long.
3. The body of the drill, 6 inches long.
                                                      4. The

The entrance strikes the mind with that awe which is the result of the magnificence arising from vastness; but I never met with any thing in the proportion of a gothic cathedral, that was either great or pleasing; the loftiness is ever too great for the breadth, insomuch, that one must bend back the head to be able to view the ceiling. What a glorious area would 220 feet long by 100 high, form, if the breadth was proportioned! But how disgusting is a disproportion in any of the dimensions! Here is much carving in stone, that is surprizingly light; particularly the canopy of a monument by the side of the east window; some of the ornaments to archbishop *Savage*'s tomb, and the decorated divisions of the east window, &c. &c. That window is amazingly executed, both in painting and masonry; the gallery across it, and the projecting frame-work of stone is uncommonly
                                                      light

4. The winch, that turns a wheel to throw the feed into the tube 5, which is a hollow cane.
6. Strings to throw round the man's neck, to support the drill by.
7. A view of the open top of the body of the drill.
(8) A circular plate of brass, fixed in by two pins, 9. 9. It is $2\frac{1}{2}$ inches diameter.
(10) A small wheel, $1\frac{1}{4}$ inches diameter, turned by the winch 4, with holes in it large enough to contain eight or ten

---

light and imperceptible at a small distance. The stone work in the upper part of the west window is also traced in a very light and beautiful manner.

The chapter-house is perhaps the most peculiar *Gothic* building in the world, for it is elegance and proportion itself. It is an octagon of 63 feet, the height in the center of the ceiling 67. No person can enter this room without being struck with the justness and harmony of the proportion. Seven of the divisions are large windows, and there is a small gallery that runs round the whole, which I should not have mentioned, but as it is observable the projection of it is so well and skilfully contrived, as not in the least to offend the eye.

The castle or prison in this city is perhaps the most airy, healthy, and *pleasant* prison in Europe;

ten grains of lucerne, rape, &c. &c. four of them.

(11) A piece of **bear-skin fixed** upon the brass plate by two small screws; the hair side downwards, and close to the wheel, to brush off as it turns all seeds but such as lodge in the small cavities, by which means no more than necessary is carried through into the tube.

I know of no invention which, in point of simplicity (the grand article in husbandry implements) exceeds this: If the more complex drill-makers do not imitate this idea, it is much to be regretted.

The

Europe; and for these circumstances it is worth seeing.

The assembly-room is reckoned the finest in *England*; the late Earl of *Burlington* (or *Kent* under him) was the architect who designed it, on the plan of an *Egyptian* hall. It is surrounded by very magnificent *Corinthian* pillars, which have a noble effect. The dimensions are 120 feet long from wall to wall, 40 broad from wall to wall, and 40 high; but as the eye commands, nor even sees further than to the pillars, these are not the proportions that we see; the pillars themselves are above two feet in diameter, and there runs behind them a space of four feet wide; so that the dimensions which appear, and consequently alone to be considered, are 108 long, 28 wide, and 40 high, which height is so totally out of proportion to the breadth, as to

destroy

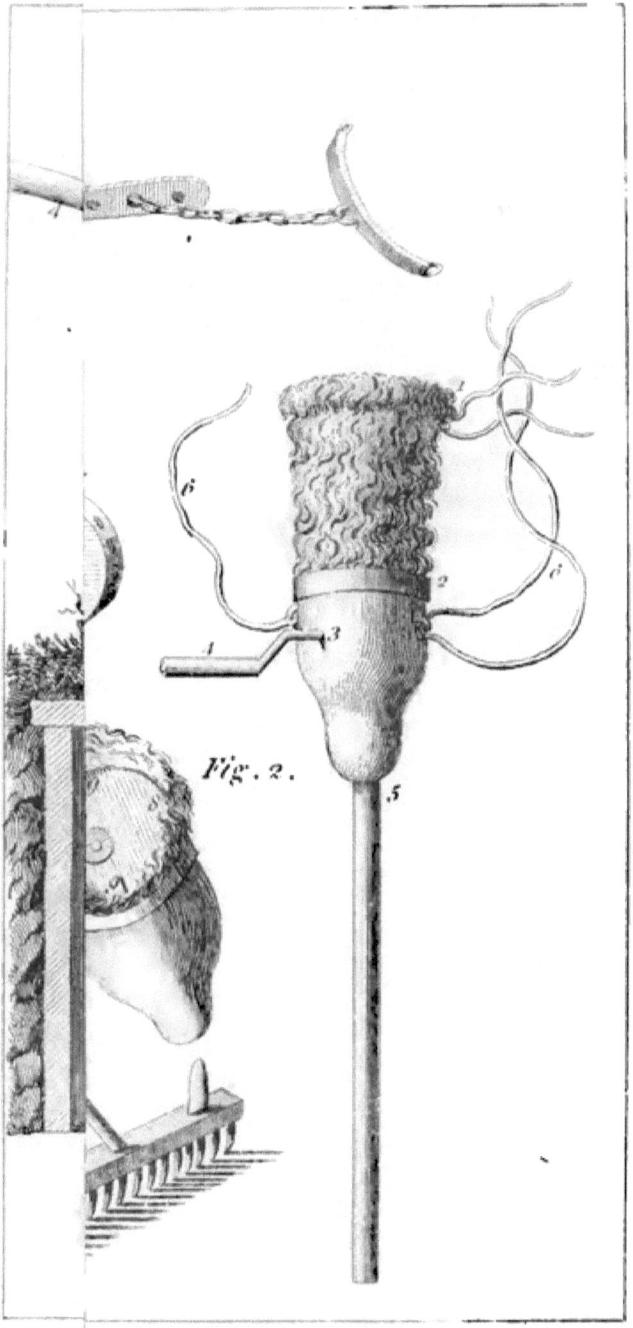

Fig. 2.

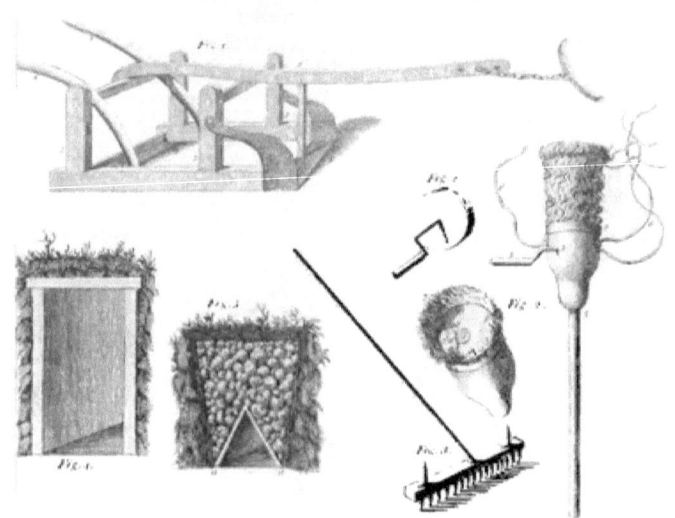

The same drill sows lucerne and rapeseed in the most convenient manner. This gentleman once contrived a rake with two broad iron teeth, for the purpose of opening the furrows; it performed very well. The back of it was set with small teeth to rake in the drills; in that manner he could sow without a horse, the land being well prepared, but he found the harrow above-mentioned a more expeditious instrument. The following is a sketch of the rake, Plate II. Fig. 3.

Dr. *Hunter* has likewise invented a bean hand-drill, and also a wheat one, upon the same

---

destroy in a great measure the elegance of the room, and gives it the appearance of a very fine passage or anti-room to some magnificent saloon. The passage behind the pillars was absurdly intended for the seats, and used so for some time; but the company was by that means quite lost, and seen no more than if they had hid themselves in the cloisters of a cathedral; this occasioned their moving the seats in front of the pillars, which was a great improvement, but at the same time not only lessened the breadth of the room, before too narrow, but likewise took off from the beauty of the pillars, by totally hiding their base, and a large part of their shafts. An assembly-room, which is always dedicated to liveliness and gaiety, should undoubtedly be adorned in a gay and elegant manner, with carving, gilding, and glasses; if a *profusion* of ornament

same principle as the turnip one, only differing in size. He has for some years past been conducting a set of experiments, upon a new system of husbandry, similar to that of the drill, being persuaded the drill husbandry will never become general in *England*: His lands are laid out in ridges nine feet wide, and every other ridge is sown, keeping the intermediate or fallow lands as clear of weeds as possible, by the assistance of the horse-hoe; upon these he sows the next year, and the stubble then becomes the fallow. In this manner the field may be

---

ment was any where excusable, it would certainly be in the temple of pleasure; but this room is so totally devoid of decoration, that the plainness of it must strike every one. The walls have no other ornament than niches, which seem calculated for *Egyptian* mummies: There are no other lights in the room than the glass lustres, (only one of which is fine) which are at present insufficient for lighting it, so that there is a darkness between the pillars quite displeasing; not a morsel of gilding is to be seen, no carving but the capitals of the pillars, and not a glass of any kind in the room; a defect which, I am sure, the ladies will agree in condemning.——But when a room that requires decoration is surrounded with pillars, they should certainly be at such a distance from each other as to admit a full view of a space on the wall behind, sufficient for a large glass or picture,

be kept under the same grain for any number of years, taking care to bestow a small portion of manures at proper seasons. An acre of middling land brings him three quarters of wheat, which for that country is a good crop. The grain is always well fed, and the land is never distressed. In this way, all kinds of land are made to produce the grain most suitable to their respective natures; it will be found from this, that the Doctor is of opinion, that all sorts of corn draw the same nourishment, and only differ in taking up more or less.

---

ture, with a spreading frame for a wreath of candles in it, which these at *York* will not; and if they would, such ornaments should certainly be in a good measure commanded from the whole room, which cannot be the case with pillars. For this reason, I apprehend, that pilasters are for an assembly-room more proper than pillars, as they admit a full view of the ornamented wall, at the same time that they assist in decorating it. It must however be confessed, that if the walls are such as should be screened, then pillars are preferable. Another objection to them is, the drowning the music. The adjoining rooms for tea, cards, &c. are nothing.

Upon the banks of the river, which is a fine one, they have a very good walk, near a mile long. In the middle it winds through a little grove of trees in a very pleasing manner, the river appearing through them in a picturesque stile;

No one can understand the principles of agriculture and vegetation better than this very ingenious cultivator, whose ideas are philosophical and perspicuous, and whose experiments are accurate and judicious.

From *York* I returned to *Risby*, by way of *Stillingfleet*, which road, though out of the way, I took for the sake of the variation; and in consequence of the kind attention of my friend Mr. *Ellerker*, who possesses at that place a large estate. The following are the minutes I made of the agriculture there: The soil is of two sorts, clay

---

stile; from this walk you look one way upon the river running through the meadow grounds, and the other up to the bridge in the city, the center arch of which is very large, and forms a fine object; the sloops, barges, boats, and business of the river, are most lively objects for this very agreeable walk.

But by far the most curious things to be seen at *York* are the copies of several capital paintings, worked by Miss *Morret*, a lady of a most surprizing genius. It is impossible to view her performances without great astonishment; for certainly the art of imitation in work is carried by her to the highest point of perfection. Exceedingly fine tapestries are often seen, and here and there a piece of flowers, or a bunch of grapes, done in a most pleasing manner; but to copy fine paintings, containing several figures, with a grace, a brilliancy, and an elegance superior to the

clay and sand, but most of the latter; the former is a strong fertile soil, which yields good crops of all sorts of corn; and the sand is mostly of a dark colour, rich, not shewing any of the signs of poor or barren land; for the spontaneous growths are large and vigorous, such as whins in the uncultivated parts and neutral grasses; even the pastures on this sand yield very tolerable crops of hay and feed; and the hedge-wood is strong and luxuriant. Some of the fields, indeed, have a lighter-coloured and a thinner sand that is not so rich, but none in which the spontaneous growth

does

---

the originals, was reserved for this most ingenious lady. The following are her principal pieces:

Two landscapes from *Zuccarelli*; they represent waterfalls, and are surprizingly performed. The nature and elegance of the colours, the glowing brilliancy, the light seen through the trees, the foam of the water, and the general effects of the clear obscure are imitated in the happiest manner.

Four ditto, by *Gaspar Poussin*. Three of these pieces are exceeding fine, the parts well connected, the general expression fine, and the colouring good: The fourth is a piece of rocks, but they are not the rocks of *Salvator*. Miss *Morret*'s copy is however evidently just; the faults, if such, are those of the painter.

The descent of St. Ignatius, by *P. da Cortona*; the

work

does not shew a larger portion of nourishment. The crops of corn on these sands were tolerably good, that is, as good as they could be with bad husbandry.

The mean rent (tythe-free) of *Stillingfleet*, is about 14 s. an acre; but if the adjoining country is, included, it is not above 10 s.

Their course of crops,

1. Fallow	1. Turnips
2. Wheat	2. Barley
3. Barley, &c.	3. Oats, pease or beans
4. Beans. And	

About

---

work good, but the original is not a pleasing picture.

A large landscape from *Bartolomeo*, very capital; the effects of the work are here surprizing. The perspective is finely imagined, the groupes of trees excellent, the diffusion of light extremely pleasing, and carried by the trees on the left side in a beautiful manner; the keeping exceedingly fine.

Democritus, in a contemplative posture, from *Salvator Rosa*; nothing can be more nobly designed, or more expressively finished, than the figure of *Democritus*: His attitude is admirable, the lean of the head on the hand fine, and the light falling across the face in the most picturesque manner; nor can any thing exceed the expression of the face, hands, and feet.

Diogenes

About *Selby*, many farmers pursue the following:

1. Turnips
2. Barley
3. Clover
4. Wheat,

At *Fuforth* and *Nabourn*,

1. Fallow
2. Wheat or rye
3. Barley
4. Pease or beans

For wheat they plough four times, sow three bushels, and reap at a medium three quarters. They stir three times for barley, sow three bushels, and reap the same quantity as of wheat. For oats they plough once or twice, sow five bushels, and reckon

four

Diogenes; his cup thrown from him; its companion by the same master; the attitude and expressive countenance of the old man with his hand in his bosom, the air of his head, and his drapery are excellent; the figure of *Diogenes* not designed in so perfect a manner, but the expression and beauty of the work in the whole inimitable.

Two large landscapes, companions; admirably done.

Figure of an old gardener holding a basket of fruit; the expression of this piece is astonishing: *Rembrandt* in his happiest stile scarcely ever exceeded the imitation of the face and hands, where the muscular traces, and the lines of age, are hit off with the most peculiar spirit.

Christ praying in the garden, from *Han. Carrach.* This work is executed most inimitably; nothing can exceed the brilliancy of the colours,

the

four quarters the mean produce. They likewise give but one earth for beans, sow five bushels broad-cast, and reckon the mean crop 2½ quarters, or three; they never hoe. It is asserted, that *Edward Smith*, of *Cawood*, once had ten quarters of beans per acre, in the broad-cast way, from five bushels of seed, and without any hoeing, which is almost incredible for an after-crop. They sow a few turnips, plough for them four or five times, never hoe them, feed them off the land with sheep and beasts, and reckon the mean value per acre at about 27 *s*. I walked over several of

---

the diffusion of light across the drapery; or the turn (or foreshortning) of the angel's arm; the countenance of *Christ* is not of great expression, but the copy I doubt not is perfectly just, for a graceful expression of the mind was not *Hannibal*'s excellency.

Boys, from *Rubens*; not finished; capitally done. The laughing expression of the countenances, and the bends and plaits of the bodies inimitably copied. To what a height of perfection may we not suppose this lady to arrive, when she has improved on such noble pieces!

Besides these, there are several others of flowers, fruit, pheasants, ducks, &c. &c. many of which are exquisitely performed.

Upon the whole, one cannot view such admirable and uncommon perfection, without a very

of their crops, and found them prodigiously thick of plants and weeds, all promiscuous. They plough three or four times for rye, sow two bushels and a half, and reap at an average three quarters; they sow it chiefly on their sands, as they find wheat on that soil very apt to be mildewed.

Tassels for dressing cloth have been cultivated in their richest clays to good advantage. They give the land a year's fallow, weed the crop by hand once, at the expence of seven, eight, or ten shillings per acre: It remains three years: They are sold by the thousand, and are reckoned very profitable, but are supposed to exhaust the land greatly. Here are likewise many potatoes cultivated, but more about *Fuforth* and *Nabourn*; the method is the same in all; they give a winter fallow for them, plant 16 bushels on an acre in rows two feet asunder, and the plants one foot, plough between them two or three times, and hand-weed the same at 5 s. an acre; 80 bushels they reckon a middling crop;

---

very great degree of surprize; and those who, after reading these imperfect notes minuted from memory, shall view these most elegant productions of female genius, will find them greatly to exceed their expectation, and to abound with beauties of the most striking and pleasing nature.

the price 1*s.* a bushel. Let us calculate the expences and profit.

Expences.	£.	s.	d.
Rent, — — —	0	10	0
Three ploughings, —	0	8	6
Planting, — —	0	10	0
Plants, — — —	0	16	0
Two horse hoeings, —	0	3	0
Two hand-weedings, —	0	5	0
Digging up*, — —	0	15	0
Profit,	£.3	7	6

Product.			
Eighty bushels, — —	4	0	0
Expences, — —	3	7	6
Profit,	£.0	12	6

It is plain from hence, that the idea of the profit and convenience of raising potatoes for their own use is false; for the return, even without manuring, is by no means equivalent to the expences; but at *Fuforth*, and the neighbourhood of *York*, the produce is greater.

* If ploughed up it will be less, but all the roots will not then be got.

Their pastures they lay down with corn, 12 *lb.* of white clover, and one quarter of hay-seeds, and sometimes four bushels of rib-grafs (plantain). They always lay them down, or rather *up*, in broad high ridges, by which means there is always a breadth of about two yards in the furrows that is good for naught, quite poisoned with water.

They have better ideas of manuring, than of most other parts of husbandry; they lay large quantities of lime on their lands with good advantage; the quantity from two to three chaldrons, sometimes one and an half, and ten loads of dung. It costs them 8 *s.* a chaldron, and 1 *s.* 2 *d.* carriage; it is generally laid for wheat or barley, and lasts three years. Paring and burning is practised among them; the paring costs 10 *s.* per acre, the burning 5 *s.* and the spreading 1 *s.* 2 *d.* They have no flocks of sheep large enough for folding.

Some clover is sown among their barley; they leave it on the ground but one year; always mow it once, and sometimes twice; get one and an half or two ton of hay at two mowings.

They reckon the product of a cow at from 3 *l.* to 4 *l.* 10 *s.* Upon a medium, two firkins of butter per cow, at 25 *s.* Cheese about one third in value of the butter, besides calf and pigs. Their method of feeding

Vol. I.   O   calves

calves and weaning them is extraordinary; for they never let any fuck above ten days or a fortnight, whether for killing or weaning, but in general only two or three days for weaning, after which they are fed with fkim-milk; and numbers of oxen, even of 60, 70, or 100 ftone, are weaned almoft as foon as born in this cheap manner, which, in the fouth of *England* would be thought impoffible. A middling cow, in the height of the fummer's feed, will give about four gallons of milk per day.

The tillage is done all by horfes, two or three in a plough abreaft, and the general quantity done in a journey is an acre. The price of ploughing, if hired, is 3 *s*. 6 *d*. per acre the firft ftirring, and 2 *s*. 6 *d*. the reft.

They reckon that 300 *l*. is fufficient to ftock a farm of 100 *l*. a year, half grafs and half arable; and 200 *l*. for the fame, all arable; which fums are very low, and would never allow of any fpirited culture.

LABOUR.

In hay-time and harveft, 1 *s*. 6 *d*. a day, and board.

In winter, 8 *d*. and ditto.

After *Candlemas*, 1 *s*. and ditto.

Reaping wheat, barley or oats, 6 *s*. per acre.

Mowing barley, &c. and binding into fheaves, 3 *s*. 6 *d*.

Mowing grafs, 2 *s*.

Making ditto into hay, 1 s.
Ditching, new, the ditch 4 feet wide, and 2¼ deep, 8 d. or 9 d. the rood of 7 yards.
Repairing ditto, 4½ d. ditto.
Threshing wheat, 2 s. a quarter.
—————— barley, 1 s.
—————— oats, 10 d.
—————— beans, 1 s.
Making faggots, 1 s. a load of 60.
Servants wages; a head man, 10 l. 10 s. to 12 l.
A ploughing lad, 8 l.
A dairy-maid, 5 l.
A common maid, 4 l. 4 s.
Women and children earn by spinning, 4 d. a day. Some only 1 d.
But little drinking of tea among them.

PROVISIONS, &c.

Bread, *per lb.*	1 d.	Mutton,	-	3¼ d.
Butter,	- -	6	Pork,	-	3½
Ditto firkin,	-	4½	Candles,	-	6½
Cheese,	-	2	Soap,	-	6
Beef,	-	3¼			

New-milk, a pint and half for 1 d.
Hay, 20 s. a ton.
Labourer's house rent, 20 s.
Repairs of their tools, 5 s.
Their firing, 20 s.

IMPLEMENTS, &c.

A new waggon, 13 l. 10 s. (two feet six inches wide at bottom, and nine feet long.)

A cart, 8 *l.*   Sharpening do. 1 *d.*
A plough, 1 *l.* 2 *s.*   Laying a coulter, 1 *s.*
A harrows, 1 *l.* 2 *s.*   Sharpening do. 1 *d.*
A roller 1 *l.* 1 *s.*   Shoeing a cart horse,
Laying a share, 8 *d.*   1 *s.* 4 *d.*

BUILDING.

Oak timber, 1 *s.* to 1 *s.* 6 *d.*
Ash ditto, 9 *d.*
Elms, 1 *s.*
Bricks per thousand, 10 *s.*
They burn in clamps; twenty chaldrons of coals burn 100,000.

The farmers here buy their sheep in at from 10 to 13 *s.* each, and sell them after a year's keeping at 25 or 26 *s.* The particulars I gained of several farms are as follows:

155 Acres in all	4 Oxen
77 ½ Grass	12 Cows
77 ½ Arable	30 Sheep
£.100 Rent	3 Servants
4 Horses	2 Labourers

He sows

17 Acres of wheat	5 Turnips
40 Spring corn	

Another:

240 Acres in all	8 or 10 oxen,
120 Grass	and young cattle
120 Arable	14 Cows
£.152 Rent	6 Servants
8 Horses	3 Labourers

He

[197]

He sows
25 Acres of wheat   25 Of clover
25 Of spring corn

Another:
107 Acres in all   2 Oxen
 30 Arable   15 Cows
 77 Grass   2 Servants
£. 75 Rent   1 Labourer
  3 Horses

He sows
 8 Acres of wheat   10 Spring corn

Another:
90 Acres in all   2 Oxen
40 Arable   6 Cows
50 Grass   10 Sheep
£. 60 Rent   2 Servants
 4 Horses   1 Labourer

He sows
10 Acres of wheat   10 Of beans and
10 Of barley   oats

Another:
115 Acres in all   2 Oxen
 75 Arable   6 Cows
 40 Grass   10 Sheep
£. 84 Rent   2 Labourers
  4 Horses   3 Servants

He sows
20 Acres of wheat   30 Of spring corn

Another:
110 Acres in all   £. 80 Rent
 60 Arable   4 Horses
 50 Grass   2 Oxen
                       6 Cows

6 Cows   3 Servants
20 Sheep   1 Labourer

He sows:

15 Acres of wheat   30 Of spring corn

Another:

160 Acres in all   2 Oxen
80 Arable   12 Cows
80 Grass   50 Sheep
£. 110 Rent   3 Servants
6 Horses   3 Labourers

He sows

25 Acres of wheat   20 Of oats and
20 Of barley   beans

Another:

130 Acres in all   4 Oxen
70 Arable   16 Cows
60 Grass   10 Sheep
£. 82 Rent   2 Servants
6 Horses   2 Labourers

He sows

13 Acres of wheat   12 Of oats, &c.
16 Of barley

Another:

122 Acres in all   2 Oxen
80 Arable   8 Cows
42 Grass   10 Sheep
£. 80 Rent   3 Servants
6 Horses   2 Labourers

In

In the whole townſhip of *Stillingfleet*, are,
    1700 Acres
       13 Farms
       60 Acres of wood
       20 Of common ſheep walk
       20 Labourers

Poor rates, 6 d. in the pound rack rent.

I know very few tracts of country enjoying greater natural advantages than this neighbourhood, they have a very fine navigable river borders their farms, which carries any or all of their products to *York*, at the ſmall diſtance of ſeven miles, and alſo keeps a conſtant communication open to the ſouthern rivers and with *Hull*; this navigation being at their very doors, ſpares them all expences of land carriage on their corn, and at the ſame time enables them to bring whatever quantities of manure they pleaſe from *York*, on very eaſy terms, and lime from other parts at as low a rate. Theſe advantages are ineſtimable.

Their ſoil contains in almoſt every farm that variety which a ſenſible cultivator would moſt wiſh for, *viz.* an excellent light ſandy loam, in ſome fields quite a ſand, but rich, and abounding with luxuriant ſpontaneous growth; and a ſtrong clay, good enough to yield beneficial crops of the moſt exhauſting vegetables. Unfortunately however, the farmers, who are in general great flovens, make very little use of thefe advantages: I fhall venture to recommend an alteration in their conduct and urge them no longer to neglect the converting their fields to the greateft profit.

All their fandy foil, of which they have a large quantity, is a good and found turnip land as any in the world; and ought beyond a doubt to be thrown into this courfe of crops,

1. Turnips
2. Barley
3. Clover and ray grafs for two, three, or four years according to their want of feed.
4. Wheat. This crop, *in fuch a courfe*, would not be liable to the mildew.

A fallow upon this land is totally ufelefs, and confequently a great lofs; but then the very foul of this culture lies in the thorough hoeing of the turnips; for the feveral ploughings for that root, greatly pulverifing every particle of the foil, gives life and vegetation to innumerable feeds of weeds, which are lodged in the land, and fpringing up with the turnips, infeft the foil to its abfolute ruin, unlefs they are totally extirpated by the hoe: By means of which the barley crop is clean; and the clover and ray-grafs laid into a proper bed to receive it. Unlefs this is

the

the case, how would it be possible in this course to have a good crop of wheat? And yet no wheat is finer than what is thus sown in many tracks of country I have viewed. The clover and ray-grass would enable them to keep good stocks of sheep to fold all the year round, and to eat off their turnips with, to the greatest profit, which would be a constant and regularly increasing improvement to their whole farms. But all this is very contrary to their present management, and totally incompatible with the wretched custom of not hoeing their turnips.

In the next place, the culture of carrots on their sands would be an admirable improvement; I examined attentively several fields in which the sand was of a dark colour, moist, and smelt and felt as if of a rich nature, which the weeds and crops from it proved to be no false conjecture; at the same time it admitted one's running in a walking-cane a yard deep; this is precisely the soil, which, about *Woodbridge* in *Suffolk*, is applied to the culture of carrots to so great profit: This root is for every purpose, infinitely superior to turnips, so that if it was substituted for them in the preceding course, the profit would be vastly greater: But such an extent cannot be expected at first, and supposing turnips to be

the

the general fallow crop, yet carrots ought undoubtedly to be directly introduced so as every farmer to have a field of them every year; for this purpose, I should advise those who attempted the culture, to pursue it nearly upon the following plan.

The corn stubble to be ploughed in sometime in the autumn; by two ploughs in the same furrow, to the depth of 18 inches: Another common ploughing before *Christmas*; and to plough and sow the latter end of *February*, or the beginning of *March*, according to the weather, but never when the land is wet or adhesive. After this last ploughing, to be harrowed fine and level, and then six pounds of carrot seed to be sown at four or five casts over each acre of land, and lightly harrowed in. When the plants are about three or four inches high, or in other words, to be seen plainly in the hoeing, they should have that operation for the first time; for which purpose, a dry season must be taken, and many hands thrown in at once for the chance of finishing before rain comes, which would set the weeds again. The people employed should all crawl along on their knees, if the young carrots are thickly surrounded with weeds, their hoes four inches wide, and the handles 18 inches long; but if the land is clean, and the

plants

plants easily to be distinguished, they may stand to hoe them, the handles of their hoes of a due length for that purpose. The plants should, at this first hoeing, be set at five or six inches asunder, and if any two plants, or a plant and a weed stand so close, that the hoe cannot easily separate them, the fingers should be used for that purpose.

About a fortnight or three weeks after, according to the weather, a dry time should be taken for harrowing over the whole field; this will not pull up one plant in twenty, but will loosen the moulds, make the carrots thrive, and if any of the weeds are set again, will displace them.

As soon as the carrots are six inches high, the first opportunity of dry weather should be taken to give the second hoeing; which should be performed with nine inch hoes, every other plant should now be cut up, and the remainder left at 16 or 18 inches asunder, the latter distance best; every weed cut up, and the whole surface carefully loosened: If any weeds grow close to a plant, the hoer should stoop and pluck them out with his fingers; the last hoeing (with the same hoes) should be given before the leaves join; or as soon as the effect of the second is fully seen, that the weeds then left may plainly appear: none should now

now be left, and the soil every where cut by the hoe, even in places where no weeds are seen. Afterwards, if any should accidentally sprout up and shew themselves above the carrots, boys should be sent in to draw them by hand; for all depends on totally extirpating them; and none of these operations must be neglected under the pretence of other business, such as hay or harvest.

By the end of *October*, they will be fit to dig up. Carrots are used two ways; they are dug up, toped, dried and cleaned, and laid up in a house for the winter to be used as wanted, or they are drawn and left in the field to be fed there by cattle: Both methods have advantages, in the first, the crop goes much the farthest, and may be applied to purposes, which it cannot in the other; in the second, the land on which they grew is greatly improved: I should, however, (unless upon a great breadth of ground) prefer the former; for besides the peculiar advantages attending it, that of raising manure may be added, as large quantities must arise from using the carrots in the farm-yard, &c. and the danger of being prevented drawing them in the other way by frosts should not be forgotten.

The

The best way of taking them up is with a three-pronged fork, they should be thrown into heaps, or left scattered about (if the weather will admit) to dry, and then carted home; there the tops should be cut off and thrown to any cattle: all will eat them greedily, especially hogs: The roots cleared from dirt and laid up in any room, house, or barn, surrounded well with straw to keep them from the frosts. Horses may be fed with them all winter instead of oats, and will do their work as well, provided it is not riding quick: They should be washed clean, chopt in pieces in a tub with a sharp spade, and given in chaff: I kept six horses so one winter; they were worked very hard, and stood it as well as they used to do with oats: Oxen will fat on them most excellently; they should have them in mangers, with a little hay now and then in the rack; and kept clean littered with straw, which will make plenty of manure. For sheep they should be scattered about a dry grass field, and will be ready for them in *March* or *April*, when turnips and all other food are gone. Nothing is better for hogs; sows will bring up large litters of pigs by this root; and pigs may be weaned upon them.

An acre of good carrots will measure about 300 bushels, and the farmer will find
them

them worth to him from 1 s. to 1 s. 6 d. per bushel, or near 20 l. per acre. But the product, like that of all other crops, will vary according to the goodness of the soil, and rise to 5 or 600 bushels. But all the sands I viewed at *Stillingfleet*, would yield good crops; the dark coloured ones the best. If the farmers there and in the neighbourhood, or any others upon light deep soils of any sort none better than loams if neither heavy nor wet) will go into this article of culture, I venture to assure them, they will find it greatly advantageous, and make their sands more profitable than their richest clays.

Another improvement much wanted in this country, is that of hollow draining the wet lands, all their clay soils and some of their light ones are much damaged by wet, which they have scarcely any notions of carrying off. Their clays, whether grass or arable, are kept up on broad high ridges; a practice seemingly judicious, but when it is remarked, that they do not take care to convey away the water which settles in the furrows, it must strike the least attentive observer, that a vast quantity of land must be lost by the overflowing of the water: Their pastures are all overrun with rushes and other aquatic weeds, the furrows quite full, and many three quarters

ters up the ridges, and all the feed and tillage in their arable lands is thrown away in the furrows, for the crop dies and is succeeded by quantities of weeds.

Instead of this mistaken conduct, they should undoubtedly plough down their ridges, level the surface, and then hollow drain the whole field, by numerous and well directed cuts, after which they might keep them on a perfect level, for grass, and use only moderate ridges of two bouts in their arable fields. It is a common complaint among them, that the manure they lay on to their fields, lasts but a very short time; which is totally owing to their want of draining, for the salts, and even the manure itself is presently washed away by the wetness of the soil; an effect which would be quite prevented by draining.

To inform these farmers that it is a very slovenly custom to let their pastures be overrun with bushes, mole and ant hills is surely needless: They must know that nothing would answer better than clearing away all rubbish of that sort; they know this, but have not the spirit, or at least the money to practise it. As to the hills and all little inequalities of the surface they should be pared off level, and nothing makes so fine a compost for all sorts of land as these turfs mixed with lime and dung;

dung; they should make a layer of them, about two feet deep, and length and breadth proportioned to the quantity, then bring a layer of lime eight inches deep over the turfs, then another layer of turfs two feet deep, then a layer of yard dung 18 inches deep, then another layer of lime eight inches deep; then a layer of turfs two feet deep; next a layer of *York* manure, cinder ashes, or mortar rubbish, 12 inches deep, and lastly, another of lime eight inches. This hill would be 12 feet high in the middle, as each layer should be made with a slope, particularly the first, for the rest to be right, that the carts might drive up easily; it should lay in this manner about two months, then it should be turned over and mixed; but on no account in the common way of doing that business. Let the men begin at one end, (or if there be a great number of them, along one side) and turn over the compost, cutting evenly through the layers, chopping to small pieces all the ant hills and turfs, mixing the pieces well with lime and dung, and when mixed, they must throw it from them parallel with the hill to have a clear space, a yard broad between the part mixed, and that to mix; when this beginning is made, some of the men should get on to the hill, and others remain the vacant space, the former to throw down the compost, and the latter to chop and mix it, and then to give it a casting throw, like corn, on to the new made heap, that is finished. By these means all the kinds of manure will be thoroughly reduced to little pieces, and perfectly mixed together: If the work is well done, the compost will do without further mixing; though, as the expence of a second turning would be a trifle after it is so well reduced, and every turning would raise a fresh fermentation, a second might be advisable: The farmer would be surprised at the vast benefit his crops would receive from a manuring of this compost after the draining; before that work is done it would be idle to do this or any other.

I have ventured these sentiments upon the improvement of *Stillingfleet* and its neighbourhood, from a sincere desire of promoting the interests, not only of agriculture in general, but that of this district in particular, that its cultivators may have objects of virtuous emulation in view, and expend their money, and give their attention to a plan, which can scarcely fail of being greatly advantageous to them: They are happy in an excellent landlord, who will never reluctantly give, either his protection or encouragement.

In an excursion I made from *Risby*, into *Holderness*, I took minutes of the present state of that large tract of country, some of which I shall here lay before the reader.

The soil is in general clay; the rent from 10 s. to 25 s. an acre, that of cars, (marshes) from 6 s. to 10 s. The farms rise from 20 l. a year to 200 l. but chiefly about 100 l. As to courses, in the open fields they run a crop to a fallow, but in the inclosures, four crops to a fallow with clover.

For wheat, they plough four or five times, but only once after clover, sow two bushels per acre, and reap at a medium, four quarters. For barley, they stir four times if fallowed; twice after turnips, sow three bushels per acre, and gain five quarters in return. They stir but once for oats, sow four bushels, and reap five quarters. For beans they give but one ploughing, sow three bushels and an half, and gain four quarters. For rape they generally pare and burn, and plough once, but sometimes after oats, when they likewise give but one ploughing; sow a peck an acre, and gain upon average, five quarters.

An acre and a half or two acres of grass, they reckon sufficient to fat an ox of 80 stone. In rearing their calves, they give them

them new milk for the firſt week, and then ſkim milk for two months. They feed their cars with young ſtock, and working cattle. Some farmers have of late begun to lime; and thoſe who live within ſix miles of *Hull*, bring manure of many ſorts from thence. The following ſketches of farms will ſhew the general œconomy of this country.

  100 Acres in all 8 Fatting beaſts
   50 Arable   100 Sheep
   50 Graſs   2 Men
£.120 Rent   2 Boys
    6 Horſes   2 Maids
    4 Oxen   1 Labourer.
    6 Cows

      Another,

  90 Acres in all 6 Cows
   30 Arable   6 Fatting beaſts
   60 Graſs   40 Sheep
 £.80 Rent   1 Man
    4 Horſes   1 Boy
    2 Oxen   1 Maid.

      Another,

  150 Acres in all 6 Oxen
   60 Arable   10 Cows
   90 Graſs   12 Fatting beaſts
£.120 Rent   16 Young cattle
    8 Horſes   40 Sheep
           2 Men

2 Men   2 Boys
2 Maids   2 Labourers.

Draining is the great improvement of the country, by means of which the land is much advanced in value, so that many acres which once yielded from 6 d. to 5 s. now are let at from 12 s. to 35 s. The great work of main drains is done by act of parliament, all the superfluous water is carried by them into the sea at *Hull*; but as the level of these waters is lower than that of the sea at spring tides, a sluice at a very great expence (about 3000 l.) is erected, containing two large doors which open in common by force of the fresh water, and let it into the sea; but when the spring tides rise, those doors are shut by the superior weight of water, and the country prevented from being overflowed. Plate III. fig. 1. 2. are sketches I took of a model of this sluice, made ¼ of an inch to a foot.

For the purpose of raising the water out of the ditches of private persons into the drains, they erect mills that work by wind, which raise it various heights. I took a draught of a small one, Plate IV. which would be of incomparable use in many countries, where these mills are quite unknown, for carrying water away, in places where

Fig. 1.

Fig. 2.

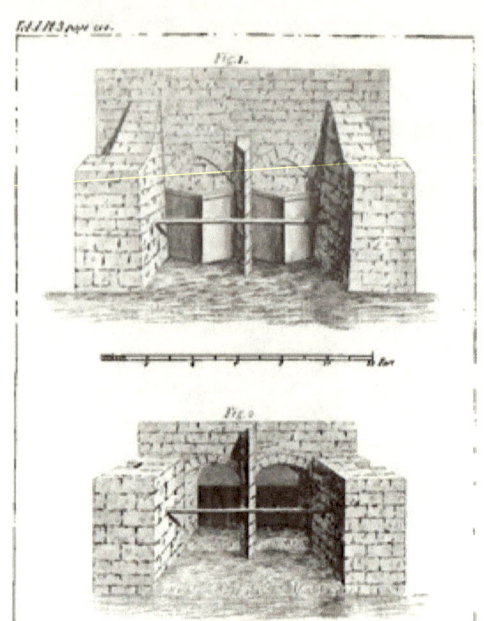

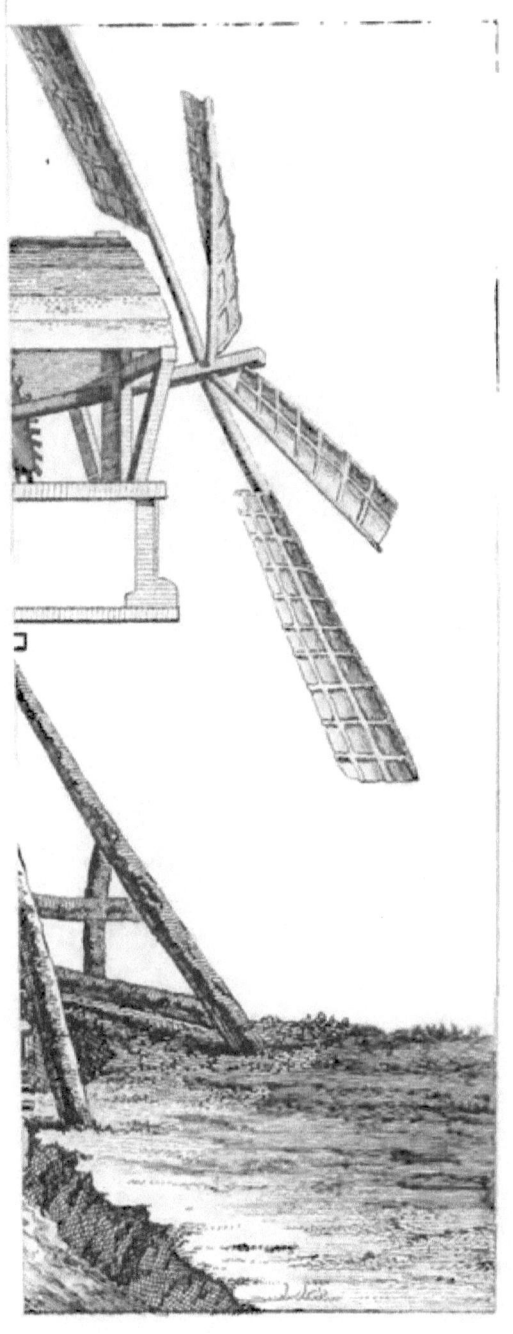

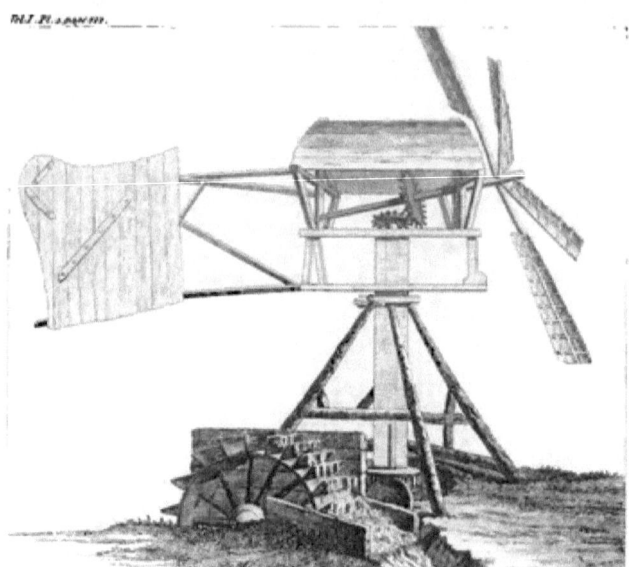

where a fall was difficult to be gained. The expence is 40 *l*. From which sum they rise in price to 400 *l*.

LABOUR.

In harvest, 10 *s*. a week, and board.
In hay-time, ditto.
In winter, 8 *s*. 6 *d*. a week.
Reaping wheat, 6 *s*. though but seldom done by the acre.
Mowing corn, 3 *s*.
———— grass, 1 *s*. 6 *d*. to 2 *s*. 6 *d*.
A drain, four feet wide at top, two deep, and three upon the slope, 8 *d*. to 16 *d*. a rood of seven yards.
Threshing wheat, 1 *s*. 6 *d*. to 3 *s*.
————— barley, 1 *s*. to 1 *s*. 3 *d*.
————— oats, 8 *d*. to 10 *d*.
————— beans, 1 *s*. to 1 *s*. 2 *d*.
————— rape, 2 *s*. a day, and board.
Head man, 12 *l*. to 14 *l*.
Next ditto, 9 *l*.
Maids ditto, from 2 *l*. 10 *s*. to 5 *l*.

IMPLEMENTS.

A waggon, 15 *l*.	Laying a share, 8 *d*.
A cart, 8 *l*.	———— coulter, 4 *d*.
A plough, 18 *s*.	Shoeing, 1 *s*. 4 *d*.
A harrow, 10 *s*.	

BUILDING.

Bricks, per 1000, 12 s.
Oak, 1 l. 15 s. to 6 l. per ton of 40 feet.
Ash, 16 s to 35 s.
Elm, 30 s. to 40 s.
Carpenter, per day, 20 d.
Mason, 2 s.*

---

* Before I take my leave of *Risby*, a place I have so much reason to remember with pleasure, I shall attempt to give you some idea of what it will be when Mr. *Ellerker* has executed his present intentions: He has begun his alterations, and when they are finished, he will have the pleasure of living in one of the most agreeable seats in this country. The house, which is a large quadrangle with three fronts, is situated on the brow of a rising ground, and overlooks to the south, west, and east, a fine inequality of soil well spread with an old growth of wood; a winding valley runs before the south front, at the distance of 2 or 300 yards, the banks of which are fringed with spontaneous thorn trees: To the north is a large lawn surrounded with plantations; to the north west, but unseen from the house, is a middling sized park, all hill and dale, and wood, exceedingly beautiful; near the house to the east, are several groves of young timber; this is the present picture and the outline of the future one.

Mr.

Having brought my visit in to this angle of country to a conclusion, I shall end this letter with a few remarks on those points of husbandry, in which this part of *East Riding* is particularly backward.

In the first place, I shall observe, that their courses of crops and general management of their arable land, are very faulty; and particularly so in a country where grass land of any goodness is extremely scarce. Artificial grass and roots for the food of cattle, are of great profit, not only by enabling the farmer to keep large stocks of cattle both in summer and winter, but likewise by ameliorating and cleaning the arable

---

Mr. *Ellerker* purposes to throw down the fences of the inclosures between the park to the house, so as to join it on one side to the garden, and in front to throw it around the water; taking in all the lawn and plantations. The valley, which runs before the house to the south, is to be floated with water, and will then have the appearance of a very noble irregular lake, winding both to the right and left into a wood to the length of a mile and half, and in many places above 100 yards wide. The underwood, in that part of the grove (to the east) which stretches down towards the valley will be grubbed up, old garden walls thrown down, and all obstructions removed, so that the lake

arable lands, and confequently improving the crops of corn.

In this part of *Yorkſhire*, the foil is in general good turnip land, and the farmers have ſhewn they are of the ſame opinion, by introducing them; but their culture is ſo wretchedly defective, that I may, without the imputation of a paradox, aſſert, they had better have let it alone. Very few of them hoe at all, and thoſe who do, execute it in ſo ſlovenly a way, that neither the crop or the land are the leaſt the better for it. With ſuch management, turnips are by no means beneficial in a courſe of

---

may be ſeen from the houſe among the ſtems of the young trees, than which nothing can have a finer effect; for as the grove will be dark, the water, when the ſun ſhines on it, will appear through the trees in the moſt picturefque manner ——— On the right ſide, the water will flow far up the valley, and be terminated by wood, with an ornamented bridge in the ſhade of it. On one ſide of the water is to be a pleaſure-ground, in a ſequeſtered hollow of varied ground, ſcattered with old thorns and large timber trees; ſome of theſe are to be thrown into clumps by the addition of flowering ſhrubs, and the graſs kept cloſely ſhaven. From many parts of it the views of the water will be various and pictureſque in ſome ſpots: It will flow up among the

of crops, as they leave the foil fo foul that a **fallow** rather than another crop ought to fucceed.

The great **benefit** of turnips is not the mere value of the crop, but the cleaning the land fo well as to enable the farmer to cultivate the artificial graffes with profit. If nine hufbandmen out of ten, give a complete year's fallow to a field, they cannot forbear taking two, and perhaps three crops of corn in confequence of it; fo that graffes cannot be fown with any profpect of benefit; but when turnips pay for the expence of the year's fallow, they are induced to fow the grafs with the firft fucceeding

---

the groves; and in others ftretch away from the eye in noble fheets, under a bold fhore finely fpread with hanging woods. A temple will be erected, commanding a moft beautiful fcenery of varied ground, wood, and water. From the houfe will be feen, over the lake, fome fine irregular flopes fcattered with a few trees and thorns, rifing to a plantation of firs, which, when fomewhat altered, will have a very elegant appearance. Embofomed in their center is to rife a little Grecian temple, juft fhowing its dome among the trees, from whence will be viewed, on every fide, a moft beautiful profpect; it will look down on the lake with an irregular fhore on the oppofite fide, rifing to the houfe, which appears in the fore ground of a noble wood

ceeding corn crop, which renders a fallow unneceſſary; and is beyond all doubt, upon turnip land, and in a country where natural graſs is ſcarce, the moſt profitable huſbandry of all.

The farmers of this country ought therefore to neglect turnips totally, or cultivate them in the clean huſband-like manner that is practiſed in many parts of *England*, of thoroughly pulverizing the land and hoeing them twice or thrice, or as often as neceſſary, to keep them diſtinct from each other, and *perfectly* free from

---

wood ſpread above it, and ſtretching away to the right and left. On one ſide from this temple, will be viewed a very extenſive country, particularly a fine vale of wood, with *Beverley* minſter riſing from the center of it; in another ſpot will be ſeen *Flamborough Head*, at the diſtance of 40 miles: To the left it will look over well cultivated hills, cut into incloſures. On the ſide oppoſite the houſe, a vaſt tract of country will be commanded far into *Lincolnſhire*, with the noble river *Humber* taking its courſe through it for many miles; *Hull* ſeen plainly on its banks, at the diſtance of nine miles. Theſe are the principal improvements which Mr. *Ellerker* deſigns ſoon to execute; I name them among many others, which will all combine to render *Riſly* one of the fineſt places in *Yorkſhire*.

weeds;

weeds: Turnips would then be found an excellent preparation for barley or oats, and for the artificial grasses sown with them.

It is in this manner that turnips and grasses are connected, the latter in a great measure depend upon the former, and their importance to this part of *Yorkshire* must be evident to every one: As to the kind, I should in the first place recommend ray-grafs and clover in the manner they have been used with so great success in *Norfolk*, for which purpose the following course upon lands rather inclinable to dryness than moisture——or quite dry, is much to be advised.

1. Turnips thoroughly hoed
2. Barley
3. Clover and ray-grafs (12 lb. of the first and two pecks of ray-grafs) for three years.
4. Wheat.
5. Turnips, &c. &c. &c.

It is impossible in this husbandry, that the land should be foul or out of heart, as in six years it gives but two crops of corn: These two crops will, on that account, be worth twice the number as taken at present; and instead of the useless expence of fallow years, very beneficial crops for the food of cattle will be had; an object,

as

as I before remarked, peculiarly important in this country.———It is by means of this courſe of crops that we ſee in *Norfolk*, upon dry ſands, great ſtocks of all ſorts of cattle, kept, and rows of hay ſtacks more like a town than a farm yard. Debar a *Norfolk* farmer from a turnip-hoe; and clover and ray-graſs, and all the wonders of huſbandry that have been performed in that country, would at once ſink to nothing.

Much of the ſoil upon the wolds in the *Eaſt Riding*, is a light dry loam on limeſtone and chalk; or, in other words, the moſt proper of any for the production of ſainfoine, a noble graſs of uncommon profit, but totally neglected, or rather unknown in this tract of country. The farmers ought beyond a doubt to cultivate a ſufficient quantity of this graſs to ſupply the place of meadows and paſtures, where ſuch are naturally wanting or deficient. For this purpoſe, turnips ſhould be ſown and well hoed, eat off with ſheep, and then barley ſown, and with that four buſhels per acre of ſainfoine ſeed.—This is the moſt improved of the *common* practice in thoſe countries where ſainfoine is general; particular experiments direct much leſs ſeed, and a different method, but I recommend nothing here to *common* farmers, which

which their brethren in other parts do not in common practife, and to great profit.—With this management they will find it laft well for horfes, cows, beafts, or hay, fifteen years. They fhould then pare and burn it, and fow turnips, keep it in a courfe of other crops for five or fix years, and then lay down with fainfoine again.

Another circumftance of bad hufbandry, (which is indeed too common in other countries) is the never hoeing of beans: Great numbers are fown upon the rich lands after wheat, and all I viewed were extremely full of weeds; this is a moft pernicious practice, and cannot be too much condemned.

Next let me obferve, that the waggons ufed in this country are fuch paltry infignificant things, that the farmers, I am confident, who ufe them for any purpofe upon the road, muft fubmit to a conftant lofs. In fome parts of *England*, they are changing narrow-wheeled waggons that contain 90 and 100 bufhels, for broad-wheeled ones; what therefore muft we think of thefe hufbandmen who content themfelves with fuch as hold no more than 40; and 50 with difficulty: this is remaining in the darknefs and ignorance of five centuries ago.

Laftly,

Lastly, let me offer some remarks on the great improvement carrying on of inclosures; but this will require a more diffusive examination. There is scarcely any point in rural œconomics more generally acknowledged, than the great benefits of inclosing open lands: some authors, it is true, have attacked them as suppositious, and asserted them to be a national disadvantage, of trivial use to the proprietors, but very mischievous to the poor. My residence in this part of *Yorkshire* brought (at first accidentally) to my knowledge some particulars respecting the merits of inclosing, and the means commonly pursued in the execution, which are not to be found in the *face* of any *acts* of parliament whatever; but which are certainly of importance in weighing and deciding the advantages of the measure. To give you a tolerable idea of these circumstances, it will be necessary to sketch the progress of an inclosure, as it generally is conducted, without any eye to legal forms, or the letter of the act.

1. The proprietors of large estates generally agree upon the measure, adjust the principal points among themselves, and fix upon their attorney before they appoint any general meeting of *all* the proprietors. The small proprietor, whose property

perty in the township is perhaps his all, has little or no weight in regulating the clauses of the act of Parliament, has seldom if ever an opportunity of putting a single one in the bill favourable to his rights, and has as little influence in the choice of commissioners; and of consequence, they have seldom any great inducement to be attentive to his interest; some recent instances of which I have heard of.

II. Any proprietor possessing a fifth of the manor, parish, lordship, &c. to be inclosed, has the right of a negative upon the measure, consequently the poorer proprietors are often obliged to assent to unreasonable clauses, rather than give up all the advantages they hope from the inclosure.

III. The attorney delivers his bill to the commissioners, who pay him and themselves without producing any account, and in what manner they please. Is it therefore any wonder, that the expences previous to the actual inclosing the ground are very frequently (unless where the township is very small) from 1800 *l.* to 2000 *l.* all which is levied and expended by the commissioners absolutely, and without controul. To this extravagant expence add, that attending the inclosure itself, the making the

the ditches; the posts and railing; buying and setting the quickwood, &c. this, added to the former expence, must surely run away with great part of the profits expected from the inclosure. But what must we think of the indolence of the proprietors, who will thus unnecessarily neglect the great improvement of their estates to advance the private interests of the commissioners, &c. For a proof of this enormous power, see the following extract from an Act, which gives an *absolute* and UNLIMITED power to the commissioners to raise *whatever sums* they please, and to assess them *in the proportions* and *in such manner*, as they think proper.

"And be it further enacted, That the reasonable costs and charges incident to, and attending the obtaining and passing this Act, and of the surveying, dividing and allotting the said lands and grounds hereby directed to be inclosed, and the preparing and inrolling the said award or instrument, and all other necessary charges and expences relating to the said divisions and inclosures, and to the fencing, hedging, and ditching, the same shall, from time to time, as such costs, charges and expences shall accrue, be borne, paid and defrayed by the several parties to whom any part of the said lands and grounds shall be allotted, in proportion to to the value of their respective shares or interests therein, *such proportions to be adjusted and settled from* time to *time, by the said commissioners or* any two *of them*; and in case any person or persons shall refuse or neglect to pay his, her, or their proportion or proportions so to be from time to time adjusted and ascertained, of such charges or expences within the time to be limited by the said commissioners, or any two of them, to such person or persons as they, or any two of them, shall appoint to receive the same, then the said commissioners, or any two of them, shall and may raise, and levy the same, by distress and sale of the goods and chattels of the person or persons so neglecting or refusing to pay the same, rendering the overplus (if any) on demand to the owner or owners of such goods and chattels, after deducting the costs and charges of taking and making such distress and sale; or otherwise it shall and may be lawful to and for the said commissioners or any two of them, from time to time, to enter into and upon the premisses, so to be allotted to such person or persons refusing or neglecting to pay as aforesaid, and to take the rents and profits thereof respectively, until thereby, or therewith, or otherwise, the share or shares, proportion or proportions of the said costs and charges so to be from

from time to time directed, awarded or appointed by the said commissioners to be paid by such person or persons as aforesaid, and also all costs, charges, and expences occasioned by or attending such entry upon and receipt of the rents and profits of the same premisses, shall respectively be paid and satisfied."

A most precious piece of delegated despotism.

IV. The division and distribution of the lands are totally in their breasts, and as the quality of the soil as well as the number of acres is considered, the business is extremely intricate, and requires uncommon attention; but on the contrary is often executed in an inaccurate and blundering manner. Nor is there any appeal from their allotments, but to the commissioners themselves, however carelessly or partially made. Thus is the property of the proprietors, and especially the poor ones, entirely at their mercy; every passion of resentment, prejudice, &c. may be gratified without controul; for they are vested with a despotic power known in no other branch of business in this free country.

V. Justice as well as common sense requires that after the *survey* and *division*, the *award* of the commissioners should be directly

rectly published, it being the record which proves the respective properties: and likewise that their accounts should, upon the conclusion of the business, be regularly arranged under each distinct head attended by every corresponding voucher, and made public to the inspection of every proprietor; but unfortunately this is so far from being the case, that the time of publishing the award is greatly procrastinated, and as to accounts they seldom show any all the particulars of that sort remain for ever a profound secret, save the particular sum demanded from each proprietor. That indeed, if they chuse it, they may communicate to each other and be able to form some judgment of the inequality of particular assessments, but as there lies no appeal from the award they are generally induced to sit down quietly, though the disproportion of the allotments and assessments should be glaringly conspicuous.

VI. There is no remedy against the impositions or blunders of the commissioners, but that which, perhaps, is as bad as the disease, *viz.* filing a bill in chancery; a remedy, which, in all probability, one or two persons must support for the good of *the whole,* but without the assistance of *half.*

VII. And if I am not greatly miftaken, even this means of redrefs is more limited than in moſt other cafes: it may compel the commiffioners to deliver in their accounts, but how can it rectify any unjuſt arrangement of the land? It lies in the breaſt of the commiffioners when to make their award, and I do not imagine, that till they have figned it, it would be prudent to file the bill againſt them. It might poffibly be two or three years before a decree could be obtained, and when any proprietor has been at the expence of incloſing his fhare, cultivating the ground, and raifing the fences, how is it poffible that even the power of the court of chancery, extenfive as it is, can in this cafe redrefs the injury, whether it arifes from the particular fituation of the allotment, the quantity, or the quality of the foil. Need I fay any thing further, to point out the real neceffity of the proprietors of land exerting themfelves to retrench this enormous power, vefted in the commiffioners. The advantages refulting from incloſures, are not to be looked upon as merely beneficial to the individual, they are of the moſt extenfive national advantage. The improvements in agriculture, that fource of all our power, muſt be trifling without them; furely therefore, every meaſure that can promote them

them should be adopted, every difficulty attending them smoothed, and every injury redressed.

It appears clearly from the above circumstances, that the proprietors of a lordship to be inclosed, give to the commissioners for executing the act, an unlimited authority of taxing their estates; and including that unheard-of power of being party, judge, and jury in the whole affair of paying themselves. If a proprietor is offended at their proceedings, and refuses to pay the sums levied on him, they are entrusted by the act, with powers immediately to distrain. Such immense confidence might be attended with few inconveniencies, if they were universally men of considerable property, and known integrity; but when the hacknied sons of *business*, are employed (which is the case nine times out of ten) the proprietors have just reason to tremble at the situation of their fortunes. It is very natural to conclude, that such causes must be attended with a very striking effect, and this accordingly is the case; for impositions, and the inaccuracy of commissioners have arose to such a height, that many proprietors who were eager for inclosures, on a sanguine prospect of benefit, have found the measure highly injurious and totally owing to the

the immense expences. There is a very false idea current, that rents are doubled by inclosing; a measure may be vastly advantageous without possessing such uncommon merit. This notion hurries numbers to inclosing, who afterwards find the expences to run away with great part of the profit. But even where the expences do not exceed the profit, it is very often the case, that the proprietor is not repaid in six or seven years, perhaps more; and when it is considered, how little able some proprietors, even in good circumstances, are to wait so long before they are reimbursed their expences; how often they are disabled (by advancing their proportions necessary for an inclosure) to provide for the settlement of their children in the world, how often they are prevented cultivating their new inclosure to any advantage, by being drained of their ready money——I think it will incontestibly appear, that the advantages resulting from this extravagant method, are trivial to the majority of proprietors, in comparison to what they might reasonably have expected, from a more equal management.

You will not think this surprizing, when you are informed the immediate rise of rent in many inclosures in this neighbourhood, has not amounted to above five or six

six shillings an acre, and in some to no more than eighteen pence and two shillings an acre. In strong rich lands, where they have some meadow lands, the rise is higher. But indeed the smallness of the rise is, in some measure, owing to their want of better husbandry; for with very few meadows, they know scarce any thing of clover and ray-grass or turnips; consequently the value of an inclosure is comparatively small to them.

But whatever cause the fact is owing to, it remains equally surprizing that the proprietors should not be more attentive to their interest, a rise of rent sufficient to pay the expences of the inclosure under the management of honest, able, and careful conductors, *may* vanish into nothing upon the mention of those who have neither integrity, abilities, or attention; and it must be strange supineness indeed that can suffer the gentlemen of a county to be duped in so flagrant a manner, as to allow even in idea the trains of imposition which are now common in the business of inclosures. It is wonderful they do not exert themselves to introduce common sense and honesty, in an affair hitherto under the cognizance of ignorance, knavery, and self-interest.

For this purpose, it seems requisite, that the following clauses should be added to the acts for inclosure.

I. That the small proprietors should have a share in the nomination of commissioners; either by a union of votes or otherwise, as might be determined.

II. That the attorney and commissioners should, before the passing the act, agree upon their several rewards, and on no account whatever be suffered to pay themselves one shilling.

III. That the commissioners proceed immediately to the survey, distribution, and assignment, and the building or forming public works.

IV. That in case any man thinks himself injured, he may be at liberty (but totally at his own expence, in case he is in the wrong) to summons a jury immediately, to view and decide the affair.

V. That as soon as the abovementioned business is concluded, the commissioners do give in their account of all sums received and expended, in the most regular manner, and with all the vouchers for payment; and that they immediately publish their award.

VI. That an action at common law be had against the commissioners for false, or unvouched accounts, &c. &c.

By

By means of these or other clauses better imagined, but of the same intention, this undoubtedly beneficial measure of inclosing would be infinitely extended, and the interests of the community, as well as individuals, greatly secured.

I am not here arguing against inclosures, the advantages arising from them are certainly very extensive; I am only saying, they are not so great as they are frequently imagined to be, and they do not always indemnify the *present* possessor from the great expence he is at in obtaining them, by the absurd and extravagant manner in which they are generally conducted.

I should extend these remarks farther, but many other points of bad husbandry will be included in the general observations, which I shall trouble you with on the conclusion of this tour.

From *Risby* I took the road to *Wentworth* house. Passing *Cave*, the seat of Sir *George Metham*, which I before described, we came to *Howden*, the soil in which neighbourhood is chiefly clay, with some fields of sandy land: lets in the open field at 10 *s*. and in the inclosures at 1 *l*. Their course is,

    1. Fallow
    2. Wheat
    3. Oats.

For wheat they plough five times, sow two bushels of seed, and reap at a medium about three quarters. For barley they plough three times, sow four bushels of seed, and reckon the mean produce four quarters. They give one or two stirrings for oats, sow four bushels, five quarters the average crop. For beans they plough but once, sow three bushels and a half broad-cast, never hoe them, and gain at a medium 2½ quarters. They sow scarce any turnips. For rye they plough once, sow 5 bushels, and 24 the mean crop. Clover they sow on spring corn, generally mow it, and gain two tons of hay at a mowing. They cultivate much flax in this neighbourhood, calling it *line*; they sow it either on a stubble in great heart, or on old grass; then weed it at the expence of from 5 *s* to 10 *s.* per acre, and they reckon that an acre, if not a bad one, will pay 5 *l.* clear of all charges.

The manure they principally depend on is lime, of which they lay two chaldrons on an acre, and it lasts a course.

They reckon 500 *l.* necessary to stock a farm of 100 *l.* a year.——The product of a cow they value at 5 *l.*

They use two, and sometimes three horses in a plough abreast, and do an acre a day. If ploughing is hired, it is 2 *s.* 6 *d.* an acre.

The

The poor women and children are much in want of employment; only a little spinning among them of line and hemp hards.

The particulars of a farm I gained were,

500 Acres in all	6 Brood mares
300 Of them grass	6 Cows
200 Arable	50 Beasts
£. 200 Rent	260 Sheep
12 Horses	5 Servants
4 Oxen	6 Labourers

He sows

40 Acres of wheat	20 Of flax
80 Of spring corn	

LABOUR.

In harvest, 9 s. a week, and beer.
A woman, 1 s. a day.
In hay-time, 1 s. 2 d. a day.
A woman, 6 d.
In winter, 1 s.
Reaping wheat, from 6 s. to 8 s.
Mowing and binding spring corn, 3 s. and 3 s. 6 d.
Threshing wheat 1 s. 9 d. per quarter.
——————— barley, 1 s. 2 d.
——————— beans, 1 s.
——————— oats reaped, 6 d.
——————— mown, 8 d.
Wages of a farming man, from 10 l. to 12 l. Of a maid, 4 l.

PROVISIONS, &c.

Bread, - - 1 d. per lb.
Butter, - - 7—21 oz.
Cheese, - - 3
Beef, - - - $3\frac{1}{2}$
Mutton, - - $3\frac{1}{2}$
Potatoes, - - 4 a peck.
Milk, - - - $\frac{1}{2}$ per quart.
Candles, - - $6\frac{1}{2}$
Labourer's house rent, 30 s.
——————— firing, 15 s.

IMPLEMENTS, &c.

A new waggon, 12 l. 10 s.
A cart, 7 l.
A plough, 1 l. 5 s.
A harrow, 12 s.
A roller, 25 s.
Shoeing a cart horse, 1 s. 4 d.
Laying a plough share and coulter, 1 s. 2 d.
Bricks, 10 s. per thousand.
Oak timber, 1 s. 6 d. a foot.

The country quite from *Cave* through *Howden* and to *Thorne*, is all low, flat, and disagreeable. At the latter place I was very lucky in meeting with information of the best kind, through the civility of Mr. *Ashcroft* and Mr. *Atkinson*. The soil is in general

neral a ſtrong clay, and many fields a peculiar ſort of earth formed by the overflowings of the tide, which left a firm ſandy kind of ſlime; the medium rent of the country is 10 s. an acre; but ſome of their common field lands let at 17 s. and 18 s. the acre; the nominal rent 20 s. to 25 s. but the meaſure is more than a real acre. Their courſe upon this land is

1. Turnips   4. Oats
2. Barley   5. Clover
3. Wheat   6. Wheat

The moſt infamous courſe I have met with ſince I have been out. On their other lands it is alſo very bad.

1. Fallow   3. Oats
2. Wheat   4. Wheat

For wheat they plough four times, ſow three buſhels, and gain at an average twenty-four. They plough but twice for barley, ſow four buſhels, and reap at a medium four quarters and a half. For oats they ſtir but once, ſow four buſhels, and gain ſix quarters at a medium. They give but one earth for beans, ſow three buſhels and a half broad-caſt, never hoe them, and get at a medium twenty-three buſhels. For turnips they plough four or five times, never hoe them, which is a fine practice when five crops ſucceed them, and the land never fallowed; the mean value

per

per acre they reckon at 18 or 20 s. and use them for sheep and beasts; they stock them with eight or ten sheep to an acre, or two beasts. They plough four times for rape, and reckon a middling crop at $3\frac{1}{2}$ quarters. Flax they sow generally on an old swarth, plough but once, weed the crop three times at the expence of 7 s. 6 d. an acre; a good one they value at 10 l. or 12 l. an acre, and worth as it grows at an average from 5 l. to 8 l. They sometimes give 4 l. rent for the flax year.

Their chief manuring is with lime, of which they lay two chaldrons on an acre, at 7 s. 6 d. per chaldron; it lasts three crops; sometimes they mix it with tide slime, called warp. They also pare and burn; the paring they do with a plough, and generally sow rape on the land.

In their tillage they use two horses in a plough, and do an acre a day. Hiring per acre is 4 s.

Some other sundry circumstances worth minuting are; the sum requisite to stock a farm of 100 l. a year, they reckon 300 l.—the product of a cow, 5 l.—the profit of sheep 4 s. per head;—poor women and children have no employment, but drink tea twice a day. The tythes are gathered, and land sells at 35 years purchase.

But

But the greatest curiosity to be met with in this country is the vast moors, which are 3, 4, and 5 miles over, and some of them near as long; they consist of a soft, spongy, loose soil, as if composed of rotten vegetables: It is all what they call turf, and is dug into square pieces for burning; when dried it is light as a feather, and burns excellently; over all the moors it lays in an even stratum, about five or six feet deep, upon a bed of stiff blue and black clay: in digging it away they frequently find vast fir trees, perfectly sound, and some oaks, but not so good as the firs; the body of a man was also found, the flesh was black, but perfectly preserved; after a short exposure to the air, it crumbled into powder; the nature of the moor is such, as to resist all putrefaction, and no kind of worm can live in it. The property of it is very remarkable; on each side, at the distance, as I mentioned before, of several miles, are many little slips of cultivated land, generally an acre (28 yards) broad, some more, and others less; the proprietors of these possess a right to all the moor which borders upon their land in a straight line, until they meet with the opposite possessors, who are in the same situation. These cultivated slips, which consist of many closes, have all, and probably most of the adjacent

(country

country) been gained in the course of many centuries from the moors; it is a good rich clay, that yields fine crops of corn and grass, but from its situation is liable to be overflowed in winter; lets at about 7 or 8 *s.* an acre. Thus a proprietor has as much land as he thinks proper; but then the expence of digging away the turf is more than the land is worth, for a man seldom cuts above four square yards a day; they give it to the poor for their cutting and taking away.

The improvement of such land is a very dubious point: To view the moor, any person would think it totally incapable of any; but I must own myself of a different opinion. In the front of the piece, I viewed where the men were cutting the turf; I observed a trench was cut on each side, and across the moor, around a square piece against the field already cleared; this trench was not above two feet deep, and yet its effect in draining was very striking; we could walk very firmly within this trench, but on the outside of it not without danger of being swallowed up; and although I could scarcely perceive any growth upon the moor in general, yet this drained part was covered with ling of a luxuriant growth, which is a sufficient proof that draining would not only be very advantageous, but the point of all others which must be first effected. The fall of five or six feet into the part cut away, which is interfected with ditches, would fecure a certainty of draining.———When this work was done, the furface ought to be burnt; but they objected to this, that it would not be allowed, as others property would prefently be on fire, and poffibly the whole country, which however I can fcarcely imagine; but if it cannot be burnt, it ought to be dug three or four times in the fummer to fweeten it, and the fucceeding fpring planted and fowed with fuch vegetables as were moft likely to fucceed. I ventured to recommend them on conjecture, potatoes, cabbages, carrots, hops, oliers, &c. &c. &c. to try them in fmall plats, that fome certainty might at leaft be gained; and as the expence would be very trifling, I believe the trial will be made.

But I fhould further have obferved, that the clay under the bog would in all probability be an excellent manure for it, both from *weight* and fertility; and with the help of lime, which they have at 7 s. 6 d. a chaldron, would enable them to reduce it to good meadow ground.

One objection occurred to me, which can only be anfwered by a lawyer: Suppofe a proprietor drains the moor in front of him, until he meets with the oppofite proprietor; *quere*, can they be ftopped by any thing but the want of turf? they would have the fame bank prefent itfelf to them as at prefent, only a poffeffor on the furface of it.

The following are the particulars of fome farms in this country; one

120 Acres in all	7 Cows
100 Arable	200 Sheep (right
20 Grafs	of commonage)
£.76 Rent	2 Servants
6 Horfes	2 Labourers

He fows

15 Acres of wheat	20 Of beans
30 Of oats	

Another:

170 Acres in all	10 Horfes
130 Arable	12 Cows
40 Grafs	3 Servants
£.56 Rent	3 Labourers

He fows

30 Of wheat	10 Of rape
60 Of oats	10 Of turnips

Another:

70 Acres in all	6 Cows
60 Arable	300 Sheep (com-
10 Grafs	monage right)
£.38 Rent	2 Servants
6 Horfes	2 Labourers

He

He sows
25 Acres of wheat   25 Of oats
Another:

87 Acres in all   6 Cows
57 Arable   200 Sheep (right
30 Grass   of commonage)
£.70 Rent   2 Servants
 6 Horses   1 Labourer
No folding in this country!

LABOUR.

In harvest, 2 s. a day, and beer.
In hay-time, 1 s. 6 d. and ditto.
In winter, 1 s.
Reaping wheat, 5 s.
————— oats, 4 s.
Mowing and gathering, 3 s.
————— grass, 1 s. 6 d.
Threshing wheat, 2 s.
————— barley, 1 s.
————— oats, 8 d.
Wages of a farming man, 11 l. 11 s.
Dairy and other maids, 3 l. to 3 l. 10 s.

PROVISIONS, &c.

Bread, *per lb.* 1 d.   Pork,   - 3¼
Cheese,   -   3   Potatoes, *p.* peck, 3
Butter,   -   5 19 oz. Candles,   - 6
Beef,   -   3½   Soap,   - 6
Mutton,   -   3½   Milk, *per* quart, 0½
Veal,   -   2½

Labourer's house rent, 25 s.
Their firing, 12 s.
Wear of their tools, 5 s.

IMPLEMENTS.

A waggon, 12 l. 12 s.   A plough, 17 l.
A cart, 9 l.   A harrow, 1 l.
Shoeing a horse, 1 s. 4 d.
Laying a share, 1 s.
Bricks, per thousand, 9 s.
Oak timber, 1 s. 6 d.
Ash, 10 d.
Elm, 1 s. 4 d.

I remain,

Your's, &c.

LETTER V.

WENTWORTH house, the palace of the Marquis of *Rockingham*, is situated between *Rotherham* and *Barnsley*, in the midst of a very beautiful country, and in a park that is one of the most exquisite spots in the world. It consists of an irregular quadrangle, inclosing three courts, with two grand fronts: The principal one to the park extends in a line upwards of 600 feet, forming a center and two wings. Nothing in architecture can be finer than this center, which extends 19 windows. In the middle, a noble portico projects 20 feet, and is 60 long in the area; six magnificent *Corinthian* pillars support it in front, and one at each end: This portico is lightness itself; the projection is bold, and when viewed obliquely from one side, admits the light through the pillars at the ends, which has a most happy effect, and adds greatly to the lightness of the edifice. The bases of the pillars rest on pedestals, in a line upon the rustics, which by some critics has been objected to, by asserting that the pedestal of a column ought to be fixed on the ground alone; but without enquiring into the propriety of such strict rules, let me remark that the effect of breaking them, is to my eye a beauty; for as it is always necessary to inclose the area of the portico with a ballustrade; when there are no pedestals * the shafts of the pillars are cut by it, which hurts the beauty of their proportion, and has in general a bad effect: but in this portico, the ballustrade extending from pedestal to pedestal, the shafts are seen complete, and the unity of the view not in the least destroyed. The timpanum is excellently proportioned; at the points are three very light statues; the cornice, the arms, and the capitals of the pillars admirably executed. A ballustrade crowns the rest of the front; at each end a statue, and between them vases; the whole uniting to form a center at once pleasing and magnificent; in which lightness vies with grandeur, and simplicity with elegance.

The rustic floor consists of a very large arcade, and two suites of rooms. In the arcade is a fine group in statuary, containing three figures as large as life, in which one of gigantic stature is getting the

* Perhaps, more properly speaking, it should be called the base, dye and cornice.

better

better of two others; the sculptor is *Foggini*; the upper parts of the two lower figures are finely executed; the turn of the backs, and the expression of the countenances, good; the forced struggling attitude of the hinder one very great, especially that of pushing his hand against the body of his antagonist. On the left of this arcade is the common apartment; first, a supping-room, 30 by 22, and 14 high; a drawing room, 33 by 25; anti-room to the dining-room, and the dining-room, 36 by 25. On the other side, offices for the steward, butlers, &c. Upon this floor are a great number of rooms of all sorts; and, among others, many admirable good apartments, of anti-room, dressing-room, bed-chamber; furnished with great elegance in velvets, damasks, &c. &c. and gilt and carved ornaments.

Upon the principal floor you enter first the grand hall, which is, beyond all comparison, the finest room in *England*; the justness of the proportion is such, as must strike every eye with the most agreeable surprize on entering it: It is 60 feet square, and 40 high; a gallery 10 feet wide is carried around the whole, which leaves the area a cube of 40 feet; this circumstance gives it a magnificence unmatched in any other hall. The gallery is supported by 18 very noble *Ionic* fluted pillars, incrusted with a paste, representing in the most natural manner several marbles. The shafts are of *Siena*, and so admirably imitated as not to be distinguished from reality by the most experienced and scrutinizing eye; the capitals of white marble, and the square of the bases of verd antique. Nothing can have a more beautiful effect than these pillars; those only on one side of the room are yet completed; but the most skilful hands from *Italy* are kept constantly employed in finishing this noble design. Between the pillars are eight niches in the wall for statues, which are ready to be placed when the pillars, walls, &c. are finished for receiving them. Over them are very elegant relievos in pannels, from the designs of Mr. *Stewart*. Above the gallery are eighteen *Corinthian* pilasters, which are also to be incrusted with the imitation of marbles: Between the shafts are pannels struck in stucco, and between the capitals festoons in the same, in a stile which cannot fail of pleasing. The ceiling is of compartments in stucco, admirably executed. His lordship designs a floor in compartments answerable to the ceiling, of the same workmanship

manship as the columns.——To the left of this noble hall is a grand suite of apartments; containing,

First, a supping-room, 40 feet by 22. The ceiling, compartments in stucco; the center a plain large oblong; at each end, a square, in which is a most elegant relievo, representing two angels supporting an urned cup of flowers resting on the head of an eagle; the divisions on each side containing scrolls. The chimney-piece very handsome; the frieze containing the *Rockingham* supporters, with a plain shield, in white marble, finely polished; the columns festooned in the same.

Second, a drawing-room, 35 by 23. The ceiling coved in stucco; the center an oval in an oblong, with medalions in the corners of the square cut by the oval, inclosed in wreaths of laurel surrounded by scrolls; the cove rising to it struck in small octagon compartments, chequered by little squares, extremely elegant. The cornice, frieze, and architrave of the wainscot beautifully carved; nothing more elegant of the kind than the scroll of carving on the frieze. The chimney-piece of white marble, polished; the cornice supported by figures of captives in the same; on the frieze, festoons of fruit and flowers; on each side a vase, on which are four small

but

but elegant figures relievo, something in the attitude of the hours in the *Aurora* of *Guido*.

Third, a dining-room 40 feet square; the ceiling of stucco; in the center a large octagon; around it eight divisions, within four of which are relievos of boys supporting a shield, inclosing a head in a blaze, by a wreath of fruit; over it a basket of flowers on a shell inverted; and under it an eagle spreading its wings. In the other division are rays in circles of fret-work: The design of the whole in a most just taste. The chimney-piece large and handsome, of white polished marble; above it architectural ornaments; a cornice, &c. supported by *Corinthian* pillars; the whole finely carved, and surrounding a space left for a picture. In the walls of the room are pannels in stucco, of a bold and spirited design, and like the ceiling exceedingly well executed. Over the doors are six historical relievos; in the center on each side a large frame work for a picture, by which are pannels, inclosing in wreaths four medalions;

Theocritus, Hector, Agamemnon, Hyacinthus.

On one side the chimney-piece, in the same stile,

Hamilcar;

  Hamilcar;
 And on other,
  Troilus.

 Returning to the grand hall, you enter from the other fide another fuite.

 Firſt, an anti-room 30 by 20; the ceiling finely finiſhed in ſtucco.

 Secondly, the grand drawing-room 36 ſquare; ceiling the ſame.

 Third, a dreſſing-room 30 by 25; the ceiling coved in ſtucco; the center an oval cut in a ſquare, elegantly decorated; the cove riſing to it moſaic'd in ſmall ſquares; deſigned with great taſte.

 Fourth, the ſtate bed-chamber, 25 ſquare.

 Fifth, another dreſſing-room, 16 ſquare, communicating with the paſſage which runs behind this ſuite of apartments.

 At the other end of the houſe behind the great dining-room is the *India* apartment, a bed-chamber 15 ſquare, with a dreſſing-room the ſame; the chimney-piece extremely handſome; pillars of *Siena* marble.

 From the other corner of the hall on the right-hand you enter by a large paſſage; the gallery, or common rendezvous room 130 feet by 18, hung with *India* paper; a moſt uſeful and agreeable room. To the right this opens into the new damaſk
       apart-

apartment, confisting of a bed-chamber and two dressing rooms, one of the latter 27 feet by 18. The chimney-piece surprizingly elegant; a border of *Siena* marble, surrounded by compartments of a black marble ground, inlaid with flowers, fruit, and birds of marble in their natural colours; most exquisitely finished. The bed-chamber, 27 by 15, the other dressing-room (both open into the gallery) 28 by 18; the chimney-piece pilasters of *Siena*, with white polished capitals supporting the cornice of white and *Siena* marble; the whole very elegant: over it a copy, from *Vandyke*, of *Charles* the First's Queen, by Lady *Fitzwilliams*, exceedingly well done; the face, hair, and drapery excellent.—— Here is one of the most curious cabinets in *England*; it is in architectural divisions of a center and two wings, on a basement story of drawers; a cornice finely wrought of ebony, the frieze of ivory, and the architecture of tortoise-shell, supported by *Corinthian* fluted pillars of tortoise-shell and ebony carved in reliefs, the capitals and bases gilt. The entrance of the building rusties in tortoise-shell, the divisions in ivory. By looking in the center on either side, is a deception of perspective; the design is very fine, and the workmanship excellent.

On the other side of the gallery, you open into a blue damask dressing-room, 25 by 24; here are two pictures by Mr. *West*, which seem to be in his happiest manner; *Diana* and *Endymion*, and *Cymon* and *Iphigene*. In the first, the most striking peculiarity is the light, all issuing from the crescent of *Diana*; this is something of the *Concetto*, but the execution is fine; the diffusion spirited and natural. The turn of her neck and naked arm is very beautiful; all the colours are fine and brilliant; and the general harmony very pleasing. In the other piece, the naked bosom of *Iphigene* is fine, and the turn of her head inimitable. *Cymon*'s figure is good, his attitude easy and natural; the colours are glowing, and consequently pleasing. Besides these pieces, here is likewise a large portrait of the late King on horseback; it is a good one, the attitude natural. Likewise a small relief in alabaster of a *Cupid* in a car, drawn by panthers: his attitude very pleasing.—Next is the chintz bed-chamber, 24 by 20.

After this comes the yellow damask apartment. The dressing-room 18 square; and the bed-chamber 25 by 18. Upon a cabinet in this room is a small *Venus* in white marble; fine, delicate, and plea-

pleafing; the drapery under her breaft beautiful.

The red and white apartment, 19 fquare; and a dreffing-room 20 by 19. Then into the laft apartment on this fide, very handfomely furnifhed, 20 by 18, and 22 by 20.

The library 60 by 20, and nobly filled*.

There are here a vaft number of books of prints, architecture and medals; of the laft

---

* The great fcarcity of the *Neapolitan* collection † of antiquities found in *Herculaneum*, will excufe a few remarks on fome of the moft ftriking of the engravings, as fome may have an opportunity of only a tranfient view; in which cafe I would recommend them to turn particularly to the following pages of the prints.

 Vol. I. 43. *Achilles*, an exceeding fine and perfect figure.
   79. Drapery, very fine.
   95. Surprizing drapery; the limbs feen through it as if of gauze.
   99. An half naked woman hanging in the air; the turn of the arms holding the drapery inimitably graceful. The beauty of the face and body exquifite; the drapery exceeding fine, difplaying the form of of the limbs through it in the

---

† Le Pitture Antiche D'Ercolano E. Contorni incife con Qualche Spiegazione: Folio.

hap-

laſt his lordſhip has one of the greateſt collections in *England*.

From the library is a direct communication, on one ſide with the preceding rooms, and on the other with the crimſon velvet apartment; conſiſting of, firſt, an anti-room, painted in obſcura in blue, in a very neat taſte, 23 feet ſquare; this opens into the bed-chamber of the ſame dimenſions, the ornaments of the bed, the glaſs frames, &c. &c. of guilt carving well executed; then the dreſſing-room 23 by 15.

The attic ſtory conſiſts of complete ſets of apartments, of bed-chamber and dreſſing-

---

happieſt manner; the whole range of painting can exhibit nothing ſo aſtoniſhingly elegant as this attitude.

103. The graceful turn of the right arm inimitable; and the drapery fine.

109. The animated ſpirit of the attitude, ſpringing upwards, ſurprizingly great: The drapery pleaſing.

119. The turn of the right arm extremely graceful; and the drapery fine.

123. The turn of the right arm very elegant; the upper part of the dra-

sing-room; including those of Lord and Lady *Rockingham*, which are four dressing-rooms and a bed-chamber: In his Lordship's anti-room hangs the famous picture of the Earl of *Strafford*, and his secretary, by *Vandyke*; and incomparably fine it is. Also the portrait of an old servant, by *Stubbs*; which appears to be most excellently done: The strong expression of the face is worthy the pencil of *Rembrandt* himself. The rooms on this floor are all spacious, many of 36 by 30, 30 by 25, &c. &c. in general well proportioned, and the furniture rich and elegant. Upon the whole

    drapery graceful, and the display of the body through all of it noble; but it bundles heavily at bottom.

129. One of the finest attitudes in the world; the profile, and grace of the head charming. The drapery inimitable.

253. Like some others of the ornamental pieces, rather *Chinese* than antique, and the drollery of the ass and crocodile truly modern.

Vol. II. 91. Correct, elegant and beautiful; the attitude and drapery fine.

113. The attitudes and drapery prodigiously fine.

131. The

whole much superior to the common stile of attic floors.

In respect of convenience, the connection of the apartments throughout the house is excellently contrived: For the grand suite of rooms on the left of the hall has a roomy passage behind it, which communicates with the offices by back stairs, and with the library and apartments adjoining, by passages. To the right of the hall the same convenience is found, for one of its doors opens into the great staircase, landing-place and passage, which runs behind the grand apartment and opens into the second dressing room; so that there
is

---

131. The attitudes and drapery and variety in the figures, very pleasing. The gardening, *Chinese*, and pretty.
267. The festoon would do honour the most elegant invention in modern taste.

Vol. III. 61. A group full of ease and nature in the attitudes: The designs very fine.
87. A spirited attitude.
97. Nothing can be finer than the back parts; the face, and attitude of the woman.
137. The naked seen through the dra-

is a double way through all this suite, to the state bed-chamber; either through the great rooms to the first dressing-room and then into the bed-chamber: or on the other side through the second dressing-room; and an immediate communication between these apartments and the staircase, which leads down to the rustic floor, and up to the attic story. All these apartments are nearly contiguous to each other, and yet you may enter almost any one of the rooms without going through another. The disposition of the other apartments is not inferior.

The passage beforementioned, or rather vestible, which connects the hall and the apartments to the right of it, likewise opens into the gallery, which as a rendez-vous room is excellently situated; to the

---

            drapery finely, and the attitude spirited.

151. Amazing drapery; the whole form seen thro' it astonishingly.

155. The attitude spirited, and the drapery fine.

Vol. IV. 117. The figure of this woman is surprizingly fine, her attitude easy, graceful and expressive, and the drapery excellent.

263. One would think this the design of a modern ceiling.

right

right it opens into both the dressing-rooms of the blue damask apartment; and on the left through the green damask dressing-room to the library and apartments adjoining, and by several large, handsome, and well-lighted passages to other apartments and staircases, which communicate with the offices, so that on every side there is a communication between all the apartments, and yet without making one a passage-room to another; which is excellently contrived *.

But the park and environs of *Wentworth* house, are, if any thing, more noble than the edifice itself; for which way soever you approach, very magnificent woods, spreading waters, and elegant temples break upon the eye at every angle. But there is so great a variety in the points of view, that it is impossible to lead you a regular tour of the whole without manifest confusion; I shall therefore take the parts distinctly, and so pass from one to the other.

Many of the objects are viewed to the greatest advantage by taking the principal

---

* His Lordship is building a most magnificent pile of stabling; it is to form a large quadrangle inclosing a square of 190 feet, with a very elegant front to the park: There are to be 84 stalls with numerous apartments for the servants attending; and spacious rooms for hay, corn, &c. &c. &c. dispersed in such a manner as to render the whole perfectly convenient.

entrance from *Rotherham*; this approach, his Lordship is at present laying out; much of the road, &c. is done, and when completed it will be a continued landscape, as beautiful as can be conceived. At the very entrance of the park, the prospect is delicious: In front you look full upon a noble range of hills, dales, lakes and woods, the house magnificently situated in the center of the whole. The eye naturally falls into the valley before you, through which the water winds in a noble stile: On the opposite side, is a vast sweep of rising slopes, finely scattered with trees, up to the house, which is here seen distinctly, and stands in the point of grandeur from whence it seems to command all the surrounding country. The woods stretching away above, below, and to the right and left with inconceivable magnificence; from the pyramid on one side, which rises from the center of a great wood, quite around to your left hand, where they join one of above an hundred acres hanging on the side of a vast hill, and forming altogether an amphitheatrical prospect, the beauties of which are much easier imagined than described. In one place the rustic temple crowns the point of a waving hill, and in another the ionic one appears with a lightness that de-

corates

corates the surrounding groves.——The situation of the house is no where better seen than from this point, for, in some places near, it appears to stand too low; but the contrary is manifest from hence, for the front-sweep of country forms the slope of a gradually rising hill, in the middle of which is the house; up to it is a fine bold rise: If it was on the highest of the ground, all the magnificence of the plantations which stretch away beyond it, would be lost, and those on each side take the appearance of right lines, stiffly pointing to the edifice. But this remark is almost general, for I scarcely know a situation, in which the principal building should be on the highest ground.

Descending from hence to the wood beneath you, which hangs towards the valley, and through which the road leads; before you enter, another view breaks upon the eye, which cannot but delight it. First, the water winding through the valley in a very beautiful manner; on the other side a fine slope rising to the rustic temple, most elegantly backed with a dark spreading wood. To the right a range of plantations, covering a whole sweep of hill, and near the summit the pyramid raising its bold head from a dark bosom of surrounding wood. The effect truly great.

great.——In the center of the view, in a gradual opening among the hills, appears the house; the situation wonderfully fine. Turning a little to the left, several woods, which from other points are seen distinct, here appear to join, and form a vast body of noble oaks, rising from the very edge of the water to the summit of the hills, on the left of the house. The ionic temple at the end most happily placed, in a spot from whence it throws an elegance over the whole landscape.

The road then entering, winds through the wood before mentioned; but here I must detain you a short time, for no grove at *Wentworth* is without its scenes of pleasing retirement.——This wood is cut into winding walks, of which there is a great variety; in one part of it, on a small hill of shaven grass, is a house for repasts in hot weather. The dining-room is 32 feet by 16, very neatly fitted up, the chimney-pieces of white marble of a judicious simplicity; the bow-window remarkably light and airy: Adjoining is a little drawing-room hung with India paper, and a large closet with book-cases; beneath are a kitchen and other offices. From hence a walk winds to the aviary, which is a light *Chinese* building of a very pleasing design; it is stocked with *Canary* and other foreign birds,

birds, which are kept alive in winter by means of hot walls at the back of the building; the front is open net-work in compartments. In one part of the wood is an octagon temple in a small lawn: And the walk winds in another place over a bridge of rock-work, which is thrown over a small water thickly surrounded with trees.

Upon coming out of this wood the objects all receive a variation at once; the plantations bear in different directions, but continue their noble appearance; for your eye rises over a fine bank of wood to the Ionic temple, which here seems dropt by the hand of Grace in the very spot where Taste herself would wish it to be seen.

The road from hence is to wind over the hill, and take a slanting course down towards the octagon temple; a very elegant little building, sweetly situated in the valley, commanding the bends of shore among the groves, and the hanging woods which crown the surrounding hills. Not far from this temple, a magnificent bridge is to be thrown over the water, and the road then to be traced through another wood, which is full of a great number of the most venerable oaks in *England*; one of which is 19 feet in circumference; and a great many of them near as large, with noble stems of a majestic height. After this it will gain an oblique view of the grand front of the house, and wind up to it in such a line, that the feet may never travel in a direction that the eye has before commanded.

Another approach from which the park is seen to great advantage, is the lower entrance from *Rotherham*, where the new porter's lodge is building. From hence the pyramid is seen upon the right, rising from a noble sweep of wood: In front the rustic temple just shews its head above a spreading plantation in a picturesque manner. On the left, along the valley, winds the lake in that waving line, which art uses to imitate the finest touches of nature: It is broken by bold projecting clumps of wood upon the banks, through which the water is in some places seen with much elegance. At a distance upon the banks of the water, which is upwards of 200 yards wide, is seen the octagon temple, in a situation fixed with such taste as to leave little for the imagination to supply. On the other side, you look upon a great extent of park, scattered with trees in the most beautiful manner imaginable, crowned with two vast woods, which here appear as one; and on every

every side fine prospects of cultivated hills spreading one beyond another.—— This approach crosses towards the lodge, where is a small but very neat room of prints on blue paper, and furnished with a harpsichord, for varying the scene of the most elegant of all amusements: The view from the windows is full upon the water, then the hills rising boldly from the shore, and terminated with a magnificent range of wood. The road winds from hence around the hill on which the rustic temple stands, and breaks at once upon the house, in a manner not only strikingly judicious in itself, but finely contrasted to the other approaches from which it is gradually seen. A part of this design was the cutting away a large part of that hill, which projected too much before the front of the house; a vast design, but not yet completed, although his lordship has already moved from it upwards of one hundred and forty thousand square yards of earth. An immense work, which required the spirit of a *Rockingham* to undertake.

Another point of view I would recommend to your attention, if ever you see this truly magnificent place, is the southern one at the top of the hill, from whence you look down upon *Rotherham*, and all the

the country around: From hence there is a prospect of valleys all scattered with villages; with cultivated hills arising on every side to the clouds: The house appears in the center of nine or ten vast hanging and other woods, which have a genuine magnificence more noble than can easily be conceived. The pyramid and temples are scattered over the scene, and give it just the air of liveliness which is consistent with the grandeur of the extent. This view is perhaps the most beautiful in *Yorkshire*; for the house, park, and woods form a circular connected landscape, equally beautiful and grand, while the surrounding country exhibits *Arcadian* scenes smiling with cultivation, and endless in variety.

From this point, moving to the left, the landscapes perpetually vary, each object taking a new appearance, and every one truly pleasing. Crossing a beautiful irriguous valley, you rise to the new plantation, at the west end of the park, from whence a new scene is beheld equal to any of the rest. You look down over a fine slope on the water, and catch it at several points breaking upon the eye through the scattered trees; the octagon temple appearing on its bank, in a situation extremely well contrasted to the elevated ones of the other build-

buildings. To the left, the woods rise in a noble manner, and joining those by the house, have a very fine effect; the *Ionic* temple just lifting its dome above them in an exquisite taste. In front, the rustic temple is seen on the hill backed with wood in the most pleasing stile, and higher still, the pyramid rising out of more lofty woods; the effect altogether glorious. To the right, the eye is feasted with a beautiful variety of cultivated hills.

Having often mentioned the pyramid, it is requisite to add, that it is a triangular tower, about 200 feet high, which was built on the summit of a very fine hill, at a distance from the house. There is a winding staircase up it, and from the top a most astonishing prospect around the whole country breaks at once upon the spectator: The house, and all its surrounding hills, woods, waters, temples, *&c.* are viewed at one glance, and around them an amazing tract of cultivated inclosures. A view scarcely to be exceeded. The following inscription is engraven over the entrance.

1748.

" This pyramidal building was erected by his MAJESTY's most dutiful subject, *Thomas* Marquis of *Rockingham,* &c In grateful respect to the preserver of our religion,

ligion, laws, and liberties, KING GEORGE THE SECOND, who, by the bleſſing of God, having ſubdued a moſt unnatural rebellion in *Britain, anno* 1746, maintains the balance of power and ſettles a juſt and honourable peace in *Europe.*"

1748.

Near it is a ſmall but very neat room, looking down upon a beautiful valley, and over a fine and extenſive proſpect, where Lady *Rockingham* ſometimes drinks tea.

At no great diſtance from the pyramid is the arch, another building, which was raiſed as an object to decorate the view from the *Ionic* temple.

The mention of that elegant piece of architecture reminds me of the exquiſite landſcapes ſeen from it; an elevated ſituation gives it the command of the valley with the water in different places, and on the other ſide of it, you look upon ſeveral of the woods before deſcribed, riſing to that noble one of an hundred acres, which hangs towards you in the grandeſt manner. In this wood, his Lordſhip propoſes building an obeliſk, which will have a fine effect, when viewed from all the oppoſite hills. Juſt by this temple is the menagery in front of the green-houſe, containing a prodigious number of foreign birds, particularly gold and pencil pheaſants, fants, cockatoos, *Mollacca* doves, &c. &c. The green-houfe is very fpacious, and behind it a neat agreeable room for drinking tea.—— Advancing from hence down the terras, the eye is continually feafted with an exceeding fine and various profpect of hills, dales, winding water, hanging woods, temples, and noble fweeps of park; and at the end of it a moft delicious view, quite different from any feen elfewhere; for you look down immediately upon a falling valley, beautifully interfected with various fheets of water, fringed with trees: Over this bird's-eye landfcape, on one fide, rifes a floping hill, fcattered with fingle trees, and on the other, a range of woods: under them in the valley ftands the octagon temple; to the left the ruftic one upon the fummit of an unplanted hill, admirably contrafted to the others, which are either decorated with clumps, or quite covered with fpreading woods.

Upon the whole, *Wentworth* is in every refpect one of the fineft places in the kingdom: In fome, the houfe is the object of curiofity; in others, a park is admired: The ornamental buildings give a reputation to one, and a general beauty of profpect to another—but all are united here: The houfe is one of the grandeft in *England*,

and

and the largest I have any where seen; the park is as noble a range of natural and artificial beauty as is any where to be beheld; the magnificence of the woods exceed all description; the temples, &c. are elegant pieces of architecture, and so admirably situated as to throw an uncommon lustre over every spot; and add to all this, the beauty of the surrounding country, which consists chiefly of cultivated hills, cut into inclosures, and well scattered with towns and villages, and you certainly will allow, that such circumstances cannot unite without forming a place at once great and beautiful.

To this slight account, I cannot but add one remark, in praise of what I must be allowed to call true taste: Nature has certainly done much at *Wentworth*, but art has heightened, decorated, and improved all her touches; in such attempts, no slight genius is requisite: Valleys may be floated with water, hills crowned with woods, and temples appear in every scene;—— riches will do all these; the money of one man may purchase the taste of another: But all that Lord *Rockingham* has yet done at *Wentworth*, as well as the noble plans he has sketched, and begun to execute, are totally his own designs: An instance certainly

tainly of his taste, though not of his compliance with fashion *.

* * * * * *

But the husbandry of the Marquis of *Rockingham* is much more worthy of attention than any palace; the effects which have and must continue to result from it are of the noblest and most truly national kind: A short sketch of his Lordship's operations, will convince you how much an extensive tract of country is obliged to this patriotic nobleman for introducing a cultivation unknown before.

Upon

---

* Certain criticks (who have objected to these sheets on account of the *stile* being disordered and diffuse, although I apologized for that circumstance in the preface, and pleaded the unavoidable necessity of writing by fits and starts at inns, farm-houses, &c.) have quoted a part of this description of *Wentworth*, and then assert, " That it is *vilely* and *absurdly* situated in a BLEAK, *clayey* country, with a hill before the principal front, that cuts off every prospect." In reply to this, I will venture to assert, That the country is not clayey: It might as well be called a stoney country;—the soil in all that neighbourhood is various, from light gravels to rich loams; but neither in stiffness, dirt, or any other circumstance, can it be called a clayey one. As to the *bleakness* of a situation where a hill cuts off every prospect, I do not perfectly understand it. But the fact is, the whole country is cut into small inclosures, the hedges are as full of trees as other inclosed countries, the woods are numerous, and throughout the environs of *Wentworth* full of great

quantities

Upon turning his attention to agriculture, his Lordship found the husbandry of the *West Riding* of *Yorkshire*, extremely deficient in numerous particulars: It was disgusting to him to view so vast a property, cultivated in so slovenly a manner; eager to substitute better methods in the room of such unpleasing as well as unprofitable ones, he determined to exert himself with spirit in the attempt; and he executed the noble scheme in a manner that does honour to his penetration.——A very few particulars, among many of the common practice, will shew how much this country wanted a *Rockingham* to animate its cultivation.

1. Large tracts of land, both grass and arable, yielded but a trifling profit, for

---

quantities of as fine timber as any in *Britain*. Let any one judge of the possibility of such a situation being *bleak:* the face of the whole neighbourhood is that of a thick woodland, rather than an open or a bleak country.——Further, *a hill cuts off every prospect:* they might have said, *did* cut off a prospect; but at present it is directly the reverse, for Lord *Rockingham* (as I mentioned in the first edition as well as the present) has cut away that hill and let in the prospect, which before was hidden.——I should by no means have bestowed this note in answer to criticisms on the stile and expression of a book of husbandry; but when the direct evidence of my senses is belied, I find it difficult to refrain from this slight remark.

want

want of draining. In wet clays, the rushes, and other aquatic rubbish, usurped the place of corn and grass; the seasons of tilling were retarded, and even destroyed; and those pastures which ought to have fed an ox, scarcely maintained a sheep.

2. The pastures and meadows of this country were universally laid down in ridge and furrow; a practice highly destructive of profit, and detestable to the eye; and the manner of laying down such lands, was as miserable as their product denoted poverty; for after many years ploughing, of numerous crops but insufficient fallows, when the soil was so exhausted as to disappoint the expectation of corn, a parcel of rubbish called hay-seeds was scattered over the surface, and the field left to time for improvement. A villanous custom, and too much practised in all parts of the kingdom.

3. The culture of turnips was become common, but in such a method that their introduction was undoubtedly a real mischief; *viz.* without hoeing, so that the year of fallow, in the general management, was the most capital one of slovenliness and bad husbandry.

4. The implements used in agriculture through this tract were insufficient for a vigorous

vigorous culture, and consequently the husbandman sustained a constant loss.

5. The general knowledge of manures was extremely imperfect, and the practice void of spirit.

These circumstances, among others, shew how much the husbandry of this country wanted improvement. Let us, in the next place, examine the means taken by his Lordship to command that most beneficial purpose. He conducted himself from the beginning, upon the soundest of all principles, that of *practising* himself those methods which *reason* told him were the best; —— well convinced that argument and persuasion would have little effect on the *John Trott* geniuses of farming, he determined to set the example of good husbandry, as the only probable means of being succesful.

In the pursuit of this end his conduct was judicious and spirited. He has upwards of 2000 acres of land in his hands; and began their improvement with draining such as were wet, rightly considering this part of husbandry as the *sine qua non* of all others. —— His method was the most perfect that experience has hitherto brought to light; that of *covered drains*.

Throughout this extensive tract of land, I found very deep fosses cut, or old ditches sunk so deep as to give in every field the command of a sufficient descent. These are kept open. Into them run the covered drains, which are cut in number proportioned to the wetness of the land, but in general at but a small distance from each other.

Of these there are three sorts, the leading or main ones of two kinds, and the branches or secondary ones. The first sort of main drains are two feet wide at top and bottom, and four or five feet deep, walled on each side and covered at top with large broad stones. Plate II. fig. 4. The expence 6 *d.* a yard running measure. —— The second are a yard deep, two feet wide at top, and 10 inches at bottom; the stones used in filling them are oblong squares of 8, 9, or 10 inches length, the edges of which are rested on the sides of the bottom of the drains, and fall on each other at their tops, in the manner represented, Plate II. fig. 5. *a. a. a. a.* the drain *b.* the tops of the stones joining; then they are filled up with bits of stone, within seven or eight inches of the top; and, lastly, the molds thrown over all.

The branches are three quarters of a yard deep, 18 inches wide at top, and nine at bottom; they are then filled up in the same manner as the others. The expence of the operation is as follows:

	£	s.	d.
A cart load of stones of 40 bushels will do 7 yards; the getting these, besides the leading, is	0	0	3½
The leading, - -	0	1	5
Digging the drains, -	0	0	4½
Fixing in the stones, and filling up, -	0	0	3
For 7 yards, it is -	0	2	4

or just 4 *d.* a yard.

The improvement by these drains (which you will observe last for ever) is almost immediately manifest; the summer succeeding the first winter totally eradicates in grass lands all those weeds which proceed from too much water, and leaves the surface in the depth of winter perfectly dry and sound, insomuch that the same land which before poached with the weight of a man, will now bear without damage the tread of an ox. In arable lands, the effect is equally striking, for the corn in winter and spring upon land that used to be flowed with rain, and quite poisoned by it, now lies perfectly dry throughout the year, and in the tillage of it, a prodigious benefit accrues

accrues from this excellent practice, for the drained fields are ready in the spring for the plough, before the others can be touched; it is well known how pernicious it is to any land to plough or harrow it while wet.

This excellent practice his Lordship experienced as he expected, some years before his example was followed by any of his tenants. But at last the advantages attending it opened their eyes, and some of the most unprejudiced executed in their farms what they were convinced succeeded so greatly in their landlords; and accordingly I viewed some fields of the tenants that were drained in this way, and in a very effectual manner.

His Lordship's management in laying down and keeping his grafs lands, is worthy of universal imitation, as a spirit of culture has brought forth a fertility and richness of pasture beyond any thing I remember to have seen. The method of laying down is this: Oats are sown (under feeded) upon land that has been exceedingly well fallowed for a year and half, by many ploughings, harrowings, &c By which operations the surface is laid most completely level, so that not the least trace of a furrow is to be distinguished; with the corn, 12 lb. of white *Dutch* clover, and eight

eight bushels of finely dressed hay-seeds are sown. At harvest the oats are reaped, and 6 lb. more of clover-seed sown over the stubble, which is then mown, and raked off, and consequently the seed pretty well buried in the ground; a very rich compost is immediately spread on the field, and well harrowed in, by which means the seed is completely covered; in this manner it is left the first winter. The crop is next year left until the seeds are ripe enough to shake in the mowing, and making, by which means the land gains a fresh sprinkling, and the whole surface ensured a total and thick covering.

The success attending this method is so very great, that in several large fields I viewed, the after-grass was 8 and 9 inches high, soon after clearing a crop of hay of two tons per acre, and this the first year of the lay. No one would have known from walking over the field that it was not of some years growth, so thick and matted on the ground was the first year's produce. This grass, in any part of the kingdom, would have let for 30 *s.* an acre, and for 40 *s.* in most: An improvement you will think of a noble kind, when you are told that the rents before this management were no more than 8 and 9 *s.* and let at their value. Adjoining several of these new lays,

some

some of the old pastures are to be seen yet in tenants hands; they are poisoned with superfluous water, and overrun with every species of trumpery and weeds, the grass of a poor sort, and the quantity trifling. In some of his Lordship's lays of three or four years old, the after-grass, had it been mown, would have yielded at least two ton of hay an acre.

It is observable upon this plan, that no part of it is beyond the reach of a common farmer; a principal view of Lord *Rockingham* in all his husbandry. Here are no two years fallow, nor any loss by laying without a crop of corn; the seeds indeed are in large quantities, and amount in total price to near 50 s. an acre *; but then it is to be considered, that the thickness of sowing gives it a most excellent crop the very first year, which in the common management is generally the very contrary; and it is incontestible that his Lordship's method pays its own expence in the first crop. Suppose the farmer's seeds cost him 20 s. the excess on the side of the better manner is then, we will say, 25 s.; a sum in the value of hay

---

		l.	*s.*	*d.*
* 18 lb. Clover,	- -	0	9	0
8 Bushels grass, at 5 s.	-	2	0	0
	£.2	9	0

that does amount to little more than a fifth of the first year's produce.

And to shew how extremely profitable it is to landlords to act in this spirited manner, let us calculate the improvement of an acre of *bad* land converted in this method into *good*.

	l.	*s.*	*d.*
Suppose 40 yards of draining, in an acre, at 4 *d.* a yard,	6	13	4
50 at 6 *d.*	1	5	0
Ploughing the old grass up; giving the land a summer fallow of six earths, in all, at 5 *s.* the price of the country,	1	10	0
Seed earth for the oats,	0	5	0
3 bushels seed oats,	0	6	0
Sowing,	0	0	3
Mowing and harvesting,	0	6	0
Grass seeds,	2	10	0
Five harrowings,	0	2	6
Sowing,	0	1	0
Mowing and raking the stubble,	0	2	0
Carting it off,	0	1	0
Manuring: suppose all expences included,	5	0	0
Threshing 8 quarters of oats,	0	8	0
Mowing and making, carting and stacking the hay,	0	7	6
Harrowing the manure; and rolling twice,	0	1	0
Three years rent, at 8 *s.* 6 *d.*	1	5	6
Total expence,	20	4	1

	Product.	*l.*	*s.*	*d.*
By 8 quarters of oats at 14 *s.*		5	12	0
By one crop of hay, suppose only 30 cwt. at 40 *s.* a ton,	–	3	0	0
By after pasture,	–	0	10	0
		9	2	0
Expence,	– –	20	4	1
Produce,	– –	9	2	0
Remains,	– – –	11	2	1

Let at 30 *s.* an acre; the increase of rent is 21 *s.* 6 *d.* which at 35 years purchase, the rate of this country, is, 37 12 6
Deduct the above remainder, 11 2 1
Neat profit on the improvement, – – – 26 10 5

Which sum, on the expenditure of 20 *l.* is above 125 *l.* per cent. On the improvement of 100 acres is 2600 *l.* And this plain calculation, I think, shews with how just an idea his Lordship undertook to improve his grass lands.

But Lord *Rockingham* in scarce any thing has acted with greater spirit, than the improvement of the turnip culture by hoeing; for the disgust he felt at seeing the common

mon slovenly management of the farmers, in respect to this crop, made him determine to introduce the excellent practice of hoeing, common in many of the southern parts of the kingdom. With this view he attempted to persuade his tenants to come into the method, described to them the operation, pointed out its advantages; clearly explained to them the great consequence of increasing the size of the roots in the luxuriance of their growth, and the equality of the crops; reminded them of the poor crops of spring corn gained after turnips, for want of a better culture; from the difference of following a crop of weeds, which will not feed cattle, and consequently not improve the land; and succeeding a large produce of valuable roots, which by their thick shade, and the quantity of cattle they maintain, enrich the land at the same time that all weeds are destroyed by the hoeing.

Uncontrovertible as this reasoning, so clearly founded on facts, must appear to the unprejudiced, yet with a set of men of contracted ideas, used to a stated road, with deviations neither to the right nor left, it had very little effect: Turnips continued to be sown, but were never hoed. His Lordship then finding that discourse and reasoning could not prevail over the obstinacy

nacy of their understandings, determined to convince their eyes. He sent into *Hertfordshire* for a husbandman used to hoeing turnips, and gave directions for his management of a large crop: This he continued several years; and by this means, by degrees, he introduced the practice, which is now (though not universal) the common practice of all the good common farmers. Much does this neighbourhood owe to so patriotic a design, which was truly planned with judgment, and executed with spirit. Much more genuine fame ought to attend such an action, than the gaining a score of battles: The senseless rabble may praise the military hero; it belongs to *the few* to venerate the spirited cultivator.

In the introduction of new implements, and the improvement of old ones, his Lordship was equally attentive: This will appear clearly enough from the following implements, which are such as his Lordship has, at different times, either had constructed by his own directions, or ordered upon the model of other counties: None of them are common in *Yorkshire*; you will easily perceive how much they merit attention. The sketches, Plate V. Fig. 1. of a drill plough are not such as I wish them; but an ingenious workman may, by
means

means of the measures, construct them with tolerable accuracy, 1. 1. The handles.

2. The hopper, 9 inches broad, 10 deep, 3 wide at bottom, with a hole at the bottom, $2\frac{1}{2}$ inches diameter, for the feed to fall through into the cavities of the roller (16), and thrown by that through a hollow in the tail of the plough (1).

3. A wheel 2 feet diameter, with an iron rim fastened to the plough by a moveable iron (5), and to the handles by a chain (4). It turns the roller (16) within the plough, by an iron (20) jointed in the middle, which goes through the hollow of it (17), and keeps the wheel a foot from the plough. By means of the chain (4), the ploughman lifts up the wheel, and stops the feed from shedding at the headlands.

6. An iron screw two feet long, which turns against the spring (19), let into the plough against the cavities (18) of the roller (16), by means of which the aperture for the feed to be thrown through is larger or smaller according to its kind or quantity.

7. The share.

8. The beam 7 feet 8 inches long, 5 inches square, one third of the length from the handles, and then 3.

9. A

9. A chain faſtened to the beam by a moving hook (22), and to the axletree (11), to keep the plough ſteady.
10. 10. The carriage wheels 3 feet diameter.
11. The axletree 2 feet from wheel to wheel.
12. The ſhaft to fix the whippletrees on for the horſes to draw by.
13. A chain from the hook (22) to the top of the ſtandards (15).
14. A ditto from the beam to the chain (9).
15. The ſtandards of carriage 20 inches high, and 15 broad.
16. The iron roller before-mentioned 4 inches long, and 2 diameter, contains 8 cavities, $1\frac{3}{4}$ inch long, and $\frac{1}{4}$ broad, for beans and peaſe, and 10 for wheat, This is drawn on a larger ſcale for greater accuracy.
19. The ſpring 4 inches and half long, and one and half broad.

The coſt complete, 3 *l.* 3 *s.*

This plough is an excellent one, for its ſimplicity and ſtrength are ſuch that it is never out of order; will bear the rough uſage of country hands, and perform its work even in the ſtrongeſt of ſoils: Many have been invented with more powers, but then the complex mechaniſm is ſuch as renders them little better than gimcracks.

It

It is excellent for wheat, or any larger grain, and never grinds the corn. Plate V. fig. 2. A turnwrift plough.
1. The beam 9 feet long.
2. The handles, 4 feet.
3. The fhare, 18 inches long, and 5 broad.
4. The coulter, 3 feet long.
5. A long circular iron which is faftened to the beam at the joint 9, and to the carriage by the chain 8, to keep the plough fteady.
6. A moveable ftick to faften the coulter either to the right or left.
7. 7. Two holes in which the irons (10. 10.) of the mould board, fig. are ftuck, to faften it on.

The carriage is the fame as the drill-plough, only the axletree fhorter, like a common wheel plough. The price complete is three guineas.

I remarked this plough in its work, and it performed with four horfes excellently, cut ten inches deep, the furrow level and true; the mould-board is fhifted from the one fide to the other in an inftant, only running the iron points into the holes, and giving it a knock with the moveable ftaff (6) This invention is of great ufe, for when the mould-board is fixed, the land muft must be ploughed different ways; to the right and to the left, with a furrow left in the middle of the ground at finishing; or else the ploughman must begin in the middle and arch up; whereas the shifting-board enables him to throw his land all one way, at the same time that it has all the powers of the fixed one.

His Lordship ordered it to be worked before me, and it is very observable that the plough would cut its furrow at the usual depth and with great truth for several perch, without holding: the strongest proof in the world of a good instrument.

Plate V. Fig. 3. A horse-hoe.
1. The beam 5 feet 8 inches long, 4 in breadth by $3\frac{1}{2}$ thick.
2. The handles 18 inches to the joining; from thence 2 feet 2 inches to the beam.
3. A wooden coulter, 2 feet 5 inches long, on a wheel.
4. The front share all of iron, which works before the middle of the other two, 19 inches long.
5. The double share.
6. The chain of the whippletree (7.)
8. The double share, a front view.

From

From a to b. 8 inches
    c to d. 8 ⎫
    d to e. 9 ⎬ ditto.
    f to g. 6½ ⎪
    g to h. 4 ⎭

The iron frame 2 inches broad, and ¼ of an inch thick.

9. Another double share to use in the same beam, for different distanced rows.

From a to b. 8½ inches
    c to d. 14 ⎫
    c to e. 10 ⎬ ditto.
    c to f. 7 ⎪
    c or f to g. 7 ⎭

The price complete, 1 *l.* 7 *s.*

This is an excellent horse-hoe, cuts the ground with great truth of what depth is chosen, and well calculated for eradicating the weeds; by means of changing the shares, which is done in a minute, it suits different spaces.

Plate V. Fig. 4. Another horse-hoe.

a. The beam, 5 feet 6 inches long, and 3½ by 3 square.
b. The handles, 3 feet 8 inches long.
c. The shares.
d. The center and wheel, 2 feet long; the wheel 9 inches diameter.
e. The share in large.

From 1 to 2. 17 inches.
    2 to 3. 4 ⎫ ditto.
    3 to 4. 11 ⎭

The iron standard 2½ broad.

f. The

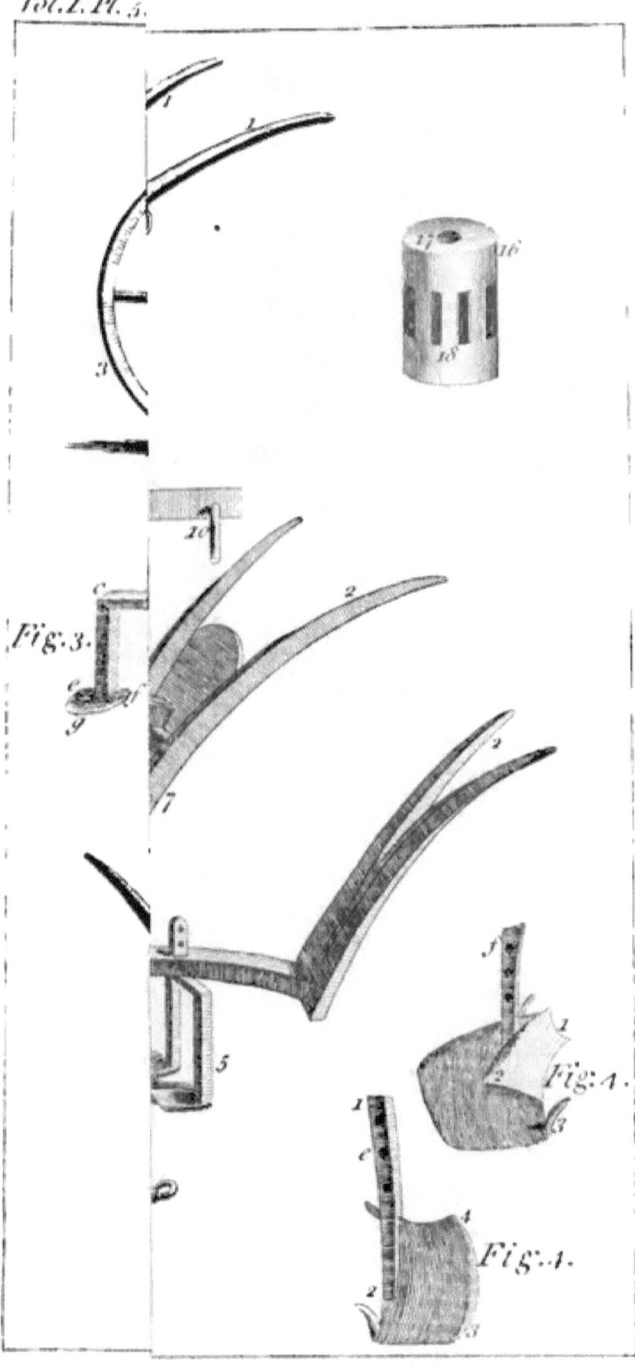

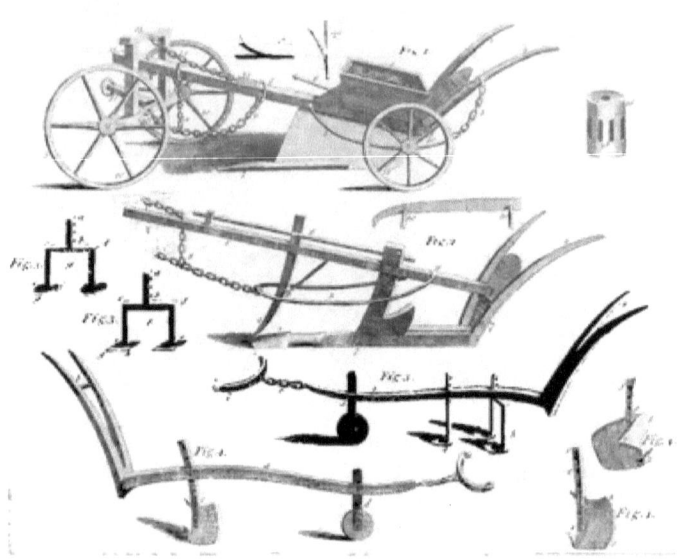

f. The same share, with the addition of a curved plate, for a mould-board.

From 1 to 2. 8 inches.
  2 to 3. 7 ditto.

It fixes on by putting the standard through a hole in it, and the little wings g. keep it steady on the sides.

The price complete, 12 s.

This machine is well calculated for narrow rows; does its work with great exactness; nothing can be more useful for horse-hoeing rows of lucerne, burnet, potatoes, &c. and the contrivance of the moveable mould iron for earthing up the rows, saves the expence of a complete implement for that purpose.

Plate VI. Fig. 1. A spiky roller.

1. The roller 5 feet 10 inches long, and 13 inches diameter; the spikes $3\frac{1}{2}$ inches long, and $2\frac{1}{2}$ or 3 from spike to spike.

2. The shafts, 11 feet long.

In the article of manuring also, this excellent cultivator gave the utmost attention to remedy the errors of the country; and to set an example of good husbandry to all the farmers around. The management of the composts at *Wentworth*, and the experiments Lord *Rockingham* has made on manures, are curious.

The composts are formed of all sorts of manures, particularly farm-yard dung, and manures purchased at the neighbouring towns; such as soap-boilers ashes, coal ashes, horn shavings, curriers shavings, &c. &c. &c. And sometimes mole-hills, turf, and lime are added, layers of these are formed one on another, and after remaining a few months are turned over; then the heap remains some time longer, after which it is mixed again, and so repeated until the substances are thoroughly rotted; which with some takes no trifling time and pains, particularly horn shavings; one compost of which manure mixed with dung, I observed, was in so complete a state of corruption, that it cut like butter, and must undoubtedly be the richest manure in the world; it had been turned over many times, that it might all be equally rotten. Many of these composts, I remarked in different fields, of various ages, successively preparing for the land, and that every acre might receive its share, and all be manured in three or four years. A management, than which nothing can be more complete.

Many other manures have been tried by his Lordship in the experimental stile. Clay he burnt, in hopes of gaining rich ashes, but it was reduced only to large hard pieces, and to glafs.

It was a common notion, that rabbit-dung was of no benefit to the land, and the opinion of a neighbouring warrener, upon which his Lordfhip agreed with him for fweeping his warren every year. By this means he got a large quantity, which coft him no more than 4 s. 6 d. a load: He tried it with pigeons dung; in a very fair comparifon: On a grafs field he laid ftripes of each, firft an acre covered with rabbits dung two loads, then an acre with the fame quantity of pigeons dung at a guinea a load; then rabbits, and next pigeons again, and fo through the field, which was a very fair trial. The rabbits dung turned out much the beft, and lafted the longeft.

Thirty years ago, a fquare piece of grafs at *Wentworth*, almoft furrounded by other pafture, was manured very well with falt; Lord *Rockingham* has remarked, that the part manured has flourifhed much better than the other to this day, no manure has been fince laid on either piece.

But this fpirited execution of a regular plan is by no means the only inftance to be produced of this Nobleman's attention to the improvement of hufbandry: as a proof of this, I fhall next mention to you a new and moſt judicious thought which is executed with uncommon ſpirit. This is the eſtabliſhment of two farms, managed, one in the *Kentiſh*, and the other in the *Hertfordſhire* method. Thoſe counties have the reputation of a very accurate cultivation; his Lordſhip therefore determined to fix a farmer from each on a diſtinct farm, to manage it in the beſt manner they had been uſed to; a moſt excellent plan, as it gave riſe to a beneficial emulation, which could not fail of being productive of the beſt conſequences. Both are ſenſible and underſtanding men. I viewed their lands with attention, and found their huſbandry to be as follows:

The ſoil of the *Kentiſh* farm is in general a rich deep black loam; in ſome fields light and excellent for turnips, and in others heavy, being nearly allied to clay. The grand principle upon which it is cultivated, is never to fallow the land; but, by means of turnips and drilled beans and peaſe, to keep it perfectly clean from weeds, and in good heart for crops of corn. For this purpoſe, the fields are thrown into the following excellent courſe:

1. Beans
2. Wheat
3. Peaſe
4. Wheat
5. Turnips or cabbages
6. Barley
7. Clover
8. Wheat

An

An ameliorating fallow crop here intervenes between every two of corn, or the exhausting ones; and when such a course is conducted with spirit, most certainly none can exceed it.

For beans he ploughs twice, sows them in equally distant drills, 20 inches asunder, with a plough marked **Plate V. Fig. 1.** among the preceding instruments; 3 bushels of seed per acre: He horse-hoes them with a **machine, Plate V. Fig. 4.** which answers extremely **well** in loosening the soil and cutting the weeds. This operation he repeats from three to seven times, according to the quantity of weeds, but always so as to keep the ground **perfectly** free from them; besides this, he hand-hoes the rows once with a small hoe, which clears away all the weeds **that grow there.** By means of this treatment, the land is in excellent order for wheat, after the crop of beans is off, which is very seldom less than 5 quarters per acre.

Pease he manages in the same manner, drills 3 bushels and an half, but they only require the horse-hoeing; the crop upon an average is 4 quarters per acre.

The tillage for the wheat is varied according to the cleanness of the land; if frequent showers have brought up many weeds after the last horse-hoeing, it is ploughed three times; if it is quite clean, only one ploughing and an half suffice. The wheat is sown broad-cast, 10 pecks to the acre, and the medium crop four quarters. For turnips he ploughs four or five times, and hand-hoes them carefully twice, by which management he raises infinitely finer crops than any common ones in *Yorkshire*. After these roots the land is ploughed but once for barley; four bushels per acre sown, and five quarters gained at a medium in return. When oats are thrown in, they receive three ploughings; four bushels sown per acre, and four quarters reaped. Clover he sows with both wheat and barley; if the latter, in the common way, but when with wheat, his management is excellent. If the weather is dry enough, he sows 16 *lb*. per acre in the middle of *March*, and then harrows the wheat thoroughly, and rolls it; and so far is it from being of any damage to the wheat, that it evidently forwards its growth.

Cabbages, his Lordship ordered him to cultivate according to the best principles of his method of husbandry, and accordingly he has planted several acres. He sows the seed the latter end of *February*, and if they run too fast, pricks them out once before the transplantation, which is about

about the middle of *June*, in rows three feet afunder, and three feet from plant to plant in the rows. If dry weather comes, they require watering. In three weeks after planting he horfe-hoes them with Plate V. Fig. 3. after which he hand-hoes around the plants; and thefe operations he repeats according to the weeds that rife; generally from three to five horfe-hoeings. The value he reckons at $\frac{1}{4}$ *d.* each to feed any fort of cattle with; ufes them chiefly for the fatting of oxen, for which purpofe they anfwer exceedingly well; but I fhould apprehend them of a greater value than that, efpecially as his foil is rich and deep. Either beans or barley come after them, according to the time they are off the land.

Of potatoes he raifes large crops; his method is to plant them in the beginning of *March*, in rows two feet afunder, and nine inches in the rows; he flices them, which is not generally done in *Yorkfhire*. The land for them is dunged with long yard dung, 32 loads per acre, and then ploughed in pretty deep, and the fetts dibbled in by a line: the rows he hand-hoes, and horfe-hoes the intervals according to the rifing of the weeds. I remarked that his crop was very free from them, and of a vigorous growth.

Besides these numerous articles, his Lordship has directed him to undertake the culture of hops according to the practice of *Kent*, and in his farm a field is planted with them. They are set in hillocks six feet six inches square; planted the latter end of *January*: there was a crop of cabbages among them; he says it is a common practice in *Kent* to have rows of cabbages or beans, or to sow turnips among them the first year, but the method must be prejudicial to the hops; for the nourishment which ought to be preserved for them, is carried off the land, and a probability of stocking it with caterpillars, grubs and other vermin, which may damage the young hops. He poles and gathers the second year, and as he has great hope from the goodness of his soil, he expects eight or nine hundred weight of hops per acre *per annum*.

His management of his manure is much better than is common in *Yorkshire*; he carries it out of the farm-yard, lays it under the hedges, and then digs up all the hillocks and rising irregular banks of earth, and mixes them well with the dung. This practice, which is common in *Essex*, is unknown among the common farmers in *Yorkshire*; of this compost he lays 50 loads (18 bushels) per acre. His method of using lime

lime is to mix it in the same manner with earth, one chaldron of lime to thirty loads of earth.

His way of feeding his horses is also uncommon among the *Yorkshire* farmers; it is to keep them all the summer in the stables, and feed them with clover fresh mown every day. He begins it the latter end of *May*, and continues it till the middle of *September*; during which time 2½ acres of good clover will maintain six horses, but they have some chaff and hay with it. This is an excellent custom; makes a plenty of manure; the clover goes infinitely further than if fed in the field, and the horses are kept in better heart (regularly worked) than in the common way; his team of six were fat and in good order. His allowance in winter is a bushel of oats and a peck of beans per horse per week. He uses three or four in a plough with a driver, and does an acre a day.

The plough he uses in common is the *Kentish* turn wrist one, Plate V. Fig. 2. of an excellent construction, cuts very deep, and goes extremely steady. He has 60 acres of arable land to six horses. Having thus gone through the œconomy of the *Kentish* farm, I shall next give you an account of the *Hertfordshire* one.

The

The soil is different; in some fields a strong clay, and in others a good hazel loam, that is excellent for turnips and barley. His courses of crops are,

1. Turnips   4. Wheat
2. Barley   5. Oats
3. Clover

This last crop of oats ought never to be suffered.

    1. Fallow   2. Wheat
    2. Wheat   3. Beans
    3. Oats   4. Wheat
And 1. Fallow

The beans in the last course ought either to be thoroughly horse and hand-hoed, or not succeeded by wheat; for no land can throw out three good crops upon the credit of one fallow, unless some of them are *fallow crops*.

He ploughs three or four times for wheat, sows 10 pecks, and reaps at a medium 18 bushels. For barley, after turnips, he gives but one earth, but if on a fallow, three or four; sows four bushels, and gains at an average four quarters. For oats he stirs but once, sows five bushels, and reckons five quarters his mean produce. The tillage he gives his beans consists only in one earth, which, considering them as a preparation for wheat, is by no means good husbandry. He sows
four

four bushels broad-cast, does not hoe them, and reaps at a medium about 4½ quarters per acre. Sometimes he drills them by hand after the plough in rows 10 inches asunder, in which method two bushels and a half of seed he finds sufficient; generally hand-hoes them but once, sometimes twice, and earths them up with the hoe when a foot high; in this manner he gets four quarters per acre. Pease he manages the same as beans; in the broad-cast way he sows four bushels, and reaps two quarters and an half; in the drilling method sows 2½ bushels; the crop the same. For turnips he ploughs three times, hoes them twice, and reckons the value at an average about 36 s. per acre. Sometimes he feeds them off the land with sheep, but when it is inclinable to wetness he draws them for beasts, scattering them over a grass close. Clover he cultivates in the same manner as the *Kentish* farmer; mows it twice for hay, of which he gets at a medium three tons per acre, and values it at 1 l. a ton. Cabbages he likewise cultivates, sows the seed the end of *February* or the beginning of *March*; pricks them out once before they are planted in the field, which is about *Midsummer*: He makes the rows 3 feet asunder, and sets the plants 3 feet from each other. In three weeks after planting he he hand-hoes them, and once more when the weeds rise: His crop this year is a very fine one. The sort used both by him and the *Kentish* farmer, is the large *Scotch* cabbage.

His yard dung he sometimes mixes with hedge earth, but oftener lays it on without; he never sows turnips without dunging, and of the vast consequence of manure for that root, he this year has a striking proof; for not having a sufficiency to cover the whole field, about a rood was left unmanured; the ploughings over the whole were the same, and sown at the same time; the field in general is a very fine crop; but just that rood is scarcely worth leaving on the ground: A pregnant instance of the consequence of manuring.

His tillage he performs with horses, four to 80 acres of arable land, uses two or three in a plough, according to the soil, and stirs an acre a day. He sometimes in his drilling practice has opened the furrows with the instrument, Plate VI. Fig. 2. which is a good contrivance enough, and would do very well in some of the operations of horse-hoeing.

1. The beam five feet long, and three inches square.

2. The handles, four feet six inches long.

3. The fhare which lets into a groove cut in the bottom of the beam, and is faftened by the iron (4).

5. The fhare at large.

```
      from a to b   16 inches.
           c to d   11 ⎫
           c to e    2 ⎬ ditto
           b to f    6 ⎭
```

One point of management of grafs, tried here with great accuracy, is the feeding off the eddifh clean. It has been afferted by many, that it is moft advantageous to leave much of it on the ground to keep the young fhoots warm in the fpring, and to rot as a manure; this his Lordfhip has tried on one field, and in adjoining ones has fed it off quite bare with *Scotch* beafts; the fucceeding year the crop has regularly been the better after the parts fed. Which refult has fince induced him always to buy in a large drove of cattle to feed through the winter, well convinced, that one great benefit of improving lands is the keeping a proportional ftock of cattle; which increafes with increafing improvement; and moft certainly, the more cattle the land maintains, the better they will make it: A much clearer pofition than the idea of letting its product rot for manure.

An

An experiment also made on clover deserves great attention: It has been often asserted, that the best time of the year for sowing this as well as other grass seeds is in autumn, without corn; his lordship tried it three times, and once failing, he continued the same field fallow another year for it, so that it was a second time sown on a fallow of two years; but, notwithstanding so great an advantage, the crop was in no degree equal to others, with corn on one year's fallow, a difference immense, and sufficient rationally to prevent any farmer from altering his present profitable custom, for one so evidently unfavourable.

The following account of the state of agriculture in the country for several miles around *Wentworth-House*, I owe to the very obliging attention of the Marquis of *Rocking* himself. The most valuable of these particulars came from his Lordship, and those of which he was doubtful were supplied by several of his tenants, who were sent for on purpose: A striking proof not only of his Lordship's knowledge, but likewise of his love of agriculture, and great readiness to forward any attempts which have the least appearance of being serviceable to the public.

The

The two general divisions of the soil, small tracts excepted, are into clay and loam; the former is strong and rich, but wet; the latter light enough for turnips, and rich enough for wheat, which I have often remarked, is the criterion of excellent land; the general average rent is about 8 s. an acre. The farms are all small, rising in general from 20 l. to 60 l. a year.—— The courses of crops are chiefly these. On the light loams,

1. Turnips   4. Wheat
2. Barley   5. Barley
3. Clover one year

On the clays,

1. Fallow   3. Beans
2. Wheat   4. Wheat

And,

1. Fallow   3. Clover
2. Barley   4. Wheat

For wheat on a fallow, they plough four or five times, sow nine pecks and an half, and reap, at an average, three quarters on clay land, and three quarters six bushels on their loams.

But one earth for wheat, on clover land.

A fallow for barley consists of four stirrings on clay; but on turnip land they plough and sow. Three bushels of seed used;

used; and the average crop on all land about five quarters. For oats they plough but once, sow four bushels, and gain at a medium, in return, about four quarters and an half: but on fresh land, six or seven quarters. They give but one stirring for beans, sow four bushels and an half broad-cast, never hoe them; the crop about 18 bushels. But Mr. *Payne* of *Warth*, in this neighbourhood, cultivates them in a much completer manner. He gives three ploughings for them besides harrowings and rollings, until it is made perfectly fine: He then in the beginning of *March* drills in the beans with his Lordship's drill-plough, described above, in rows 14 or 15 inches asunder. He horse-hoes them four times, besides hand-hoeings, and hand-weedings of the rows, and from 10 pecks of seed generally reaps 30 bushels. This is an imitation of the *Kentish* husbandry, introduced by his Lordship.

Pease are not a common crop, but when sown they plough for them but once; sow three bushels and an half, use the common rouncival, and get 24 bushels an acre, at an average. For rye, they plough four or five times, sow **nine** pecks, and gain in return 24 bushels. Their culture of turnips is from four to six earths; hoeing, through the attention and example of the

Marquis

Marquis of *Rockingham*, is coming into practice, infomuch that many farmers now hoe their crops, who formerly had fcarce any notion of it. Perhaps a quarter or a third of the crops are now hoed: They reckoned the medium value of crops not hoed at 20 *s.* an acre, and of thofe that are hoed, at 40 *s.* a moſt ſtriking proof of the excellency of the practice: They uſe them both for ſheep and beaſts, generally draw them and feed on paſtures; ſometimes in ſheds, and reckon that a middling acre of hoed turnips will fat two beaſts of fifty ſtone each; that is finiſh their fatting, if half fat by grafs. They give both hay and ſtraw with them. Of rape the ſow very little; generally on freſh land, and feed it off with ſheep, ſowing wheat after it.

Clover they ſow with barley, chiefly for mowing; they cut it twice, and get three tons of hay at the two mowings: They find no crop whatever to anſwer better, but ſome land begins to grow tired of it, the culture having been common theſe 40 years. The wheat they find better after that which is mown, than that which is fed.

The management of their manure chiefly conſiſts in the foddering their farm-yards with the ſtraw of the crop; the excellent cuſtom of cutting ſtubble for that purpoſe is almost unknown among them: In the spring they lead the dung on to a hill, some few, in imitation of his Lordship, turn it over, but it is not common; they lay it upon turnip land, and wheat fallow. Lime is much used on turnips and wheat fallows. They lay a chaldron an acre, which costs them 7 s. besides the leading, all together 12 s. by the time it is on the land: To carry a chaldron 12 miles they reckon worth 20 s.

Pigeon dung they lay on all sorts of land, a chaldron per acre, which they value at 30 s. In the neighbourhood of *Sheffield*, bones are a very common manure; they lay a chaldron per acre on grass, and find them excellent.

Some malt-dust is used, of which they lay a chaldron per acre.

Soap ashes are a favourite manure for grass lands, and some are laid on a fallow for turnips, three chaldrons per acre at 8 s. per chaldron; they are reckoned to last three or four years.

Coal-ashes they likewise lay on their grass lands, five or six chaldron per acre; cost 1 s. 6 d. per chaldron.

Rape-dust they generally use with lime, but not mixed; five quarters of lime and 15 bushels of rape-dust to an acre. It is an excellent manure, but declining in use, on

account

account of the high price, being got up to 13 *s.* a quarter. Soot they get for 4 *d.* a bushel, lay it on grass and barley, a chaldron to the acre; it lasts one or two crops.

The grass lands in this neighbourhood are applied rather more to the breeding of stock than either to dairying or fatting: They have scarce any notion of a good dairy for the profit of butter and cheese. Indeed, as the prices of lean stock have been of late, indifferent grass, like theirs, unimproved, may probably pay best in rearing young cattle. They allot two acres to the fatting of a beast of 50 stone, or to the keeping a cow: A good one gives, in the height of the season, three gallons of milk per day, and yields product by the year about 4 *l.* The profit of keeping a beast of 50 stone a year, and fatting him does not exceed 4 *l.* They keep very few hogs in proportion to their cows; a dairy of six cows does not maintain above three or four pigs. The winter food of their cows when milked consists of nothing but hay. In the rearing their calves, they let them suck only two or three days, after which they give them new, and then skim milk: But for the butchers, they let them suck four or five weeks. In the wintering a cow, they reckon she eats, between *Martinmas* and *May-day*, two tons and an half of hay. The price of joisting a cow in winter at straw is 6 *d.* or 8 *d.* a week, and to keep them from *May-day* to *Michaelmas* 30 *s.* for the keeping a fatting beast 5 *s.* less than for a cow.

As to sheep, the whole country has nothing that deserves the name of a flock; the number kept by the farmers rising only from ten to thirty, and yet the profit they make on them is by no means trifling; they reckon 8 *l.* or 9 *l.* a score, their gain by keeping them a year. The joisting price is 3 *d.* a week in winter; but any farmer would readily give 6 *d.* a week through the month of *April*; five sheep give about a stone of wool.

Respecting the tillage of this neighbourhood; they rekon six horses necessary for the culture of 60 acres of arable land; in ploughing, at strong work, they use four at length, but afterwards only two a-breast; and do three rood or an acre a day. Their allowance of corn consists only of half a peck of oats each horse per day in feed-time: The price of joisting from *May-day* to *Michaelmas* is 25 *s.* and they reckon their teams to cost them yearly, upon the whole, (shoeing included) 7 *l.* 10 *s.* a horse. Their oxen they winter in common upon straw,

straw, but, when they work, upon hay: Horses for tillage, they reckon best.

The price per acre for ploughing is 5 s.

They reckon 150 *l.* absolutely necessary for a farmer who hires 40 acres at 20 *l.* a year, about half arable and half grass; but if it is well stocked, 170 *l.* will be requisite: Which sum they divide as follows,

	l.	*s.*	*d.*			
Three horses, —	30	0	0			
Two cows, —	18	0	0			
A sow, — —	2	0	0			
Harness, — —	3	0	0			
A cart, — —	8	0	0			
A plough, —	1	10	0			
A pair of harrows,	1	10	0			
Sundry small articles, spades, shovels, screen, ropes, &c.	10	0	0			
Dairy utensils, —	1	10	0			
				25	10	0
Furniture, —	20	0	0			
Seed, — —	7	10	0			
Rent, — —	20	0	0			
Tythe and rates, —	7	0	0			
House keeping, &c.	40	0	0			
				94	10	0
				£. 170	0	0

Land

Land sells in general from 30 to 40 years purchase. The employment of the poor women and children is chiefly among the farmers, but many spin worsted: All drink tea.

The general oeconomy of the farms will be seen from the following sketches.

180 Acres in all	6 Cows
60 Ditto arable	2 Beasts
120 Grass	6 Young cattle
£. 80 Rent	2 Servants
7 Horses	1 Labourer.

Of another,

145 Acres in all	8 Cows
70 Arable	4 Beasts
75 Grass	6 Young cattle
£.60 Rent	18 Sheep
7 Horses	3 Servants
2 Oxen	1 Labourer

Another,

80 Acres in all	3 Cows
40 Arable	4 Young cattle
40 Grass	10 Sheep
£.35 Rent	2 Servants
6 Horses	1 Labourer

Another,

60 Acres in all	30 Arable
30 Grass	£.30 Rent
	5 Horses

5 Horses   60 Sheep (a right
4 Cows   of commonage)
4 Young cattle   2 Servants

Another,

100 Acres in all   8 Cows
 50 Arable   6 Young cattle
 50 Grafs   10 Sheep
£.40 Rent   2 Servants
 10 Horses   1 Labourer

Another,

70 Acres in all   6 Horses
40 Arable   4 Cows
30 Grafs   14 Sheep
£.25 Rent   2 Servants

Another,

50 Acres in all   5 Horses
35 Arable   2 Cows
15 Grafs   1 Servant
£.22 Rent   1 Labourer.

LABOUR.

In harvest and hay-time, 1 s. a day, victuals and drink.
In winter, 1 s.
Reaping, per acre, 5 s. 6 d. or 6 s.
Mowing corn, 2 s.
——— grafs, 1 s. 6 d.

Hoeing

Hoeing turnips, 4 s. an acre the first time, and 2 s. the second.
Ditching, the reparation 2 s. and 2 s. 6 d. the acre, of 28 yards.
Threshing wheat, 8 d. a load of 3 bushels.
———————— barley, 1 s. 6 d. a quarter.
———————— oats, 8 d. ditto.
Wages of the head man, 9 l. to 10 l.
——————— ploughman, 7 l. to 8 l.
——————— boy of 10 or 12 years, 4 l.
——————— maid servants, 2 l. to 4 l.
Women a day in harvest, 8 d. and 10 d. with ale twice, small beer, and a dinner.
——————————— in hay-time, 6 d. and beer.
——————————— in winter, 5 d.

IMPLEMENTS.

A waggon, 14 l. A spade, 3 s. 9 d.
A cart, 9 l. Laying a share and
A plough, 1 l. 10 s. a coulter, 1 s.
A harrow, 1 l. 10 s. Shoeing a horse, 1 s.
A stone roller, 1 l. 10 s. 2 d.
A scythe, 3 s. 9 d.

BUILDING.

Bricks per 1000, 9 s. or 10 s.
Oak-timber, 1 s. to 2 s. 6 d.
Ash, 1 s. 2 d.
Carpenter, per day, 1 s. 4 d. and 1 s. 6 d.
Mason, ditto, 1 s. 4 d. and 1 s. 6 d.
Stone walling, 3 s. 6 d. and 4 s. a rod.

PRO-

PROVISIONS, &c.

Bread,	1 d. per lb.	Veal,	$2\frac{1}{2}$ d.
Cheese,	$3\frac{1}{2}$	Milk,	$0\frac{1}{2}$ a pint.
Butter,	7 18 oz.	Potatoes,	4 a peck.
Beef,	$3\frac{1}{4}$	Candles,	$6\frac{1}{2}$
Mutton,	$3\frac{1}{2}$	Soap,	6

Labourer's house rent, 25 s.
——————— tools, 4 s.
——————— firing, 12 s.

Upon this system of husbandry, it is in general to be remarked, first, That the rent, 8 s. per acre, must certainly be a rent of favour, not of value, since the disproportion between that and the products is obvious. The courses——1. turnips, 2. barley, 3. clover, 4. wheat; and 1. fallow, 2. barley, 3. clover, 4. wheat, cannot be too much commended. But 1. fallow, 2. wheat, 3. beans, 4. wheat, is very bad; and execrably so, where the beans are not hoed: Eighteen bushels per acre of that pulse from such good land speaks sufficiently the evil of the conduct. Mr. *Payne*'s imitation displays much better husbandry; this wretched culture of beans, when designed as a preparation for wheat, was one cause of Lord *Rockingham*'s being anxious to set an example of the *Kentish* husbandry; so much superior

superior to the common method of *Yorkshire*: Farmers are slow at imitating new practices, but the continued success which will undoubtedly attend his Lordship's improvements, cannot fail of effecting a reformation in time; the consequences of it give one peculiar pleasure to contemplate: For *Wentworth* is in the center of an immense tract of many counties that never hoed a bean: so that if the improvement spreads, here is field enough. Greater crops of beans will be produced, and the benefit to those of wheat will be immense.

The introduction of turnip hoeing (owing also to the same noble cultivator) is at present more generally apparent in its utility, than from the number of common farmers who have followed the method: It must undoubtedly become general, for the value of hoed turnips *to sell*, being double that of the unhoed ones, is a circumstance that must operate, and powerfully.

There is something both to commend and disapprove in the management of manures; but their beginning to follow the Marquis's example, in turning over their dunghills, predicts a more perfect conduct.

Their grass lands they manage in a very defective husbandry; the mere riding through

through the country, is sufficient to see this: Their manure is laid on grass very sparingly; they take scarce any care in cleaning them from trumpery and rubbish; such as bushes, briars, molehills, and even thistles and docks: they have as little notion of keeping old pastures level by smoothing all inequalities of the surface; and as to the laying arable land down to grass, they do it in the ridge and furrow-way, sow a very scanty measure of seeds, and attend very little to the soil then being in good heart.

And here I cannot but remark, the singular judgment with which Lord *Rockingham* has practised agriculture. He first first took a general and comprehensive view of the common husbandry of his neighbourhood, and then applied his attention peculiarly to those points in which that common husbandry was most defective.

I cannot take my leave of these pursuits, so truly worth of a *British* nobleman——of a philosopher——and of a man, without remarking how greatly the example calls for imitation. Those who have declined the employments and amusements of agriculture under the false idea of their being mean and unworthy of great

riches

riches and high rank, fhould, if reflection is infufficient to undeceive them, confider the example I have in thefe pages endeavoured to fketch; will they find the character of a ftatefman and a patriot, fullied by the addition of that of a farmer?

LETTER VI.

FROM *Wentworth-House*, we took the road to *Kniveton*, the feat of his Grace the Duke of *Leeds*. From *Rotherham* to *Kniveton* the land is of various forts; near that town, as I remarked in another place, the rents are exceedingly high; but towards *Ashton*, the foil grows but indifferent, the fandy parts let from 2 *s*. 6 *d*. to 5 *s*. an acre; and good inclofures at 12 *s*. About *Kniveton*, rents vary from 1 *s*. to 20 *s*. an acre, but run at an average about 8 *s*. or 9 *s*. fome few farms of 200 *l*. a year and upwards, but in general from 20 *l*. to 60 *l*. throughout this road. Paring and burning is a common practice; they cut the turf with a paring plough, which appears a very good invention. Fig. 3. Plate VI. gives an idea of its conftruction.

1. The beam, fix feet long.
2. The handles, five feet fix inches long.
3. The fhare, one foot broad, and nine inches long.

4. The coulter and wheel, ten inches diameter.

5. The coulter frame work, which shifts it by means of sliding the frame.

6. The ear.

7. Ditto in large, 10 inches from a. to b. and 12 from b. to c.

8. The coulter frame in large, thirteen inches from a. to b. and twenty-two from b. to c. *

From

---

* At *Kniveton*, you first enter the hall, 50 feet by 30, painted by Sir *James Thornhill*. Around it it are several antique statues, some of which are very finely executed.
Cupid.
Lucretia; the drapery admirably light and fine; and the air of the head beautiful.
Hercules.
Venus.
Paris.
Diana. Her drapery good, but the folds rather too small.

In the anti-room, among other pictures, are,

Holbein. Portrait of the Earl of *Worcester.*
Lord *Cecil.* The hands and face very fine.
Vandyke. Marquis of *Montrose*, inimitably fine; the features and countenance noble, and the attitude easy and elegant.
King and Queen of *Bohemia.* Good.

Drawing-

From *Kniveton* to *Workfop* and *Welbeck*, the foil is chiefly fand; lets at a low rent, of from 4 s. to 8 s. an acre; the latter place, the feat of his Grace the Duke of *Portland*, is very well deferving the attention of the curious traveller; in the park are feveral noble woods of very antient and venerable

---

Drawing-room, 24 fquare.
Bed-chamber.
Clofet. A mufic-piece by *Titian*. The drapery pretty.
Dining-room, 36 by 25.
Rubens. The four parts of the world. The figures are thofe of *Rubens*, a pure flefhy female, but the beafts furprizingly fine; the panther equal to any thing ever painted, and the crocodile admirably done. The groupe vile.
Titian. The four Evangelifts; heavy and inexpreffive, but the diffufion of light good, the air of the heads is fine, and the hands appear to me very well executed.
Paul Veronefe. Marriage of Cana. A ftrange groupe; the drapery very bad; nor is there any propriety of action: The expreffion is however ftrong.
Solomon receiving his wifdom. The figure of *Solomon* is that of a fleeping clown. The attitude of the Deity in the air, and the expreffion of his countenance are fine: The colours bad.

venerable oaks, of an extraordinary size; the remains of one are to be seen, yet living, with a passage cut through it large enough for a coach to drive through; and another with seven vast branches growing from one body: These are both real

---

David and Nathan, by the same master, but unknown. The colours and *manner* the same.

Reynolds. The late Duchess of *Leeds*; a most sweet attitude and the eyes exquisitely done.

Drawing-room, 25 square.

Vandyke. Earl of *Stafford*; fine.

Rubens. Sea goddesses; the figures, attitudes and colours are not pleasing.

Ditto. *Venus and Cupid.* By no means agreeable.

Schalken. Old woman with a candle. The expression of the light strong and fine.

Bassan. The creation.

The landscapes: Fine.

Adoration of the shepherds; ditto.

Lucretia and Tarquin; the picture of an old hag, pulling a letcher by the nose.

Carlo Marrat. Virgin and child.

Wise men's offerings. Figure of the Virgin, good.

Holbein. Erasmus and Sir Thomas More; very fine.

Ostend. A man reading a paper. The minute expression strong.

Vandyke

real curiosities; though by no means equal in beauty to many of the other oaks, that are not in decay.

A fine winding valley leading from the house through the **woods**, whose bottom was of a boggy nature, **his Grace** has dug out

---

Vandyke. Earl *of Derby*; fine.

On the right of the hall is the stair-case, painted by *Le Guere*, 32 square by 60 high.

The falcon 54 by 34; here are the following antiques.

Nero. The head and attitude very fine.

Venus and Cupid. The head and turn of the neck exquisite; and the attitude elegant.

Cleopatra Nothing can be finer than this drapery; the turn of the head is good, but the attitude wants expression.

The pictures are,

Guido. Death *of St. Sebastian*; fine. The colours, naked, and lights expressive.

Titian. Ditto *tying to a tree*, fine colouring, but no expression.

The vestibule, 23 square.

Canalletti. Six views of *Venice*; of a fine and blooming brilliancy.

Poussin. Landscape; fine. The figures excellent, the hills and trees noble, but the sky appears to be of too deep a blue.

Vol. I.   Y   *Ancona.*

out to a proper depth, and floated with water; by which means he has gained a moſt noble lake, of a great length and breadth, which winds in an eaſy, but bold courſe, at the foot of ſeveral very fine woods; through which, from many points of view, the water is ſeen in a pictu-reſque

Ancona. Two views of *Rome*; the architecture fine.

Dreſſing-room, 25 by 21.

Titian. *Philip the ſecond of Spain:* Exceeding fine; the ſame as at *Devonſhire Houſe.*

Bed-chamber, 23 by 21.

Vandyke. *King Charles on horſeback.* The horſe by *Wooton;* fine.

Dreſſing-room, 25 by 24.

Bed-chamber, 25 by 22.

Cloſet. *A nun,* the drapery excellent.

A landſcape; a waterfall; good.

Bed-chamber, 34 by 24.

Portrait of the Duke of Florence and Machiavel; excellent.

Drawing-room, 33 by 31.

Bartolomeo. *Armida and Rinaldo.*

Danae and the Golden Shower, the colours are pretty good, but the drawing appears to be bad.

Other pictures not hung in order, are,

Holbein. *Alderman Hewet;* very fine.

Vandyke. *Earl of Strafford, and his Secretary.*

Earl

resque manner. At a distance from the house, but in sight of it, was built not long since a very elegant, as well as magnificent bridge, of three arches; the center 90 feet span, and the side ones each 75; but ―― cruel to think of! no sooner finished than undone!―― the center arch dropped in, having just exhibited the beauty of the design, to add to the mortification of the loss.―― Mr. *Mylne* the architect *.

The

Vandyke. Earl of Arundel.
David with Goliah's head.
Titian. Himself at music. The colours, drapery and attitude good, but the diffusion of light quite unnatural.
Titian. Lot and his daughters; vile.
Portrait of the Duke of Newburgh; very fine.

* The collection of paintings in the house contains several capital pieces highly worth attention. The hall of 36 feet by 30, is hung round with several family portraits by the best **masters**, among which those of *Horace*, Lord *Vere*, and Sir *Francis Vere*, appear to be particularly well done.

The library 30 by 20.
Old Frank. Six pieces of architecture with figures; admirably done, the colours extremely brilliant, and the finishing excellent.

A large

The great stable at *Welbeck* is one of the finest in *England*; it was built for a riding-house by the Duke of *Newcastle*. It is 130 feet long by 40 broad, and contains 40 stalls.

Relative to husbandry, his Grace was so obliging as to give me some information, which merits great attention.

The soil of the park and the fields his Grace keeps in his own hands, consists of clay and sand. The latter I examined with some attention, and found it of a deep staple; and from the spontaneous growth of grass, &c. I apprehend it not to be deficient

---

A large landscape with architecture; very fine, but the colours appear rather faded.

Rubens. *Venus and Cupid.*

King Charles the First on horseback, the same as that at *Kniveton*, where the horse is said to be by *Wooton.*

Drawing-room, 27 by 22. In this room and the adjoining closet are several very fine bronzes. On the other side of the common hall is the *Gothic* hall, 44 by 30. The doors, door-cases, window-frames, chimney-piece, &c. &c. are all *Gothic*, and in a very light taste.

The dining-room, 67 by 25: Among other portraits, here are

William

cient in richness. Carrots, I am confident, would thrive admirably in it, and turn out to immense profit. One very remarkable circumstance relative to it is, its being particularly subject to the attack of the coc-chaffer grub, which in this country is sometimes an absolute plague, from their immense numbers: These vermin breed in the sandy lands, and eat away all the roots of the grass, corn, &c. &c. They come in their insect state in such swarms as to darken the sun, and when they light on trees, eat off the leaves to perfect nakedness

---

William Cavendish, first Duke of Newcastle; admirable.
Holles, first Earl of Clare; very fine.
Thomas Wentworth, first Earl of Strafford, inimitable; the face and hands surprizingly painted.
Blue drawing-room, 34 by 19.
Guido. A Magdalen, exceeding fine.
Rubens. A head; admirable.
Vandyke. Sir Kenelm Digby; fine.
Rubens. Music piece, ditto.
Salvator Rosa. A landscape; a water-fall; beautiful.
Holbein. Sir Thomas More, exquisite.
Carrache. Venus risen from the Bath.
P. Laura. Four small pieces, companions, very fine. The subjects, which are chiefly rural business,

nefs. When the Duke dug away the moory bottom of the valley, in order to form the lake, fome of the loofe boggy earth was fpread on this fandy foil, by way of an experiment to try its nature; the effect was very remarkable; for the land fo manured has been ever fince perfectly free from thefe vermin, although the adjoining parts, not manured, were attacked in the ufual manner. —— The farms around *Welbeck* are all fmall, from 20 *l.* to 70 *l.* a year, and land lets from 4 *s.* to 8 *s.* an acre. Improvement is greatly wanting

in

---

bufinefs, are treated in a manner not ufual with this painter; the defigns are elegant, and the colouring good.

Albano. Chrift and the Woman of Samaria.

Blue bed chamber, 30 by 18, and two dreffing rooms adjoining.

In the attic ftory are feveral pieces, which fhould by no means be overlooked.

In the crimfon bed chamber, the landfcape over the chimney, though in a peculiar ftile, has merit.

Two pieces of fruit and flowers; fine.

In the dreffing-room to the crimfon damafk bed chamber, are;

Lagraine. A battle; fine.

Guido. St. Michael and the Archangel.

A large battle; very expreflive.

Several

in this country, for the worst of the sands I viewed would, in many parts of the kingdom, let at 10 s. or 12 s. and if judiciously cultivated, would be well worth 15 s. to any industrious man; nor will good husbandry ever be found in them till the rents are greatly raised; till four or five farms are laid together throughout the country, and some tenants brought from other parts

---

Several on glass, very fine; particularly a *Diana*, inimitably done.

In the *Gothic* closet, which is very prettily fitted up in that taste, are,

The Descent from the Cross, admirable. Its companion, very fine.

A small Venus on a pedestal; most sweetly delicate.

A small clump of trees; excellent; but the ground is of amber.

An old woman's head; surprizingly expressive, *Borgognone*. *Two small battles*; fine.

Three pieces of flowers; exceedingly well done.

Several of figures; in the stile of *Rubens*.

Cattle and two figures, fine.

Christ and the Woman of Samaria; admirable.

An old woman with a candle, and other figures; well done; the light in the stile of *Schalken*.

In the chintz bed-chamber.

Fair Rosamond, very fine and delicate, but no tempting piece.

In Lady *Oxford*'s bed-chamber is a very large cabinet, made out of the great oak in the park; the veins are very beautiful.

of the kingdom where such soils are managed as they ought to be.

His Grace was so obliging as to write to the Duke of *Norfolk*, that I might not meet with any difficulty in seeing *Worksop*, as I had been informed it was not shewn; this procured me a certain admission to view that edifice, celebrated not only for its beauty, but the surprising expedition used in raising it. If finished upon as large a scale as begun, it would be, I apprehend, the largest house in *England*; for the part already done is only a fifth of the design*.

In

---

* The front that is finished, is 318 feet long, and very light and beautiful; the center of it is a portico, which makes a small projection; six very handsome *Corinthian* pillars, resting on the rustics, support the tympanum; the whole extremely elegant. Upon the points of the triangle are three figures, and a balustrade crowns the building from the tympanum to the projecting part at the ends, which mark the terminations in the stile of wings: Upon these are vases which are in a proper taste, but the double ones at the corners have the appearance of being crouded. This front, upon the whole, is undoubtedly very beautiful; there is a noble simplicity in it which must please every eye, without raising any idea of want of ornament.

The

The farm-yard at *Workſop* will be juſtly thought very well worth viewing. It is a quadrangular range of buildings, ſurrounding a ſquare of 60 yards: See plate VI. fig. 4.

- a. The houſe, in the back part of which her Grace has a room fitted up in the *Gothic* taſte for drinking tea in; it opens into the park.
- b. b. Two barns.
- c. An open ſhade for the cattle to run under in bad weather.
- d. d. d. Stables, hog-ſties, poultry apartments, &c. &c.

The entrance is into a veſtible, in front of which is the ſtair-caſe; the grand apartment to the left and the following rooms to the right: Firſt, an anti-room 25 feet ſquare; the chimney-piece of white marble, and handſome; over it a painting in freſco, an imitation of a baſſo-relievo of boys, by *Bruin*, a *Flemiſh* artiſt, at preſent employed by his Grace to execute ſeveral works in the ſame manner; they are incomparably well done, and the deception complete.

Bed-chamber, 25 ſquare; *Vulcan* boys by the ſame hand; excellently done.

Dreſſing-room, 22 by 25; the chimney-piece, eagles in the white marble taking a twiſted ſnake; handſome.

Chintz

e. A drain for carrying off the water.
f. A pump and cistern.
g. g. g. g. The surrounding wall, against which the above-mentioned offices (except the barns and house) are built in the form of sheds.
4. The entrance.

The whole cost 7000 *l*. But as others may be induced, and at a considerable expence, to similar undertakings, I shall venture a few observations upon this, which may in such cases have their use. The barns (which are not large ones) are out of all proportion to the size of the yard;

Chintz bed chamber, 25 square; chimney-piece of black and white marble, very elegant; a fruit-piece, fine.

The grand apartment consists of, first, a drawing-room, 36 by 30, very elegantly furnished with crimson damask, and magnificent slabs of *Siena* marble. Secondly, the grand drawing-room, 53 by 30, hung with most beautiful tapestry of the *Gobelines* manufactory, which, for colours, and an exquisite imitation of nature in several of the animals, is beyond all praise; the colours are amazingly brilliant, and the tints of painting in some parts most happily imitated. The chimney-piece of *Siena* and white marble polished, the pier and chimney-glasses large and magnificent. Third, the din-
ing-

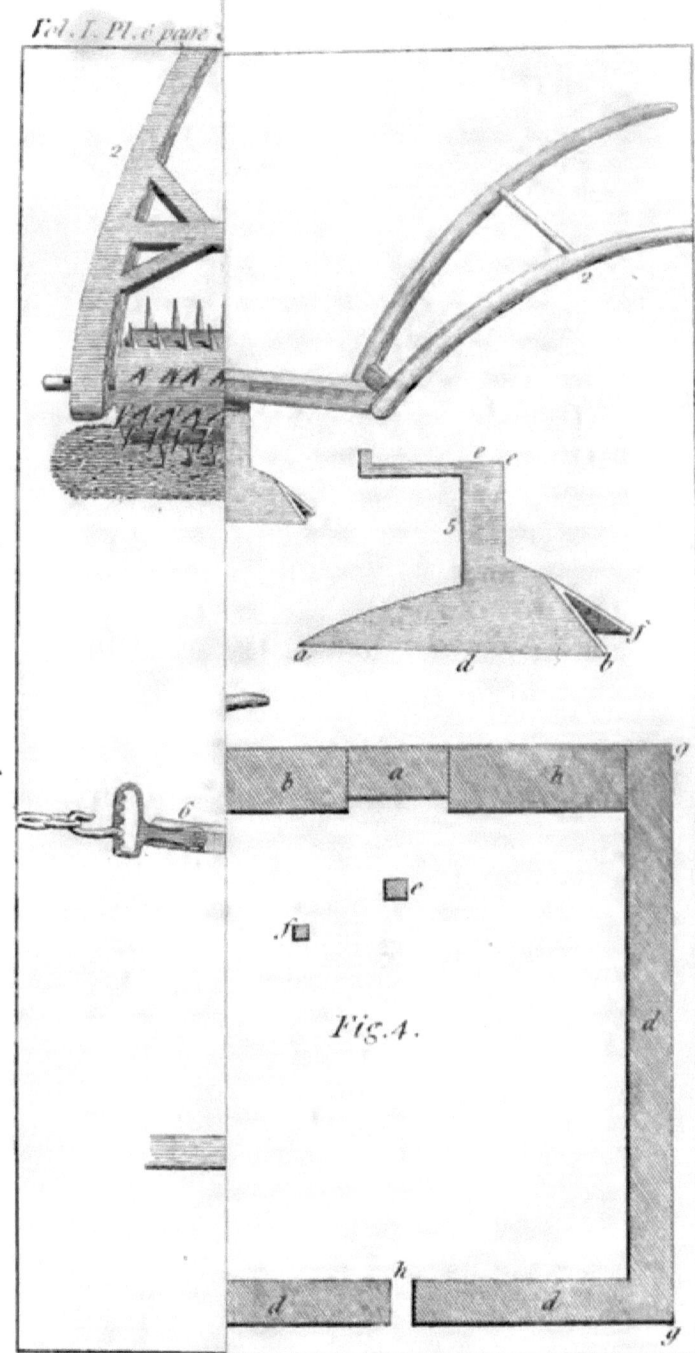

Fig. 4.

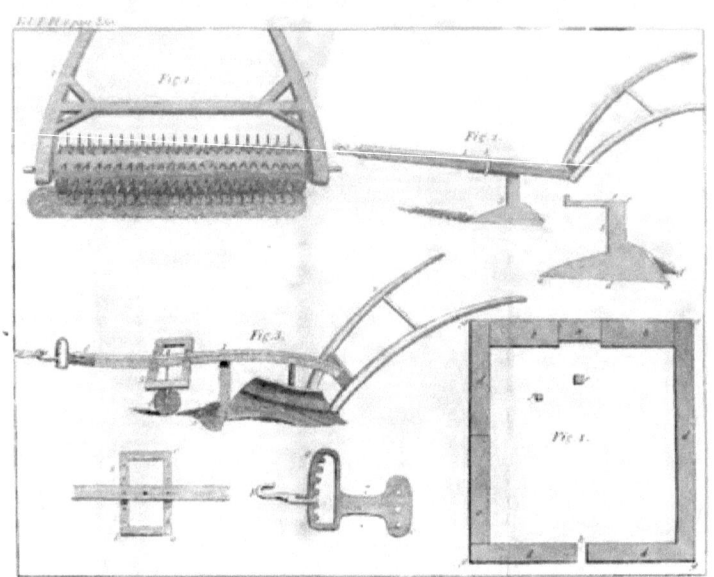

yard; they ought, for foddering with straw the number of **cattle** proper for such a yard, to be six times as large, and certainly should be four in number, one on each side, for the convenience of distributing the straw as the corn is threshed.

The **sink** for carrying off the water exhausts the manure of its greatest riches, for all the urine runs off with it. Instead of this, **the** surrounding buildings **ought to be raised so** high, **as** to admit a layer **of marle,** chalk, or clay, two feet deep, over the whole area, then the foddering; **by which**

---

ing-room, 42 by 28; here **are** two large landscapes, brilliant and pleasing:

Cain and Abel; dark, but expressive.

Dido and Æneas.

The area of **the** stair-case is 37 by 25; it is painted in pannels of fresco, in imitation of relievos, by the above mentioned *Fleming*, and most excellently done; the lights and shades are so happily tempered, as **to give the** rotundity of nature to the objects, and place them almost **in full** relief: Many of the designs have merit, **the** attitudes and expression good.—Over the chimney in the anti-room is a picture of **St.** *Rocque*, which appears to be fine; the dog admirable, but the lights unnaturally diffused.

A dead Christ; very fine.

Not

which means the urine would be retained, and the mixing the whole together in *May*, would make an admirable compost ready for the land. If it does run off, it should be into a well, for pumping up.

A pump is a very insufficient method of supplying a large (or indeed any) farmyard with water: All points of business, and especially the care of cattle, that depend absolutely upon the memory of servants, will undoubtedly be, at times, in jeopardy; for which reason, conveniencies should be so contrived, as to render memory unnecessary. In this case, the mouth of a pond, or a stream flowing into a very.

Not far from the house is a pleasure-ground, laid out and decorated with great taste: An artificial lake and river are made, in which nature is very happily imitated, and the ground surrounding laid out in a very agreeable manner. Near the entrance is a *Gothic* bench, in a shady sequester'd spot, looking immediately on a creek of the water, over-hung with wood; the shore broken and rocky: At a little distance the banks spread themselves, and open a fine bend of the water, surrounded with trees; and at a distance, in the very bosom of a dark wood, the water winds through the arches of a most elegant bridge; the effect as happy as can be conceived; for the sun shining upon the bridge,

very long cistern should always be taken into a farm-yard. I would give treble the price to joist my cows in a yard wherein the water ran, than in one where it was pumped.

While I was viewing this yard, a waggon came in loaded with malt grains for the hogs; they were thrown down in the cleanest places for the swine to feed on them. This shews the great want of sufficient conveniencies for the hogs, *viz.* spacious cisterns to hold such food, that when plenty, it may be kept against times of scarcity; pipes should be laid into such
cisterns

---

bridge, gives it a brilliance which contrasts admirably with the brownness of the surrounding groves. Plate VII. will give some idea of this little enchanting scene.

From this view, a walk winds to the left through the wood, to a lawn, at the bottom of which to the right, flows the water, which is seen as you move along very beautifully; on the left, at the upper part of the opening, is a *Tuscan* temple, properly situated for viewing a part of the lake. Other serpentine-walks lead from hence to different parts of the ground; one to the new menagerie, and another down to the bridge, which is in itself very light and pretty; but the termination of the water being seen at no greater distance than
four

[334]

cisterns from the dairy and the scullery sink, and around them spouts into troughs communicating with all the hogs' apartments, for the conveniency of feeding them with little trouble, and without waste: with distinct ones for those that are fatting, that they may always be able to help themselves, and without waste.

A yard upon so large a scale as this, should have sheds with racks, mangers, and stalls for fatting oxen, with spaces for stacks of hay and straw, and back-rooms for turnips, carrots, cabbages, &c. &c. to be thrown directly into the manger

---

four or five yards, is rather unlucky, because it destroys the idea of all propriety to build a bridge over a water which may be coasted round in half a second; but I apprehend it is intended to carry the water further, to remove the conclusion out of sight. After crossing this bridge, you find the banks' rising ground scattered with trees and shrubs; the effect truly beautiful. At a little distance is a slight trickling fall of water in the midst of wood, just sufficient for the neighbourhood of a temple in a sequestered spot, where the water is heard but not seen. Upon the whole, this shrubbery will amuse any person whose taste leads them to admire the soft touches of nature's pencil, scenes of *the beautiful* unmixed with *the sublime.*

through

through sliding doors, at the head of every ox.

I purpose taking some other opportunity of laying before the public a plan for a farm-yard, so contrived as to obviate these and many other objections; as I apprehend, nobility and gentlemen of large fortunes, who are desirous of building these offices completely, may not always chuse to give the time requisite for examining the very imperfect plans that are so often laid before them.

His Grace keeps many hundred acres of land in his own hands; the soil chiefly sand. He has tried carrots more than once, and found them to answer incomparably: His method has very justly been to hoe and weed them thoroughly. Cabbages he has likewise tried, and with great success; finds that one acre is better than two of turnips (hoed) even on sandy land. Rents run from 3 *s.* to about 7 *s.* 6 *d.* Farms in general small, from 20 *l.* to 100 *l.*

Returning towards *Doncaster*, in the way to *Pontefract*, the principal objects worthy of notice are the experimental agriculture of *Selwood Hewett*, Esq; of *Bilham*, and *James Farrar*, Esq; of *Barnborough Grange*, to both which gentlemen I was introduced by the obliging attention of the Marquis

of

of *Rockingham*. They were so kind as to give me the following account. Mr. *Hewett*'s experiments have been chiefly upon carrots, lucerne, and burnet. He began the culture of the first in the year 1765, with one acre, which he ploughed seven times as a winter fallow; the soil a fine light hazel mould, about a foot deep, upon a limestone rock. They were sown the middle of *April*, by hand, in drills one foot asunder, with 4 *lb.* and half of seed. As soon as they came up they were horse-hoed, which a man and boy did in five hours; the weeds that grew among the plants were drawn out by hand; after this they were horse-hoed a second time, and again across the rows, which cut away the plants to the distance of about six inches asunder. The crop was begun to be taken up in *October*, and continued drawing, as wanted, till the middle of *March*; the quantity sixteen cart-loads, of forty bushels each, or 640 bushels, which is an immense crop. Six horses were kept on them through the winter (except when absent from home) without oats; performed their work as usual, and looked equally well. Some beasts were fatted on them and turnips, which evidently preferred the carrots, insomuch that it was soon difficult to make them eat the turnips

at

at all. A lean porker was fatted by carrots in ten days time; eat nothing else, and the fat when killed was very fine, white and firm, nor did it boil away in the dressing: The quantity of carrots eat, 14 stone; for all were weighed. Hogs in general feed upon them with great eagerness.

In 1766, Mr. *Hewett* cultivated another acre, which he managed in the same manner, and applied to the same uses, with the same success; the crop nearly as before.

In 1767, a third acre cultivated, cleaned, and used as before; the crop equally good.

In 1768, he sowed two acres, but one of them has failed, and are ploughed up again; nor is the remaining one equal to former crops.

This ingenious cultivator is in general of opinion, that carrots may prove of very great use; for turnips being subject to the fly, and cabbages to rotting, these roots being liable to neither, may be much better depended upon. But he thinks the care and expence of cultivation too great to be profitable to a common farmer. To this opinion, however, I can by no means subscribe; I have found by experiment, that carrots applied to any use, are well worth more than 1 s. a bushel.

	l.	s.	d.
Now 640 bushels at that rate amount to	32	0	0

Let us in the next place confider the deductions to be made.

	l.	s.	d.
Suppose rent, &c.	1	0	0
Seven ploughings,	1	8	0
Seed, 4¼ lb. at 1 s. 4 d.	0	6	0
Sowing,	0	1	6
Harrowing,	0	2	0
Three horse-hoeings cannot amount to	0	7	6
Hand-weeding,	1	10	0

This is certainly an high allowance.

	l.	s.	d.
Digging up,	2	0	0
Total expence,	6	15	0
Amount of crop,	32	0	0
Expences,	6	15	0
Neat profit,	25	5	0

Which fum per acre, I fhould apprehend fufficient to fatisfy any man. Nor can I poffibly fee why fuch culture fhould not anfwer in common, for if the expence and care attending five acres of corn, or any common crop, be thrown to the account

account of one acre of carrots, yet the farmer will find, it is evident, more than five times the profit upon the latter than he will ever receive from the former.

Lucerne, Mr. *Hewett* cultivated for some time. It was sown in drills 9 or 10 years ago, by Mr. *Miller*'s direction in the Gardener's Dictionary, upon the same soil as the carrots were raised in; for the first four years it was kept perfectly clean from weeds, but after that the natural grass got the better of it. Mr. *Hewett* does not mention it as a perfect experiment, because the seed was sown after four crops without a fallow intervening, upon which account it certainly had not fair play: cows, he observed, would eat any spontaneous growth rather than lucerne when full grown.

Of burnet he sowed two acres in drills two feet asunder, and kept perfectly clean for two years; but he found that nothing would eat it unless absolutely forced by hunger, though he tried all sorts of cattle: This induced him to let it stand for seed, of which, the product of only one acre, he sold as much as brought him 4 *l*.

Of bird-grass, he sowed a rood with 3 lb. of seed at 16 *s*. *per* lb. the land perfectly clean; it was sowed alone, and turned out quite worthless.

Sainfoine he sows after a fallow or turnips with half a crop of barley, four bushels of seed; it lasts in common 12 or 14 years. It is never mown the first year, but fed with all cattle except sheep: After the first year, always mows the first growth for hay, and generally gets 50 Cwt. per acre, worth 30 *s.* a ton: He gives it to his beasts, cows, and horses; and it is reckoned a very great improvement.

The large *Scotch* cabbage he cultivates in the following manner: Sows them in *May*, transplants them twice; the last time into the field in *August* in rows, three feet asunder, and two feet from plant to plant; uses them for feeding cows, and fatting beasts and sheep. The butter, if used immediately, is good, but will not keep 12 hours. Six cabbages weighed 10 stone 7 lb. and half. But the average weight from 8 to 12 lb.

Mr. *Farrer*'s husbandry consists chiefly in attempting to perfect the common method of culture; which will be seen by his way of managing his fallows. He breaks up the old stubble at *Michaelmas*; in *March* or beginning of *April*, stirs again, makes it very fine by the middle of *May:* After every ploughing he rolls it, sometimes with a spiky roller, which he finds of great use in breaking the clods in a dry season; it is

upon

upon the same construction as the Marquis of *Rockingham*'s, only the spikes with blunt ends instead of sharp ones. After the rollings, he rakes the field with a horse rake; which is made the same as a common rake for clearing stubbles of corn, only of a considerable length and strength to work by a horse in shafts: This machine he draws across the land to clear it of twitch, and finds it to answer greatly. Upon this fallow, he lays his manure in *October*, consisting of his yard dung mixed in heaps, and ploughing it in, leaves the field for barley in the spring, when he ploughs and sows at once. He never gets less than six quarters per acre; with it he sows clover, which he mows for hay twice, and gains $3\frac{1}{2}$ tons at twice; wheat upon the clover, of which he seldom reaps less than three quarters. The soil is excellent, a fine rich loam worth 30 *s.* an acre.

Upon land not light enough for turnips, nothing can exceed this husbandry, which every where deserves imitation; the making the fallow fine by the middle of *May*, is an admirable plan, and cannot fail of great success, as it is the only method of rendering the land perfectly clean from seed weeds. But I should apprehend the laying the dung on before the winter, would endanger the salts being washed from it by the winter's rains, notwithstanding its being turned in by the plough, for the weight of the snow and rain certainly act through the loose moulds. Their method in *Essex* seems to be preferable, which is to throw the land up in narrow ridges in *October*, and to carry the manure on the first frost that comes in the spring, and they leave it in heaps on the land till they sow, which is always the first dry season that comes, even as soon as *February*.

This gentleman's way of breaking up grass lands is an excellent one; first with a common plough he strikes a furrow, and then with a paring one turns into that furow a slice of the turf two inches thick; after this comes the common plough in the same furrow, and turning the moulds on to the turf, buries it; upon this tillage he harrows in oats, and gets from 7 to 10 quarters per acre: After which he fallows. The public is much indebted to both these gentlemen for their attention to such judicious experiments.

From *Doncaster* to *Pontefract*, the soil is of various sorts, and lets from 7 *s*. to 20 *s*. an acre; farms continue small, in general under 100 *l*. a year. I made many inquiries into the culture of liquorice around *Pontefract*, and found the quantity of land planted with it, not so considerable as I had been

been informed: It never amounts to 100 acres, and oftentimes not to 50. The crown of the bud and the runners (the horizontal shoots from the root) are what they plant, and these they procure in taking up an old crop. The method of planting is this:

The land is first dug three feet and half, or four feet deep; but I should inform you, that the soil is a fine rich hazel loam, rather inclined to sand than clay, but not visibly to either. Then a covering of rotten dung is spread on the land, which is directly dug in one spit deep. After this it is formed into arched ridges, three feet wide. Upon every ridge they plant three rows, one upon the crown, and one on each side of it. The plants on the best land, four inches from each other; but on that which is indifferent, only three inches.

The first year they sow the ground with onions or carrots; but this practice, they allow, rather hurts the crop. The carrots are exceeding fine; all weeds are carefully pulled out by hand, so as to keep the ground perfectly clean. In the winter, the tops of the liquorice are cut off.

The second and third years, the plantation is hoed several times, so as to extirpate all weeds and keep the soil loose, the hoes six inches wide. It always stands three years, sometimes four.

When they dig up the crop, they cut a trench as deep as the land was before dug (for so deep the liquorice roots will run) and this trench they continue directly across the land; when cleared, and the roots all picked up by women and children as the men proceed, they begin a second by it, throwing the moulds into the old one, and so continue through... the whole field, by which means it is all dug over to the old depth; and is ready with the former management for a fresh crop of liquorice; by which means one digging (after the first) serves both for the old and new crop. And this is so great an inducement to continue the plantation upon the same ground, that many fields have been continually cropped with it as long back as the oldest man can remember: In this case, however, the land requires much manuring; new land is the best.

Upon raising the crop, the plants are cut off, and the roots separated into three sorts; they sell all together upon an average, at 3 s. 6 d. or 4 s. a stone of 15 lb.; and their crops rise from 150 to 400 stone; many about 250.

All

All the people employed about *Pontefract* in the liquorice plantations are paid by the day, and not as in hop-gardens, &c. by the piece: This circumstance made it difficult to discover the expences and profit of an acre of liquorice; but from the best intelligence I could gain, it is not far from the following sketch:

	l.	*s.*	*d.*
Their rents rise from 4 *l.* to 8 *l.* per acre; commonly about	5	0	0
The cost of the plants from 2 *s.* to 5 *s.* per 1000, say 3 *s.* 6 *d.* 90,000 plants, at that rate, amount to	15	0	0
The first digging the land costs	12	0	0
The common digging, we cannot estimate, in proportion to the price of the first, at less than	2	0	0
Manuring, I calculate at	3	0	0
Striking into beds	0	10	0
Planting	2	10	0
Wheeding the first year	2	12	6
Cutting off the tops	0	2	6
Hand-hoeing the second year	2	2	0
Cutting off the tops	0	3	6
Hand-hoeing the third year	2	2	0
Cutting off the tops	0	5	0
Digging up, &c.	14	0	0
£.	61	7	6

Suppose

Suppose the crop 250 stone, this at 3 s. 9 d. amounts to

£. 61 7 6
46 18 0

Loss, - - - 14 9 6

If the crop is 300 stone, the account will stand thus:

300 at 3 s. 9 d. - - 56 5 0
Loss - - - 10 2 6

If 350 is the crop, the profit will be as follows:

350 at 3 s. 9 d. - - - 65 13 0
Expences, - - - 61 7 6
Profit, - - 4 5 6

From hence we find that the first crop must be considerably above the medium to ... expences: With the second, third, ... so forth, the case is different. The expences then are these,

	l.	s.	d.
Rent, - - - -	5	0	0
Digging, - - -	2	0	0
Manuring, - -	3	0	0
Making the beds, - -	0	10	0
Planting, - - -	2	10	0
Weeding and hoeing, - -	6	16	6
Cutting the tops, - -	0	11	0
Digging up, &c. - -	14	0	0
	34	7	6

250 stone,

250 stone, at 3 s. 9 d.	-	46	18	0
Expences, - - -		34	7	6
Profit, - - -		12	10	6
Profit, *per annum*, - -		4	3	6

And this, I believe, is not exceeded in common in the liquorice culture. The soil in general about *Pontefract*, is very rich and fine, lets much of it so high as 40 s. an acre, 20 s. a common rent, at an average; farms very small *.

The

---

* *Methley*, the seat of Lord *Mexborough*, about six miles from this town, is fitted up and furnished in so rich a manner, as to attract the attention of travellers. The ground-floor consists of a vestibule, a dining-room, and a drawing-room; the first 37 by 7, and a large bow-window; the second 37 by 25, hung with crimson damask, the ornaments carved and gilt: The ceiling in compartments, ornamented in green and gold and white. The chimney-piece very handsome, the cornice, &c. of white marble, the frieze of *Siena*, with white scrolls on it; and supported by Ionic pillars of *Siena*: The door and window-cases of white and gold; the cornice of the same, and the frieze green and gold, very elegant. The frames of the glasses, settees, chairs, &c. carved and richly gilt.

Upon

The soil from *Pontefract* to Methley is rich, and lets at a high rent, generally above 20 s. an acre, and some as high as 40 s. The farms are all small, from 20 l. to 80 l. a year; very few rise to 100 l.

Upon the first floor are three apartments: The green velvet bed-chamber, 19 by 18. The chimney-piece, corinthian pillars of *Siena* marble, with gilt capitals. The crimson damask room, 23 by 18; the ceiling white and gold in compartments, with festoons of gilding in them in a light and elegant taste; the chimney-piece white and *Siena* marble; in the center, doves in bass-relief, very fine. The ornaments of the bed gilt carving; and the window curtains covered with scrolls of the same: Adjoining, a small dressing-room, the ceiling gilt scrolls on a lead white, light and pleasing.——The chintz-room, 25 by 18, the ceiling in compartments with flight scrolls of gilding. Here are two large and very fine *India* figures, above a yard high, in glass-cases. A dressing-room, 18 by 12, neatly as well as richly fitted up. I should remark in general, that the articles of carving and gilding are done throughout the house with much elegance; the doors, door-cases, window-frames, pannels, &c. are ornamented in this manner; the ceilings are in general very well executed, the scrolls of gilding not crowded

From *Methley*, we went to *Temple Newsham*, the seat of Lord *Irwin*; the roads in many places are even worse than before, but the soil better. Rents run up to 50 s. an acre, but on an average between 20 s. and 30 s.; farms the same. Of wheat they get from 30 to 40 bushels per acre: Of barley, four, five, and six quarters *.

From

---

crowded, but light and neat as well as rich, and the furniture equally well chosen. The house, you doubtless observe, is not a large one, but it is, upon the whole, much better finished than most of its size in the kingdom, and than many more capital ones. One remark, however, I should add, which is, that those who go to *Methley* by *Pontefract*, must be extremely fond of seeing houses, or they will not recompense the fatigue of passing such detestable roads. They are full of ruts, whose gaping jaws threaten to swallow up any carriage less than a waggon. It would be no bad precaution, to yoke half a score of oxen to your coach, to be ready to encounter such quagmires as you will here meet with.

* Lord *Irwin*'s collection of pictures is not only capital, but very numerous. The following are those which struck me the most. I cannot add the masters, as the person who shews the house, knows neither the subject, or painter of scarce any; a circumstance to be regretted, when

when a catalogue is so easily written for the information of the traveller; one advantage however attends it, which is, the certainty that one's remarks are mere feelings, and never the praise or censure which the world attaches to *names*.

In the breakfast-room, 32 by 27, are,

A Bacchanalian piece: The attitude of the naked woman, in the front ground, fine; and the figures well designed.

An Astrologer. Very fine.

In the crimson damask bed-chamber.

Countess of Ossory; a portrait. The whole figure excellent. The attitude astonishingly spirited and elegant; the air of the head, the beauty of the face and hair, inimitable. An exquisite piece.

Landscape with figures. The woman in white, good; the water very bad.

In the dressing-room.

Large landscapes. Very fine.

Dead game. Excellent.

Landscape. I apprehend by *Bassan*. Strong but ugly expression.

Sea-piece. Fine.

In the green dressing-room.

Landscape. Rocks, and every thing green.

A storm. Fine.

A large battle-piece. Strong expression; I suppose by *Borgognone*.

land lets, at an average, for about 20 s.

an

Group of horsemen, with rocks. The wild manner of *Salvator Rosa.*
Lot and his daughters. Colours and attitudes very fine.
Battle-piece. Spirited.
Ditto. Ditto.
Sleeping woman, satyrs, &c. Good: In the stile of *Rubens.*
Landscape. Middling.

In the blue damask dressing-room.

Boys. Charity and her three children introduced; the brilliancy of the colours exceeding fine; the boys very well done.
Cephalus and Procris. Fine.
Two battle-pieces. Round ones; amazingly spirited.
Two pieces of dead game. Inimitable.
Two small pieces on copper. In one a decolation by a female figure, with a scimitar in her hand: Perhaps *Holophernes.* The colours and finishing exquisite.
Landscape. A water-fall; very fine.
Group of boys. Inimitable.
Sea-piece.
Two small pictures, groups of horsemen. Very fine: The spirited manner of *Salvator* and *Borgognone.*
A calm. Pretty.
A large landscape. Rocks and trees dark, but expressive.

In

an acre; the arable about 10 *s*. Farms in general

In the gallery, a very fine room, 108 by 28, are

Two large battle-pieces. Exceeding fine.

Landscape, under one of the above, a calm evening. Very fine; the boor on an afs, exquisitely done; colours, expression, attitude, and cattle excellent.

Ditto. Its companion. The figures, rocks, and broken trees admirable.

Group of horsemen on a bridge. The lights strong, and the expression spirited.

Its Companion. Ditto.

Storm among rocks; and the companion. Surprizing expression.

Fruit. Excellently done.

A baptism. Very fine colours.

Descent from the Cross. This is in the stile of *Albert Durer*: The minute expression resulting from high finishing, amazing; but the draperies (except the gauze linen) very bad.

Battle at sea. Very fine.

Two rocks with figures. Very wild and dark, but nobly touched: If they are not by *Salvator*, they are worthy of him.

Large piece of birds. Spirited; the colours excellent.

Two large pieces, a storm among rocks, and a raging torrent. A wild and very noble expression.

Holy family. In the stile of *Carlo Marrat*; the boy

general small, but one man occupies eight

---

boy admirably fine. Her countenance good, but the draperies heavy and disgusting.

Large landscape. In a dark stile; but the light through the trees, and the woman very fine: The general blueish cast unnatural.

Hunting the wild-boar. Strong expression.

Two pieces of fruit, &c. Very fine.

Two landscapes. In the stile of *Poussin.*

Landscape with rocks and buildings. The tree on the left side, exquisite: The keeping fine.

Its companion. Trees and buildings excellent.

Prometheus. Great.

A large shipwreck. Amazingly spirited in the figures; and a general horror nobly expressed.

A waterfall. Its companion: The figures, trees, and general wildness, exceedingly fine.

A landscape; under ditto. Admirably fine. The general effect of the clear obscure; the calm majesty of the scene; the spirit of the figures, architecture, &c. incomparable: Worthy the pencil of *Poussin.*

Portrait of a Scotch Lord. Excellent expression.

Ditto of Mr. Scarborough. Good.

Ditto of a man writing. Great expression; in the manner of *Rembrandt.*

Fruit-shop. Excellent.

Jane Shore. The minute expression of the naked, and the gauze drapery is astonishingly fine. The finishing of the breasts and limbs, surprizing.

Vol. I. A a *Europa.*

eight hundred acres; an instance, however, very

Europa. It seems in the stile of *Rubens*; fine. The colours excellent.

A supper. The lights, and ugly expression, fine: It is in the manner of *Schalken*.

Moses striking the rock. The colours bad; the group and figures quite *Dutch*.

Seadrech, Meshach, and Abednego. Prodigious fine.

Two boys heads. Amazingly fine; the turn, attitude, and expression great.

Two pieces of horses. Fine.

Portrait of the Earl of Holland. Admirable.

Holy Family. A large picture in the stile of *Rubens*. Nothing can be finer than the boys; the principal one is inimitable; the head and face of the *Virgin* very fine, but somewhat too elegant for *Rubens*.

Two small battles.

A dead Christ. Amazingly fine.

Two sea-pieces. Fine.

Architecture. An arch and a landscape through it. The arch fine.

A priest holding a crucifix. Excellent.

Joseph and our Saviour. Fine; something in the manner of *Carlo Marratt*.

Rachel, Joseph and Benjamin. Fine, but unpleasing.

Architecture and figures. Exceedingly fine.

Christ praying in the garden. The colouring and attitude inimitable; but the lights unnaturally

very unusual *.

I observed about *Byrom* much sandy land, which

---

rally diffused: I should suppose it of the school of *Carrach*.

Its companion. A figure praying, vile drapery; but the rest fine.

Lord Irwin. Very good.

A group of dancing boys. Finished with a glow and brilliancy beyond expression. The attitudes exquisite: The colours astonishingly fine; the landscape beautiful; but the lights strangely diffused.

Diana, in two pieces. Clumsy as ever *Rubens* painted.

Portrait of Sir Arthur Ingram. Good; but a wretched attitude.

A fruit-piece. Fine.

A small picture of many figures. It somewhat resembles the manner both of *Borgognone* and *Bassan*; fine.

Its companion, a woman riding. Quite *Dutch* ideas, figures and drapery.

Cattle-piece (over the library door). Fine.

Architecture (under the large sea-piece). Very fine and bold.

The library is a very handsome room, divided by Corinthian pillars. It is 24 square. In the chapel is an altar-piece, somewhat curious: A last supper. The figure of *Christ* has the countenance of a clown; the group is wretched; one of the apostles is in a tye-wig, and another's hair would do exceedingly well for a bag.

* At *Byrom*, the seat of Sir *John Ramsden*, are

which seemed of an excellent staple, and great quantities of turnips. Sir *John Ramsden* uses the same machine for hoeing them as I have already described near *Grantham*: It is better than no hoeing, and that is all that can be said for it. I should not, however, forget to remark, that this gentleman once raised a turnip in the field that weighed 42 lb. a size which, I suppose, was

---

are several pictures, which will give no slight entertainment to those who are fond of painting: Among others here are, in the dining-room, 36 by 25,

Rubens. Boys, with a festoon of fruit by *Snyders.* Most capital; nothing can be finer than the attitudes and sweet expression of the boys: The group is sketched with all imaginable elegance. The faces and hair incomparable.

Spaniels on the scent. An admirable spirit in the attitudes of the dogs. The partridge in the air very fine.

A water-fall with rocks. Amazingly fine. The foam of the water incomparable; the rocks nobly majestic; the colours excellent; the figures fine and well placed; their attitudes striking; and the general keeping and brilliancy very pleasing. I should suppose it by *Pousin.*

Water-fowl. Fine.

A Musi-

was never equalled. The sand is excellent, lets at 20 *s*. an acre, and would yield immense crops of carrots; which would be found by far the most profitable use it could be applied to. Cabbages, Sir *John* has cultivated with success: His present crop is of a vigorous growth, large size, and bids fair for yielding an immense produce.

The

A Musician. It is *Titian* in that character; said at *Kniveton* (where is another) to be by himself. The colours and attitudes are good: The diffusion of light bad.

An hunting-piece. The spirit of the dogs excellently catched; the colouring is likewise good. But the figures are thrown into a corner, as if they had nothing to do with the sport; but cattle was the painter's *forte*.

In the drawing-room, 30 by 16,

A large landscape. Cattle going over a bridge; incomparably fine: The colours very lively, without being tawdry. The general brilliancy excellent. The tree amazingly fine: The cattle good: The figures elegantly grouped: The bridge, water, &c. inimitable. It may be called, *La belle Nature.*——Under it,

Dead Game. The partridge very natural.

Landscape. A glowing heat; very fine: The finishing exquisite; light through the trees, fine.

Fruit

[358]

The soil between *Ferry Bridge* and *Howden*, (which is in the road I before travelled) consists chiefly of sand; it is very indifferently cultivated: Turnips they sow in some quantities, but seldom hoe them.

Fruit with a Tankard, &c. Very well done.

A Fox with a dead Fowl. Excellent.

A dead Hare, &c. Fine. The greyhound's head good; but not curiosity enough in his nose.

Two Landscapes (over the doors). Fine. The figures elegantly grouped: That of the lake and trees very pleasing.

A large Battle. Great fire and spirit.

Two small Landscapes. Colours admirable; the rocks and forest sublimely grand.

Butterflies and Leaves. Exceedingly well finished.

A Nativity. Very graceful and pleasing; the Virgin's countenance fine, and her attitude easy and natural. If the hands are any rule to judge by, I should suppose this piece by *Parmagiano*.

A Venetian Prospect. Brilliant and fine: It is in *Canaletti*'s manner.

Two Pieces, Companions; one of *Fruit-women*: The colours very good. The other *A Woman milking a Goat*, &c. Fine; but not so brilliant. But the cattle very well done.

Marchioness of *Rockingham* (over the chimney). The attitude elegant, and drapery good.

Two Heads; *Oliver Cromwell*, and another, its companion.

And

And now, Sir, as I am setting off for the *North-Riding*, you will here allow me to conclude this long letter.

I am, &c.

END of the FIRST VOLUME.

Just published, written by the same Author,
Handsomely printed in Octavo; Price 5s. sewed; 6s. bound;
The SECOND EDITION, corrected and enlarged,

OF

A SIX WEEKS TOUR

THROUGH THE

SOUTHERN COUNTIES of ENGLAND and WALES,

DESCRIBING PARTICULARLY,

I. The present State of Agriculture and Manufactures.
II. The different Methods of cultivating the Soil.
III. The Success attending some late Experiments on various Grasses, &c.
IV. The various Prices of Labour and Provisions.
V. The State of the working Poor in those Counties wherein the Riots were most remarkable.

WITH

DESCRIPTIONS and COPPERPLATES,
Of such new invented IMPLEMENTS of HUSBANDRY, as deserve to be generally known:

INTERSPERSED

With Accounts of the SEATS of the NOBILITY and GENTRY, and other Objects worthy Notice.

☞ In this Second Edition, the Author has inserted some fresh Informations he received, of new Improvements in Husbandry in the Neighbourhood of the Rout, with other considerable Additions, which he hopes will render it more acceptable to the Public, and be found to co-operate entirely with his original Design of extending the Knowledge of British Agriculture.

⁎ "The Design of this Tour is to spread useful Knowledge of all Sorts, to display to one Part of the Kingdom the Practices of the other, to remark wherein such Practice is hurtful, and wherein it is commendable; to draw forth *spirited Examples of good Husbandry* from Obscurity, and display them as the proper Objects of Imitation.

"The Farmers in one Place grow rich by Methods that would enrich their Brethren in another, but remain quite unknown.

The following Passage, characteristic of this Work, is translated from a foreign Literary Journal.

"The Title of this Work is long, but we find the Work itself too short. It is full of useful and interesting Observations upon divers Subjects mentioned in the Title. The Author, who is profoundly versed in every Thing that concerns rural Oeconomy and Agriculture, is also a Man of Wit and Taste; and the Descriptions which he gives of many fine Seats in the Country, shew that he has a great Knowledge of the fine Arts, and particularly of Architecture."

Biblioth. des Scien. &c. *Tom. vingt-neuvieme; prem. part. p.* 215.